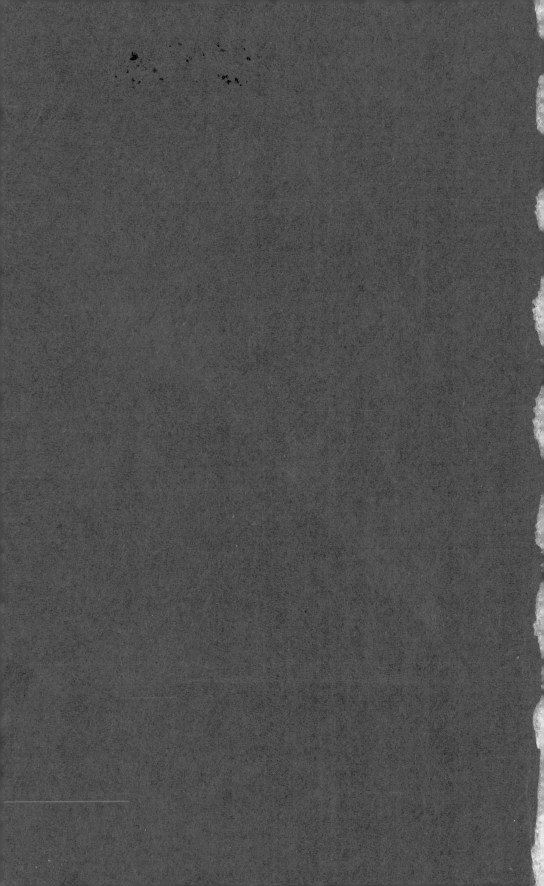

TEENAGE IDOL, TRAVELIN' MAN

HYPERION
NEW YORK

TEENAGE IDOL

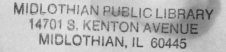

The Complete Biography of ***Rick Nelson***

Philip Bashe

TRAVELIN' MAN

"Poor Little Fool," by Sharon Sheeley, copyright © 1957, Matragun Music, all rights
reserved; reprinted by permission.

"It's Late," by Dorsey Burnette, copyright © 1958 and 1959, Ring A Ding Music ‖
Chrysalis Songs (BMI); all rights in the U.S. and Canada administered by Ring A
Ding Music ‖ Chrysalis Songs (BMI); all rights reserved; used by permission.

"Lonesome Town," by Baker Knight, copyright © 1958, Matragun Music, all rights
reserved; reprinted by permission.

"Tryin' to Get to You," by Rose Marie McCoy and Charlie Singleton, copyright ©
1983, Elvis Presley Music & Gladys Music; all rights on behalf of Elvis Presley Music
administered by Unichappell Music, Inc., and all rights on behalf of Gladys Music
administered by Chappell & Co.; all rights reserved; used by permission.

"Travelin' Man," by Jerry Fuller, copyright © 1960, renewed 1988 Acuff-Rose Music,
Inc.; all rights reserved; used by permission; international copyright secured.

(Acknowledgments continue on page 306.)

Library of Congress Cataloging-in-Publication Data

Bashe, Philip.
   Teenage idol, travelin' man: the complete biography of Rick
Nelson/Philip Bashe.—1st ed.
     p. cm.
   Includes bibliographical references and index.
   Discography: p.
   ISBN 1-56282-969-6: $22.95 ($27.95 Can.)
   1. Nelson, Rick, 1940–1985. 2. Singers—United States—Biography.
I. Title.
ML420.N3826B4   1992
782.42166'092—dc20
[B]   92–2829
                                         CIP
                                       MN

First Edition

10 9 8 7 6 5 4 3 2 1

Dedicated to my
Be-Bop Baby,
Patty Romanowski Bashe.
For everything.

Acknowledgments

Between this book's inception in summer 1988 and completion in fall 1989, I was fortunate to benefit from many people's cooperation. I'd like to thank them here.

For research assistance above and beyond the call of duty: Irving Adelman, Marcia Blackman, Loretta Kelleher, Margaret Cincotta, Iris Quigley, and Kris Rus of the East Meadow Library reference department, who tirelessly retrieved microfilm and periodicals; Marcy Zuckerman, Nassau County Library System; New York Public Library, including Reading Room; Lincoln Center for the Performing Arts Research Center's Music Division, Theatre Collection, and Rodgers & Hammerstein Archives of Recorded Sound; Beverly Taylor, Hollywood High School Library; Ronald L. Becker, Rutgers University Libraries; Museum of Broadcasting; and B. George, Archive of Contemporary Music.

Also: Jeffrey P. Kranzdorf; Susan Bluttman, formerly of the Disney Channel; Paul Grein, *Billboard* magazine; Tina Hopkinson and Jim Schumacher, EMI Records; Bill Inglot, Rhino Records; John Koenig and Jeff Tamarkin, *Goldmine* magazine; Andy McKaie, MCA Records; Bill Peterson, American Federation of Musicians; Tim Rogers, PolyGram Records; David Schwartz, *Mix* magazine; Bill Hathaway, Record Research; Lloyd and Stu, Mr. Cheapo Record Exchange; Fred Kaplan, Memory Lane Records; Lewis Lorenz, Esq.; Russ Wapensky; David Peck; Mary MacDonald and Jann S. Wenner of *Rolling Stone* magazine; and for his musical expertise, George Constantine Ploska.

A great deal of appreciation is due the following persons for consenting to speak with me. Listed alphabetically they are: Eric Anderson, Oscar Arslanian, Parley Baer, John Beland, Bruce Belland, Dick Bensfield, Shelly Berger, Peter Bogdanovich, Ivan Bonar, Dick Bremerkamp, Charley Britt, Al Brown, Jr., Jack Brumley, Tom Brumley, Dave Burgess, Alberta Burnette, Billy Burnette, Thurley Burnette, Ronnie Burns, Paul Cameron, Joe Campbell, Pete Candoli, Hubcap Carter, Stephen Chambers, Lorrie Collins, Mary Jo Collins, Georgeann Crewe, Mary Jane Croft, Richard Cromelin, Mike Curb, Charles Bud Dant, Bill Davenport, John Davis, Fred DeCordova, Don Defore, Jud DeNaut, Marti Ditonto, Steve Duncan, Jack Ellena, Bob Ellison, Robert Emmett, Frenchy Falik, Douglas B. Feaver, Kenneth Ferguson, John Fogerty, Pete Fornatale, Allen Fox, Sandy Friedman, Richie Frost, Jerry Fuller, Gene Garf, Peter Garrison, Larry Geller, Mr. and Mrs. Ben Gershman, Leonard Goldenson, Vincente Gomez, Billy Gray, Ty Grimes, John Guedel, Jack Halloran, Willard B. Hansen, Glen D. Hardin, Dotty Harmony, Iris Harris, Dick Heckmann, Bill Hollingshead, Bill Hoyt, Sally Hughes, Holly Humphreys, Walter Hutchinson, Jack Iannarelli, James Intveld, Plas Johnson, Ray Johnson, Allen Kemp, Barney Kessel, Karl Kindberg, Baker Knight, Glen Larson, Greg Leach, Don Lewis, Bob Lock, Stephen Love, Robin Luke, Neal Matthews, Billy May, Randy Meisner, Lee Miller, Scotty Moore,

Dave Morgan, Sean Morgan, David Morse, Richard Nader, Phyllis Neal, Al Nelson, Connie Nelson, Deanna Nelson, George Nelson, Rich Nelson, Robert Nelson, Gary Olsen, Joe Osborn, Earl Palmer, Carl Perkins, Bill Pitman, Bill Putnam, Patricia Reed, Barbra Reinecke, Howard Roberts, Bunny Robyn, Larry Rogers, Johnny Rotella, Mark Sandrich, Jr., Richard Schnyder, Esther Schuster, Patrick Shanahan, Del Shannon, Greg Shaw, Sister Zita Marie, David Skepner, Hal Smith, Joanie Sommers, James Stacy, Joan Staley, Gordon Stoker, Alvin Stoller, Bill Straw, George Stuart, Mike Sullivan, Joe Sutton, Lyle Talbot, Miles Thomas, Eddie Tuduri, Pat Upton, Randolph Van Scoyk, Jack Wagner, Ray Walker, Ed Ward, Duane West, Paul West, Jay White, Stephanie Wolfberg, Anita Young and Skip Young.

While all were very helpful, James Burton, Alan Bush, Jimmie Haskell, Paul Rose, Sharon Sheeley, Dennis (Larden) Sarokin, and David Nelson must be singled out for their insight and generosity of time.

I am especially grateful to Rick's friend and manager, Greg McDonald, and to his devoted cousin and former manager, Willy Nelson.

Finally, very special thanks to my editor, Bob Miller; his assistant, Mary Ann Naples; Nancy Nicholas, who understood Rick's importance and first shared my vision of a book about his life; my agent, Sarah Lazin; Sarah's assistants Meg Jeffrey and Laura Nolan; Holly George-Warren; Jed Mattes; Leila Barconey; Colleen Swank; Robert and Rochelle Bashe; and the late Evelyn Bashe.

About the Author

Philip Bashe has authored or coauthored the books *You Don't Have to Die: One Family's Guide to Surviving Childhood Cancer; That's Not All Folks!; How to Keep the Children You Love Off Drugs; Dee Snider's Teenage Survival Guide; Heavy Metal Thunder;* the *Rolling Stone Rock Almanac;* and the forthcoming *Dog Days: The New York Yankees' Fall From Grace and Eventual Redemption.* A former magazine editor-writer and radio announcer, he lives with his wife, author Patricia Romanowski, and son Justin in Baldwin, New York.

Contents

Preface

I was a generation too young to appreciate Rick Nelson in his commercial prime. By the time I became aware of him in the early 1970s, the onetime child star and teenage idol's rock & roll records had stopped selling, his film career was behind him, and *The Adventures of Ozzie and Harriet*, the television series in which he'd starred with his family from 1952 to 1966, was in syndicated reruns.

What drew me to this musician on the comeback trail was his valiant determination to remain a vital, contemporary artist. Most stars from his era, the so-called Golden Age of Rock & Roll, either had been forced into retirement a decade earlier or now recycled their moldy hits at revival shows. Having witnessed one or two of these memoryfests, it struck me that it wasn't so much the music that needed reviving as the performers, most of whom sounded passionless and seemed obsolete.

Then there was Rick, refusing to be led to pasture, driven to recapture his winning form. His efforts were impeded, however, by the public's deeply ingrained image of him as the wholesome kid brother and teenage singer they had watched grow up on TV. This image, distorted over time, now seemed laughably incompatible with early-1970s' rock music and its culture.

In 1972 Rick wrote and recorded the autobiographical "Garden Party," a true recounting of a concert where the audience had jeered him for looking and sounding different from the Rick Nelson they knew, the Rick Nelson of their pasts. He expressed what the painful experience taught him in the song's stirring refrain: "You can't please everyone, so you got to please yourself."

"Garden Party," Rick's first hit in nearly a decade, sold several million copies. What moved listeners even more than its gentle country gait was the singer's resoluteness and integrity, not to mention his sheer nerve, expressed in the line, "If memories were all I sang, I'd rather drive a truck." That song succinctly and powerfully expressed the philosophy that guided Rick's four-decade career as one of rock & roll's most unlikely, yet enduring, stars.

The third-generation scion of a wealthy show-business family, Rick's roots were light-years from those of his rockabilly favorites—Elvis Presley, Carl Perkins, Johnny Cash, Jerry Lee Lewis— whose music he and millions of other teenagers grew up with. The most obvious difference between Rick and other fans is that while they may have sung at local talent shows, Rick, beginning at sixteen, made records and lip-synced them on his parents' television show for a weekly home audience of eighteen million.

His auspicious circumstances and his dreamboat looks often obscured Rick's considerable talent and led some to unfairly label him a fraud. In fact, Rick was a genuine rock & roll hero who never placed profit above artistic fulfillment. This was no less true late in his life when his bitter, protracted divorce from Kris Harmon Nelson left him in financial ruin.

Although the onetime star enjoyed only a handful of hits after 1965, Rick stubbornly sidestepped trends and created the music he believed in, whether his records sold or not and whether he performed in front of thousands or hundreds. On December 31, 1985, he was on his way to play yet another one-nighter—the last of some two hundred fifty that year—when a fire broke out aboard his private plane, killing Rick, his fiancée, and five others.

Strong-willed professionally, in his private life Rick was passive and reserved, the loyal son of a domineering, ambitious father. Ozzie Nelson, creator and star of an unprecedented radio and television dynasty, directed Rick not only on *The Adventures* but offcamera as well, and was the most influential person in his life. Rick felt forever torn between his devotion to Ozzie and his desperate need to establish an identity separate from father and family. He became an escape artist, always seeking his independence—from Ozzie; from an unhappy marriage; from celebrityhood; from adulthood, which Rick resisted like Peter Pan by singing rock & roll; and most of all from the Boy Next Door image that plagued him through the years.

Despite his five decades in the American consciousness, Rick's story has never been fully told. A performer from the age of eight, he cherished his privacy. For Rick it was as much one of life's staples as hamburgers and his beloved Sun Records 45s. Thus he has remained misunderstood, enigmatic, and the subject of countless factual inaccuracies even after his death.

The most glaring misconception is that because Rick wound up performing in comparative isolation, he died bitter and unhappy. Perhaps it would be understandable if he had, but it is not true. Serene and basically secure, Rick had lived with waxing and waning popularity his entire adult life and did not measure his self-worth by public acceptance. Although his career's destination was uncertain at the time of his death, for Rick the journey was satisfying enough.

To me and to many others, the real misfortune is the perpetuation of that tragic-figure image and Rick's shamefully unsung role in popular-music history. In the 1950s he recorded some of the era's most vibrant rockabilly sides, and through his family's TV series introduced more Americans to rock & roll than anyone except possibly Elvis Presley. In the 1970s his Stone Canyon Band joined the vanguard of the country-rock movement, one of that decade's dominant trends.

Threads of unfulfilled promise run through Rick's forty-five years, but these are overshadowed by his many accomplishments: his approximately sixty million records sold; his posthumous election to the Rock & Roll Hall of Fame; his twenty-two years on radio and television in one of the most culturally influential programs of its time; and his four children, three of whom now follow in his footsteps professionally.

Certainly his death at such an early age was a tragedy. Yet even though The Road ultimately killed him, it was where Rick most wanted to be, doing what brought him the greatest contentment he knew, making music. To the end, this escape artist eluded fans' expectations and made good on the promise pledged in "Garden Party": He pleased himself.

Prologue

Something's wrong. Like the instant cameras discharging—*pop!-zhirr*—all over New York's Madison Square Garden, the thought flashed through his mind.

Leaning into the mike, head cocked, Rick Nelson howled a relatively obscure blues number he'd once recorded, "My Babe." Though his eyes were closed in concentration, he felt from the audience a chill as hard and cold as the steel strings of his electric guitar.

With a few measures to catch his breath, Rick glanced at lead guitarist Allen Kemp, whose eyes met his as if to say, What the hell is going on? The three other members of his Stone Canyon Band were all hunched over their instruments, seemingly oblivious. Rick replied with an imperceptible shrug and returned his gaze to the fans completely surrounding the stage, positioned like the hole in the center of one of Rick's many million-selling 45s.

In an arena as vast as the Garden, peering out into the crowd is like looking up into a nighttime sky: absolute darkness broken by shimmering constellations of lit matches and those damn blinding flashbulbs. All you can make out are the first several rows, and as Rick scanned their faces he read disappointment, disbelief, and dismay.

Something's wrong. The audience of twenty thousand had already reached the same conclusion. They'd packed every seat for this nostalgic evening of rock & roll oldies. It was 1971, and the golden era being celebrated the late 1950s and early 1960s, when Rick, then teenage Ricky, was rock's crown prince to Elvis Presley's king, scoring a staggering twenty-seven Top Twenty singles.

So why, the fans wanted to know, wasn't he singing his old hits? Lord knows, Rick could have filled several hours onstage with nothing but. Acquiescing to the evening's spirit, he'd opened with his debut recording, 1957's "I'm Walkin'," and followed it with "Be-Bop Baby," a song now so foreign to him that he'd had to relearn it note by note during rehearsals.

From there the set had proceeded chronologically: "Poor Little Fool," from 1958, when Eisenhower occupied the White House and the New York Yankees held an annual monopoly on World Series pennants; "Hello Mary Lou," from 1961, when Kennedy was boldly leading the country into the New Frontier and Cold War paranoia raged. Each song met with enthusiastic clapping and excited female squeals, a momentary return to when Rick's fans screamed so loudly that he could scarcely hear himself sing.

The final chords of "My Babe" shimmered through the Garden and the group quietly struck up "She Belongs to Me." Rick's 1969 hit interpretation of this Bob Dylan song had broken a five-year dry spell, but its introductory notes elicited only a smattering of applause. As the singer-songwriter chiefly responsible for transforming rock & roll into a more literary and politically conscious medium, Dylan was no favorite of this crowd (although, coincidentally, this night he happened to be hidden in it). The fans, mostly in their twenties and thirties, had come to hear musical memories evoking simpler times of puppy love, sock hops, and hot rods. Rick had betrayed them.

More than most performing arts, rock & roll trades on the interplay between musician and spectator, turning both into participants. When artist and audience connect, notes seem to ricochet from the stage to the far wall and back again, sweeping up the musicians. But when that connection fails, sounds hang limply in midair, as if projected into a vacuum. The physical act of playing becomes laborious. Painful. The drummer's wrists ache, and the guitarist's fingertips sting.

The singer's burden is analogous to transmitting messages that dissipate before reaching their destination. He feels removed from the words leaving his lips, as if he were somewhere else. Certainly in the middle of "She Belongs to Me," with the audience unmistakably displeased, Rick wished he were anyplace else but on that stage.

There was more to the crowd's antagonism, though, than repertoire. Not only didn't their Ricky sound the same, he didn't look the same. The other acts had costumed themselves appropriately in ancient artifacts: penny loafers, cardigans, sparkling lamé. Women lacquered their hair until it could deflect bullets; men combed theirs into heavy, glistening pompadours. But Rick refused to look the part of a wax-museum figure. Instead he wore bell-bottom pants and a livid purple rhinestone-embroidered Western shirt that glowed iridescently under the stage lights.

Then there was his hair. His hair. *His hair.*

As America's favorite child actor since Shirley Temple, he'd worn it in a distinctively skewed crewcut; and later, as a rock & roll idol, moderate in length, neatly side-parted and lifted off his forehead. Now, in keeping with the times, Rick's dark locks brushed his shoulders, partially obscuring his flawlessly sculpted face, and further confounding those fans who hadn't followed his (and its) growth since both they and Rick escaped adolescence.

For the finale, Rick hoisted off his electric guitar and sat down at a grand piano. Adjusting the microphone, he announced, "We'd like to do one of the greatest rock & roll songs ever written . . ." The audience stirred in its seats while taking a silent inventory of his many records. Apparently the boy had come to his senses.

". . . the Rolling Stones' 'Honky Tonk Women.'"

The heckling and hissing ensued.

How ironic that Rick should choose to invoke *their* name and to perform *their* recent music: Had it not been for the Stones and other English groups such as the Beatles, the performers on tonight's bill—Chuck Berry, Bobby Rydell, Bo Diddley, the Shirelles, the Coasters, and Gary U.S. Bonds—might not be regarded as relics from a bygone era. This was no less true for Rick, displaced along with the rest of them by the mid-1960s "British Invasion."

Rick nailed "Honky Tonk Women" to a close. His eyes still on the piano keys, he heard the boos, first a mere ripple in back. Then it surged forward like a wave toward the shore, building in intensity. To appease the crowd, instead of introducing his band members as planned, Rick slung the guitar back on and rushed into "Travelin' Man," a number-one smash from 1961. Then he quickly left the stage.

Back in the dressing room Rick sat dejectedly on a wooden bench, his hands braced on either side of him, shaking his head. "I knew I shouldn't have come here," he mumbled. Rick had resisted oldies programs for years, but the opportunity to play the Garden for the first time in front of twenty thousand people had seduced him, and he was angry at himself.

The catcalls? Rick could endure them, just as he had the cancellation of his family's TV series in 1966 and the downward spiral his recording and acting careers had taken since then.

What truly bewildered him was the audience's implicit warning that they would accept him not as he was but only as he had been. But of course Rick wasn't Ricky anymore; he was a thirty-one-year-old husband and father with greater aspirations than peddling memories.

Rick sat on that hard bench for a long time before slipping out a side door into the brisk night air.

When I was a young boy,
My mama told me, "Son,
You gotta keep it together,
You know you're the only one."
So I tried to see the sunshine,
And tried to feel the rain,
But I just couldn't get it together,
I was feelin' too much pain.

So I got myself a guitar
When I was just a kid.
I played rock & roll music
And I'm so glad I did.

—*FROM "GYPSY PILOT,"*
BY RICK NELSON

One

The hostile Madison Square Garden crowd, like most of us, knew Rick as part of "America's Favorite Family," to quote *The Adventures of Ozzie and Harriet*'s opening credits. For three decades, on radio and television, the blissful, strifeless Nelson household stood as an archetype against which we measured our own and inevitably found ours wanting. But not even the Nelsons could live up to their portrayal. They were, in fact, the antithesis of domestic normality: a show-business family. It was only on the set of their long-running series that Ozzie, Harriet, David, and Rick could act as the "average" nuclear unit.

The Nelson performing tradition, now in its fourth generation, had begun at the turn of the century with Rick's paternal grandparents, George and Ethel. George Waldemar Nelson, a bank clerk, was also an amateur thespian and song-and-dance

1

man, well known around his New Jersey hometown as "Jersey City's Honey Boy" (nicknamed after Welsh-born blackface minstrel-show star "Honey Boy" Evans). Son of Swedes Anders Magnus Nelson and Anna L. Johnson, and the first of his clan born in the United States, George entertained at local minstrel shows, which is where he met his wife to be.

Petite Brooklynite Ethel Irene Orr, the last of Jackson and Mary (Wright) Orr's nine children, sang in a startlingly husky voice and energetically played ragtime piano. Rick always said that his own syncopated keyboard style was a combination of rhythm & blues great Ray Charles's and his grandmother's. Soon after they met, George and Ethel were singing duets on stage as "Nelson and Orr," and in a pattern that would be repeated with Rick's parents, professional ties led to marital ties. On March 4, 1903, Nelson and Orr became Nelson and Nelson.

The second of their three sons, Oswald George, better known as Ozzie, was born in Jersey City on March 20, 1906. He, his parents, and his two-year-old brother, Alfred, lived in a narrow two-story house on Virginia Avenue. Today tumbledown dwellings and abandoned, burned-out shells infest the once middle-class neighborhood. The Statue of Liberty, clearly visible to the east, seems to taunt the impoverished, predominately minority, population. But to the George Nelson family and to the ethnic mix that comprised Jersey City in the early 1900s, she stood for unlimited opportunity.

The promise the statue represented remained with Ozzie long after the family moved to Ridgefield Park, New Jersey, in 1911. Located just across the Hudson River from Manhattan, the town is still a picture postcard of suburban America, with tranquil, shady streets and a pervasive sense of community and national pride. On holidays George always unfurled an American flag across the front porch of the Nelsons' three-story shingled Gothic house.

Ozzie's childhood home was as warm and loving as the one he later depicted on *The Adventures of Ozzie and Harriet*. Music

2

and acting both played a big part in Nelson domestic life. Before his sons reached their teens, George conscripted them into the *olio*: theatrical parlance for the minstrel-show segment in which performers sang downstage, in front of the curtain, between acts. With Ethel accompanying them on piano, George, Ozzie, and Alfred put on skits and warbled popular tunes as the Four Nelsons.

A voracious reader, Ozzie dog-eared copies of *David Copperfield, Tommy Tiptop*, the Rover Boys, and especially Horatio Alger's rags-to-riches boys' stories. The latter's recurring theme of infinite possibility had an immense impact on him, as it did on such young men as Henry Ford, David Sarnoff, John D. Rockefeller, George Eastman, and Thomas Edison. That they and Ozzie all wound up millionaires might be coincidence. Then again, maybe not: for the honesty and virtue of Alger's protagonists weren't their only rewards, but were usually supplemented by cash.

Though the public would come to know Ozzie as the indolent, bumbling father he played on the air, in reality he displayed Algeresque drive and ambition his entire life. In addition to becoming the youngest American Eagle Scout on record at thirteen, Ozzie went on to excel in scholastics, debating, cartooning, and sports. Fellow students at Ridgefield Park High School sensed his potential, captioning his 1923 senior yearbook picture, "All things are possible to a willing heart."

Ozzie followed his brother Alfred to all-male Rutgers University in New Brunswick, New Jersey. "He was very popular, one of the big men on campus," said David Morse, Class of 1929. Ozzie belonged to the prestigious Ivy Club fraternity, quartered in a handsome house on Rutgers's ivy-covered campus. His roommate, Alfred G. Brown, Jr., today a retired Navy Commander, remembered Ozzie as "just the grandest guy, with all kinds of ability."

Brown and Morse both describe a basically serious student. "Very straight and frank," said Morse, who went on to a distinguished law career, "and very much his own man." It's a charac-

3

terization borne out by yearbook photographs of Ozzie the undergrad. In every one his somber face seems to stand out from the others. He sits rigidly, spine ramrod straight, gazing not at the camera but above it, as if setting his sights on the future.

Despite weighing a slight one hundred thirty pounds, Ozzie played running back and quarterback at Rutgers, where football was central to campus life. The school's battle cry, "I'd die for dear old Rutgers," was attributed to a Class of 1895 fullback named Frank Kingsley Grant, who allegedly broke his leg on a play, limped to the sidelines, lit a cigarette, and uttered heroically, "I'd die to win this game."

Such fanatical dedication, whether factual or not, suited the five-foot-nine Ozzie as snugly as his scarlet jersey and knickers. To him, football wasn't merely a game, it was a metaphor for life itself, and would continue to be. Speaking at a dinner honoring a local high school's championship football team in 1926, he told the young players, "As in football, life is full of possibilities and chances. It is the man that takes advantage of these that will eventually succeed in the game of life."

Ozzie was two months from completing his Bachelor of Letters degree in literature when his strapping father had to be hospitalized with Paget's disease, a rare and painful form of chronic bone cancer he'd been battling for three years. Forty-seven-year-old George Nelson finally succumbed to complications a few weeks later, with Ozzie at his New York Hospital bedside. Cruelly, the date was March 20, 1927, Ozzie's twenty-first birthday; furthermore, Ethel had only recently given birth to a third son, Donald.

Though devastated, Ozzie assumed responsibility for his mother and newborn brother. To help meet tuition at the New Jersey Law School, he headed a dance band comprised of five other Rutgers alumni. Ozzie played only passable banjo and saxophone, and had once been rejected by the university glee club, but he was a natural leader and organizer. It was these abilities, more than musical or comedic talent, upon which Ozzie

4

would build his phenomenal entertainment career. Even then his need to exert control was evident.

The sextet proved highly successful, performing five or more nights a week at parties, proms, and debutante balls. "He even played in a speakeasy," recalled David Morse. "The kids from Rutgers snuck there to dance and to have a glass of beer, which was the deviltry at the time." During music breaks Ozzie pulled up a chair on the bandstand and completed his law-school assignments for the next day.

Thanks to commercial radio, by the early 1920s Americans could hear their favorite jazz orchestras at home by tuning in to live remote broadcasts from elegant ballrooms such as the Avalon in Chicago and the Palomar in Los Angeles. Ozzie was a great fan of these popular dance-music shows. One night in 1930 he sat listening to *Roemer's Homers,* sponsored by the Rudolf Roemer Furniture Company on New York's WMCA.

A rival bandleader's dreadful voice set him to thinking, *Even I can sing better than that.* "I have a funny quirk in my character," he said when he was twenty-seven, "I always think I can do anything anyone else can." Soon he was presiding over the program every Sunday at 7:00 P.M.

Liberally borrowing its sound and style from Rudy Vallee's Connecticut Yankees, the Nelson Orchestra became an immediate favorite. Ozzie shamelessly crooned through a megaphone, a Vallee trademark, promoted his Rutgers association the way Vallee touted his with Yale, and substituted a cheery "Hello there, everybody!" for Vallee's "Heigh-ho, everybody!" With his collegiate good looks, thick, wavy, russet brown hair, and shy, boyish smile, Ozzie even resembled Vallee, a fortuitous coincidence he freely exploited.

In 1931 Ozzie's group won a New York *Daily Mirror* contest to determine the most popular local dance band. First prize was a June-to-September stint at the Glen Island Casino, the legendary "cradle of name bands." Tommy and Jimmy Dorsey, Charlie Barnet, Glenn Miller, Woody Herman, and Les Brown all got their starts there; Ozzie preceded them.

5

A sprawling, southern-style building, the Casino sat perched on the edge of the Long Island Sound. Inside were soft lights, tiny tables, and room for one thousand. The actual audience was far greater, including the small boats that moored just outside the sea wall, where the music spilled over the water and was carried out on the night air. Add to that countless listeners picking up the live nationwide broadcasts.

Opening night brought out luminaries such as bandleaders Vallee, Paul Whiteman, Fred Waring, and Vincent Lopez. By evening's end Ozzie had a record contract with Jack Kapp's Brunswick label. The summer wasn't over before his rendition of "I Still Get a Thrill (Thinking of You)" became a national top-ten seller and the first of thirty-eight chart hits for the Nelson orchestra over the next ten years.

Ozzie had recently earned his Bachelor of Law degree, but the prerequisite for taking the state bar exam was one year's clerking in a law office. George Nelson had always told his boys, "Work for yourselves and start as close to the top as you can." A bandleader, Ozzie reckoned, got to do both. Plus, here he was, not yet twenty-five, and earning more money than most attorneys; even more than a Supreme Court Justice. So he continued with his now eight-man group, assuring family and friends that once all this heady musical success ended—as he believed it inevitably would—he would settle down and resume his law career.

Ozzie never did get around to sitting for that exam.

On New Year's Eve 1932, he was booked at Manhattan's famous Hollywood Restaurant, located at Broadway and Forty-eighth Street. During Prohibition the cabaret was popular with the hip-flask crowd and with the federal agents who charged in there to arrest them. For the price of dinner, club-goers were treated to a lavish revue featuring gorgeous showgirls and chorus girls. So many revelers were expected at the Hollywood this particular night, its manager rented the larger Edison Hotel Grand Ballroom. There Ozzie first met Harriet Hilliard.

She too came from a musical-theatrical background, but her

parents were professionals. Hilliard was the middle name of her father, Roy Snyder, son of onetime Hagenbeck-Wallace Circus general manager Jacob Snyder and his wife, Ella Harris Snyder. Roy, born in Wooster, Ohio, got his show-business start in 1898 as a three-dollar-a-week prop boy with the W. B. Patton repertory company. Within four years he graduated to stage manager and as Roy E. Hilliard went on to star in and to direct stock-theater companies throughout the Midwest.

One of those companies, the North Brothers Stock Company, based in Topeka, Kansas, launched the stage careers of Pat O'Brien, Ralph Bellamy, Warner Baxter, and many other esteemed actors. Its female lead at the turn of the century was a soft-featured, doe-eyed Iowa girl nine years Roy Hilliard's junior, Hazel Dell McNutt.

"Repertory-company actors had to commit to memory about twenty plays and be able to play any one of them on a moment's notice," explained actor Lyle Talbot, who in the 1920s performed opposite Hazel and Roy in the Winninger Brothers Repertory Company and, coincidentally, later played meddlesome neighbor Joe Randolph on *The Adventures of Ozzie and Harriet.* "There were probably three or four hundred of these traveling companies, mostly in the Midwest, because there wasn't much other entertainment in rural places."

As had happened to George and Ethel Nelson, the professional relationship between the North Brothers' leading man and woman turned personal, and Hazel became Mrs. Roy Hilliard. Their only child, Peggy Louise—later known to the world as Harriet—was born at the McNutt home on July 18, 1909.

She was just six weeks old when she made her theatrical debut, carried on stage by actor Harry Minturn in a Western comedy called *Heir to the Hoorah.* At age three Peggy Lou notched her first speaking role, in *Mrs. Wiggs of the Cabbage Patch,* and after that continued to appear in various productions with her parents.

From ages five through sixteen she attended public and pri-

7

vate schools in Kansas City, Missouri, while the Hilliards tripped the boards across the heartland. She spent most of those years at St. Agnes Academy, established at the turn of the century as a convent boarding school for working-class girls, many from underprivileged homes. At Christmas and during the summer, while the other students returned home to their families, Peggy Lou went on tour with hers.

"She was beautiful," remembered Lyle Talbot, who first met the teenager when she visited her parents on the road. A long-distance love affair developed between the two. "My parents were also actors and were in companies with Roy and Hazel Hilliard, so our families knew each other and thought that she and I might become an item. We started a romance by correspondence." This lasted until Talbot went to Hollywood and became one of film's steadiest-working actors.

Peggy Lou's upbringing was hardly conventional, but Hazel did her best to make the Hilliards' nomadic life as normal as possible. Harriet once recalled: "With us on every tour went the little trunk with our own pictures, handmade doilies, flower vases, and bedspreads that were really ours," to render the anonymous rooming-house and hotel rooms more homey. "Whenever we got into a new town, these were the first things we unpacked."

This illusion of a normal, stable home ended in 1925 when the Hilliards permanently separated, though, oddly, they never divorced. "In those days, a husband and wife could generally get jobs in the same company," said Lyle Talbot, "because it was always cheaper to hire a couple. But sometimes they couldn't, so Roy and Hazel worked in different companies. They weren't estranged from each other, it was just that kind of relationship."

Mother and daughter moved to New York, where after school Peggy Lou pursued acting. Along the way, she adopted the stage name Harriet Hilliard. So it appeared in the playbill to her Broadway bow at seventeen: playing the "Charleston maid" in *The Blonde Sinner,* a "Smart Farce With Music in Three Acts,"

8

staged atop the New Amsterdam Theatre. At the same time, she studied with ballet master Chester Hale and danced in the line of his New York's Capitol Theatre Corps de Ballet.

Able to sing, dance, and act, versatile Harriet was a natural for vaudeville, that popular form of American entertainment. Joseph (Jack) Doncourt had been a leading vaudevillian in the early 1900s, and a generation later his comedian son Ken was successfully following in his footsteps under the last name Murray. Two shows a day, seven days a week, Harriet played his straight woman, a professional role she would spend most of her career perfecting. In addition to Murray, Harriet also worked opposite actor Bert Lahr in the *Harry Carrol Revue* and with comic-actor Danny Duncan in, of all things, a family situation-comedy sketch.

But Harriet was an ascending talent in an art form on the wane. Vaudeville's death knell had been sounded in 1927 by the coming of talking motion pictures. Like vultures swooping down upon a carcass, film studios snatched stage stars from this rich talent pool. Universal Pictures signed Harriet and cast her in a short titled *Musical Justice,* forgettable to most viewers but not to Ozzie Nelson.

If Ozzie had been impressed by Harriet Hilliard on screen, he was bowled over when he saw her in person at the Edison Ballroom, emceeing the New Year's Eve extravaganza. Always quick to recognize opportunity, Ozzie wanted to hire her on the spot, figuring that the novelty of a girl singer would distinguish his orchestra from the competition. Through a mutual friend, artist Ham Fisher (creator of the *Joe Palooka* comic strip), introductions were made one night in 1932 at the Hollywood Restaurant, and over lunch at Sardi's the next day Ozzie persuaded Harriet to join his band at less than the $150 a week she was earning at the Hollywood.

Like most entertainers Ozzie possessed a healthy ego, but one of his strengths was acknowledging his weaknesses, among

9

them his voice. When he allowed his resonant tenor to flow freely, it was quite appealing. Too often, though, he affected the rounded tones and vibrato of his idol Rudy Vallee and sounded reedy and strained. No songster herself, Harriet chirped more than sang but compensated for her technical shortcomings with charm and good humor. "We each have some talent," Ozzie told her. "I sing pretty good with a bad voice, and you sing pretty bad with a good voice. Put us together, and we're a team." If they couldn't do justice to torchy ballads, they could sing "cute songs," as he called them, "trick stuff." He had in mind the very type of boy-girl duet his parents had trilled in turn-of-the-century minstrel shows.

For a personalized touch, Ozzie composed many of these specialty numbers himself, such as "Hey, Hey, Harriet." He had a weakness for wordy titles ("I'm Looking for a Guy Who Plays Alto and Baritone and Doubles on a Clarinet and Wears a Size 37 Suit") and coy humor. The couple developed a natural onstage rapport and incorporated comical, lyrical banter into the tunes, such as this exchange from "As Long as You're Not in Love With Anyone Else, Why Don't You Fall in Love With Me":

OZZIE: Would you like to go out on Friday? I've got tickets for the fight.

HARRIET: Oh, I'm getting married Friday; how about Saturday night?

OZZIE: You know, I can tell at a glance that I'm using the wrong approach. I'm not being taken seriously.

HARRIET: Oh, you're being taken all right, only you don't know it.

It was to be the basis of their comedy for the next forty years; Ozzie playing the earnest, perplexed foil, and Harriet the relentless but always playful tease.

Now numbering fourteen, the Nelson orchestra had developed into a relatively well-regarded pre–Swing Era Big Band.

Ozzie took no exception to the common critical descriptions "suave swing" and "middle of the road," for his music was deliberately sedate, characterized by tidy ensemble playing, muted trumpets, soothing woodwinds, and cautious rhythms.

"It was music for the old folks to dance to," explained first trumpeter Holly Humphreys, who joined the orchestra the same day as Harriet in 1932. "Ozzie used to call it 'going-to-the-grocery-store tempo': *ump-chink, ump-chink.*" With the country mired in the Great Depression, Ozzie intuitively sensed that the Roaring Twenties' frantic tempos and celebratory tunes were inappropriate. Still, he was intrigued by the hot jazz sounds bubbling out of Harlem's Cotton Club and other uptown night-spots. A song archivist with impeccable taste, Ozzie occasionally set his musicians loose on some surprisingly adventurous rhythm & blues, such as the frenzied, risqué "Reefer Man," which he sang in mock black dialect.

The band became a fixture at the Hotel New Yorker's swank Terrace Restaurant. Ozzie, dapper in a midnight blue dinner jacket, would close his eyes and sway to the beat as he wielded the baton, while at a downstage microphone "the lovely Miss Hilliard" quickened the pulses of the men clustered before the bandstand. Petite but well proportioned, Harriet stood five foot four and a half in heels, had penetrating blue-gray eyes, a porcelain complexion, cheeks rouged a soft raspberry, and blond hair worn in an elegant bun. Prominent newspaper columnist Nils T. Granlund cited her as "the perfect example of showgirl beauty."

In September 1933 the couple added another facet to their career when the NBC radio network signed them to provide the music for *The Baker's Broadcast*, a weekly half-hour comedy sponsored by Standard Brands. The first of its three hosts was the popular Joe Penner, a short, squat Hungarian-born comic with a globular head, which he topped with a derby and plugged with a cigar. He is best remembered for one line, "Wanna buy

11

a duck?" delivered when least expected and, inexplicably, always to explosive laughter.

During summer hiatus, Ozzie, Harriet, and their musicians took to the road, playing everything from automobile dealerships, to showboats, to dilapidated roadhouses where collecting the evening's percentages from unscrupulous owners could prove hazardous. Once, at a Batavia, New York, "dance hall"— actually a grease-stained garage in which a tiny bandstand had been erected—the two gangsterish brothers running the joint refused to hand over the orchestra's $1,200 fee.

"I suggest you boys pay us what you owe us," Ozzie said loftily, "unless you want to be blacklisted with the union." Although he was referring to the musicians' union, the pair thought he meant the violent Black Hand of the Mafia. They glanced at each other wide-eyed and quickly paid Ozzie in cash, as several menacing accomplices looked on. It wasn't until the bandleader had ambled out the door, puzzled by their abrupt change of heart, that the two thugs realized they'd been conned.

Ozzie, Harriet, and the band's baggage man raced off in a Marmon 16, with the hoodlums in hot pursuit. At least, that's what Ozzie thought when he saw a pair of fast-gaining headlights in his rearview mirror. Spotting a dirt road ahead, he cut his lights, jerked the steering wheel and plowed into a cornfield, just as the other car streaked by. The three of them huddled inside until daylight, then proceeded to the next "jump," in Buffalo.

By now, Ozzie and Harriet's time spent together had changed their relationship. Initially it had been strictly business. Not once during her first six months in the band did Ozzie so much as offer to drive her home from work. "We were just friends," Harriet later said. "Then we became close friends, and then we discovered it was a little difficult to do without one another." The problem was Harriet was already married.

When she was twenty-one and on the vaudeville circuit, Harriet had become the second wife of her partner Roy Sedley, a little-remembered vaudevillian with a penchant for wedding

12

female entertainers more famous than he and for dropping his pants in search of laughs. That, it seems, ended Sedley's brief union with Harriet. According to this 1933 story in the New York *Daily Mirror,* " 'Striped Panties Killed Romance,' Dancer Declares":

> It was Roy Sedley's "awning-striped" underwear that disrupted her married life, Harriet Hilliard Sedley, star dancer and singer with Ozzie Nelson's orchestra at the Hotel New Yorker, said yesterday after filing a suit for annulment . . .
>
> "The underwear was terrible," she told a *Daily Mirror* reporter. "It wouldn't have been so bad, perhaps, if he hadn't insisted upon displaying it whenever he could. Why, we'd have company . . . and he'd peel off his clothes and run around in those terrible striped things. They got a laugh—but not from me."

Harriet left the comic after just one year and in 1933 was granted an annulment, thanks to Ozzie's legal expertise. He'd found that as the guilty party in an earlier adultery decree, Sedley was legally forbidden from marrying again in New York State at the time he wed Harriet in the town of Solvay on August 19, 1930. (Sedley repeated this scheme with his third wife, comedienne Betty Kean, whom he illegally married in 1934. Before he got to kiss his new bride, she was in court filing papers.)

Even with Roy Sedley out of the way, Harriet rebuffed Ozzie's proposals for two years, worried that marriage might impede her career. And both were concerned about whether the public would accept them as man and wife.

On October 8, 1935, Harriet finally became Mrs. Ozzie Nelson, though she didn't officially discard Hilliard until the early 1950s. The small Tuesday-afternoon ceremony took place in Ethel Nelson's new home in Hackensack, New Jersey, amid white chrysanthemums, palms, and autumn foliage. Pressing career obligations postponed their honeymoon, however—for four years. Just five days after exchanging vows, Harriet was on a twenty-four-hour flight to Hollywood, to make her first feature film, RKO's *Follow the Fleet,* with Fred Astaire, Ginger Rogers, and Randolph Scott.

The three-month separation was hard on Harriet. "I hated it," she said. "I counted the days until I could join Ozzie." When it finally ended, she told her close friend Ginger Rogers, "I'm going home and having a baby." A month later she was pregnant.

For Harriet, 1936 was "the most fun year of our lives. It was a regular ball." She and Ozzie took a luxurious suite at the Hotel Lexington, having only to ride the elevator downstairs to work in the evening at the Silver Grill restaurant. When not performing around town or up and down the East Coast, the expectant couple still enjoyed New York's glamorous night-life, barely slowing down despite Harriet's condition.

David Ozzie Nelson was born on October 24, 1936, at Doctors Hospital in Manhattan. His parents named the ten-pound infant after press agent Dave Green, who'd sent the mother-to-be a furious telegram that read in part, "A fine way to louse up a motion-picture career."

Assisted by a nurse, a maid, and a driver, Harriet remained home with David only temporarily. Not that motherhood didn't fulfill her, but she was a determined career gal who'd worked hard to get where she was. Give it all up now? She couldn't, and by mid-December Harriet was singing alongside her husband again. However, when it came time to shoot *New Faces of 1937* and *Life of the Party* in Hollywood, she didn't know what to do.

After all, she'd been separated from her own mother as a child. But she'd survived and perhaps been made stronger by it. Ultimately Harriet decided to honor her contract, returning to California for three and a half months. Ozzie and the orchestra, meanwhile, were bound to New York and *The Baker's Broadcast,* now hosted by the fascinating Robert L. Ripley, world adventurer and originator of *Believe It Or Not.*

In 1937 NBC matched Ozzie and Harriet with cartoonist Feg Murray for a celebrity-interview program to broadcast from

Hollywood, which was fast replacing New York as the industry's capital. Since David was just an infant, and Harriet spent months filming on the West Coast anyway, it made sense to move there. So that September the Nelsons took the train to California and rented a Tudor-style house in North Hollywood. But *The Feg Murray Show* was canceled at season's end.

Without a regular radio program, Ozzie and Harriet went on the road again. Only things had changed. As the Swing Era progressed, its audience matured, now as interested in listening as in Lindying. The favored setting switched from dance hall to concert hall, and the bandleader's role changed too, from convivial entertainer to serious virtuoso. Benny Goodman, Glenn Miller, Artie Shaw, Duke Ellington, and Count Basie were each, at the very least, first-rate instrumentalists accompanied by only the finest players.

The Nelson Orchestra, and particularly Ozzie, simply could not compete on that level. Billy May, onetime trumpeter for Miller and Ozzie's bandleader in the mid-to-late 1940s, remarked of his abilities, "As a musician, Ozzie was a good lawyer." He and Harriet were reduced to playing up to four shows daily on the dwindling vaudeville circuit. Little blue-eyed, golden-haired David often accompanied his parents' troupe of jugglers, gymnasts, comics, tap dancers, and the like, and celebrated his second birthday on the road, in Columbus, Ohio.

In 1939 the Nelsons rented an apartment in Englewood, New Jersey, just blocks from Ozzie's brother Alfred, now a dentist. Ozzie's mother Ethel and baby brother Donald lived a short distance away, and Hazel Hilliard in the next building. Ozzie always remained exceptionally close to his family, and Harriet equally close to her mother. It was also convenient to live near relatives when you were pregnant, which Harriet was again.

Unable to work by her seventh month, she stayed home with David while Ozzie went on the road with vocalist Roseanne Stevens replacing Harriet. The baby, expected April 15, 1940, repeatedly missed its cue; twice Ozzie darted back home, only

15

to return to the Midwest both times without cigars for his band-mates. He was in Milwaukee when Harriet's labor began the morning of May 8, so Alfred Nelson rushed her to Holy Name Hospital in Teaneck, New Jersey, where he supervised the dental staff and his wife, Kay, worked as head nurse. A second son was born at 1:25 P.M.

Ozzie took Alfred's congratulatory phone call in his dressing room at the Riverside Theater, and he and Harriet named the child Eric Hilliard Nelson. This time press agent Dave Green hit the roof. "A second child," he told Harriet, "will put you out of business. This baby will positively wreck your career!" He couldn't have been more wrong.

Two

With Harriet having decided to remain in Englewood with her newborn son, Ozzie now assumed the role of absentee parent. Because of orchestra commitments, it was four days before he could first hold Eric, called Ricky from birth. And no sooner had the bandleader murmured tenderly into the boy's ear that he would one day carry the ball for dear old Rutgers than Ozzie was off on a jumbled summer-1940 itinerary: June, Chicago; August, Dallas; October, Syracuse.

To create some semblance of family life, the Nelsons purchased a rambling two-story Colonial on a wooded three-quarter acre in Tenafly, New Jersey. Ozzie also bought the charming nineteenth-century farmhouse next door, which he remodeled for his mother and thirteen-year-old brother, Donald. Hazel lived nearby, so whenever Harriet and David accompanied the band on jaunts, Rick had two grandmothers to care for him.

17

Despite Harriet's original intentions, the baby-faced Nelson's first year virtually duplicated his older brother's. Rick's first birthday party was thrown in San Rafael, California, attended by musicians and their wives. Even when his mother was home, servants basically ran the household anyway, although Harriet pointed out at the time, "I have to do all the thinking."

Today with dual-income families and children cared for by nannies or relatives or in day-care centers, this isn't unusual. But in the early 1940s, when only one in ten mothers worked outside the home, it was a highly unorthodox arrangement.

Six months after moving to the Tenafly house, three-fourths of the Nelsons were relocating to Hollywood again. NBC had offered Ozzie and Harriet a slot on *The Raleigh Cigarette Program,* starring comedian Red Skelton. Anxious to get off the road, Ozzie took it. He knew full well that once the C. E. Hooper ratings were in, he and Harriet might wind up back in Jersey like last time, so to avoid uprooting Ricky they left him with his paternal grandmother.

The couple's two years with Robert L. Ripley, an alcoholic eccentric, barely prepared them for working with the moody Skelton, often cited as the embodiment of the tortured artist. Skelton himself has dismissed comparisons to Pagliacci, yet a sad clown is a recurrent image in many of his paintings. And perhaps it is only symbolic, but as a poor boy unable to afford a brush, Richard Skelton used cut-off hanks of his own cinnamon-colored hair for swabbing the paint around.

Skelton, a brilliant pantomimist, was not fully appreciated until he moved to television in the 1950s. Still, he could sell a gag as well as any radio comic—his infectious laugh usually preceding the punchline—and on his own show created a host of memorable characters. Harriet, originally hired as vocalist, appeared in so many skits, she emerged as Skelton's costar. Their best-remembered pairing cast Harriet as the exasperated "Mummy," and Skelton as her scheming "mean widdle kid," Junior, who cries "I dood it!" after each transgression.

The Tuesday-night show was one of the 1941–42 season's

runaway hits, with Skelton voted Outstanding New Star by *Motion Picture Daily*. That November Ozzie, Harriet, David, and Grandma Hilliard moved into what would become their permanent home. Ozzie's eyes lit up the moment he saw it, tucked away on a wide dead-end street above Hollywood Boulevard.

Eighteen twenty-two Camino Palmero reminded him of the dream house they'd left behind: a two-story, fourteen-room Cape Cod Colonial with a rolling green lawn and not a palm tree in sight. You could snap a picture and caption it "Tenafly." Or "New Haven." It looked right out of Anywhere, U. S. A.— anywhere, that is, except Los Angeles. This seems only fitting, as Ozzie would forever be a Hollywood outsider. Whereas most stars' homes screamed opulence, the Nelsons' whispered comfort.

Harriet, denied a house of her own for so long, made up for lost time. She decorated the interior to her Early American taste: antiques, needlepoint cushions, wallclocks, rocking chairs, and oil lamps with beribboned shades. Many of the pieces were acquired from her years with the orchestra, when she passed time in transit longingly clipping pictures of furnishings from women's magazines.

The Nelson residence was to become The Most Televised Home in America, a distinction its current owners proudly acknowledge with a small brass plaque erected in front. Today the house is shingled blue and shuttered white, but in 1942 when Rick finally joined the others, it was white and green, and the tree coverage was not nearly so dense.

Rick was a small, sickly child who suffered with severe asthma. He and his brother shared a bedroom until Hazel Hilliard moved into her own house nearby. David still recalls having to endure the pungent aroma from a vaporizer used to aid Rick's breathing at night: "My parents would put tincture of evergreen into this long tube, heat it up, and the steam would fill the room."

The brothers experienced essentially the same disordered upbringing during their early years, yet while David acted outwardly calm and well adjusted, Rick seemed high-strung and insecure. His worried mother ingeniously lowered book shelves and painted a child's eye-level line all around his spacious playroom, reasoning that its size made him feel dwarfed and anxious.

"He was an odd little kid," said John Guedel, producer of *The Raleigh Cigarette Program.* Guedel describes Rick as likable "but shy and introspective. There was always a little mystery there. You never knew what he was thinking." Most family portraits from Rick's youth show a towheaded, wiry boy who appears distant from his parents and his brother. Much like Ozzie the college undergrad, Rick rarely focuses at the camera. But whereas his father always stared fixedly at tomorrow, Rick looks lost in thought.

When the Army drafted Red Skelton in May 1944, the Nelsons could have easily found themselves another star to support, but John Guedel felt they should capitalize on their newfound popularity. "Let's sell a show with you and Harriet in it," he suggested. Thinking the producer meant one in the same vein as Skelton's, Ozzie asked, "Who'll be the comedian?"

"No, not that type of show."

Guedel envisioned a domestic situation comedy like the long-running hit *Fibber McGee and Molly,* produced just across the hall at NBC. What's more, he told Ozzie, it could be drawn from the Nelsons' colorful real lives, which even the most inventive scriptwriter would be hard-pressed to equal.

No bandleader had ever starred in his own regular-season series before, but Guedel, Ozzie, and a writer set about recording an audition acetate, radio's equivalent of a TV pilot. Guedel eventually sold the new show to sponsor International Silver, "the solid silver with beauty that lives forever."

The original concept called for the Nelsons to play themselves: a bandleader and his vocalist wife. But they were also to inherit a small-town drugstore, which would facilitate writing new characters—"customers"—in and out at will. When the Sunday-evening program premiered on Ozzie and Harriet's ninth wedding anniversary, October 8, 1944, that idea had been scrapped. Instead most action took place in their fictional home at 1847 Rogers Road.

Another significant change had also been made, at Ozzie's behest. Guedel's working title was "Harriet and Ozzie." Taking his producer aside, Ozzie said, "I like it very much, John, except for, uh, one thing . . ." Ozzie had a paradoxical way of speaking; forcefully, yet impeded by a slight stammer. "I think 'Ozzie' should come before, uh, 'Harriet.' You know, the man always comes first."

So it became *The Adventures of Ozzie and Harriet* starring "Young America's favorite couple," an odd introduction considering Harriet was thirty-five and Ozzie nearly forty. Broadcast over CBS, second largest of the four national networks, it aired opposite NBC's *Catholic Hour,* Mutual's *Quick as a Flash,* and ABC's *Radio Hall of Fame.*

Many successful programs require a season or two of fine-tuning. This was certainly true of *The Adventures,* which initially reflected less the sensibilities of its two stars than of its two main writers, radio-comedy veterans John P. Medbury and Jack Douglas. Their joke-filled scripts may have suited ex-employers Bob Hope and Eddie Cantor, but not Ozzie.

The balance between the Nelsons and their supporting cast was also off, with the characters drawn so broadly that they overwhelmed the comparatively mild-mannered Ozzie and Harriet. Particularly memorable were Bea Benaderet as the Nelsons' slothful, whining maid; Francis "Dink" Trout as meek, henpecked Roger Waddington; and Englishman John Brown as obstreperous neighbor Thorny Thornbury.

Even flawed, *The Adventures of Ozzie and Harriet* attracted favorable press. *The New York Times*'s Jack Gould called it "a pleasant and frequently funny show" but suggested the writers devote "a little more attention to the comedy inherent in the 'situation'—i.e., the Nelson household."

Ozzie must have read that review, for Medbury and Douglas were gone after the first season, replaced over the next two years by Sol Sax, Sherwood Schwartz, Rupert Pray, Paul West, and Ben Gershman. With them, and with Ozzie taking charge as head writer, the show changed appreciably. "It went from slapstick to a more plausible sitcom," said Gershman, who as storyman wrote each week's three-page single-spaced plot synopsis. " 'Homey shit,' we used to call it."

All Ozzie really did was to draw from life at 1822 Camino Palmero. A talented writer himself, he knew that scripting a family comedy required not so much a vivid imagination as an observant eye. Increasingly, he found himself watching his two boys, whose antics and brotherly enmity provided a wellspring of inspiration.

David is remembered by relatives and visitors to the Nelson home as a quiet, serious boy. "Very undemanding of attention," said his cousin George Nelson. By age nine David's blond hair had darkened several shades and was invariably covered by a Cub Scouts cap. He'd filled out, was almost stocky, a development that either aroused or coincided with an interest in sports.

Rick, though also quiet, was more happy-go-lucky and prankish, craving attention. While vacationing with his parents at an elegant hotel, he made his grand entrance into the formal dining room by sliding down a banister. Rick was wearing his little suit and tie, as Harriet had instructed, but no shoes or socks. He was quickly hustled upstairs.

With such dissonant dispositions, Rick and David clashed. The pugnacious younger boy started most of the fights, relentlessly teasing David about a mole on his nose and especially his weight. "How's your fat?" he'd inquire sarcastically. Because one of Rick's front teeth slanted, David took revenge by calling him "Fang" and crooking a finger in front of his mouth.

David, like many dutiful older siblings, wondered at times why his younger brother received a disproportionate amount of parental attention. "Rick was always the fair-haired one," said cousin Rich Nelson, conjecturing this was due to his asthma and small size. Whatever the reason, their Aunt Kay favored good-natured David, "because she felt he wasn't treated the same."

22

The Nelson boys attended Gardner Street Public School, a charmless institutional green building at Hawthorn and Vista streets. Walking the two-and-a-half blocks to and from classes, they passed their grandmother Hazel's small mustard-colored house. Returning home, they were greeted by their English setter, Nicky.

"Hollywood was a wonderful place to live then," David reflected. "We didn't think of it as *Hollywood*, stardomville, it was just our home. Every Saturday Rick and I dressed up in our cowboy outfits and took the streetcar down Hollywood Boulevard to the Hitching Post, this theater that played Westerns and serials for a quarter. All the kids, of course, would take their cap pistols. The theater had a policy that you had to check your guns at the door, so we carried two: one to give to the theater manager, and the other to fire at the bad guys when they came on the screen."

It was the very picture of normal family life, but with a crucial difference. Even the most trifling daily occurrence at 1822 Camino Palmero was potential grist for the radio program, which Jack Gould hailed in 1947 as "head of the class in the field of domestic humor." Gould saw as the show's backbone its writers' "awareness that the life of a pair of young parents can be hectic enough without superfluous embellishment." His New York *Herald Tribune* colleague, John Crosby, was moved to marvel about that very point: "The problems that beset the Nelsons are so minute," he wrote, "you sometimes wonder how in the world they'll last half an hour."

The Adventures of Ozzie and Harriet was a family program in more ways than one. For the 1948–49 season, twenty-one-year-old Don Nelson joined the fold as an apprentice writer. Two months old when his father died, Don was raised in New Jersey by his widowed mother, a strong, resilient woman her family nicknamed "Little Napoleon," and by brother Alfred and his wife Kay Nelson, to whom he became a sixth son. Alfred had purchased Ozzie's Tenafly home and every evening went next door to look in on Ethel and his youngest brother.

23

Don was the most artistic of the three brothers, an accomplished writer, painter, and musician. Following his exit from the service he enrolled in the University of Southern California. Then, in the first of many nepotistic moves throughout the years, Ozzie drafted him onto the *The Adventures of Ozzie and Harriet.*

There were two other family members to consider adding to the cast: Rick and David, now ages eight and twelve. Initially they were only referred to in the scripts, but midway through the maiden season, Ozzie hired child actor Joel Davis to play David, replacing him the next year with Tommy Bernard. And in 1945 Henry Blair, a twelve-year-old who ably mimicked a much younger child's voice, began portraying Rick.

Ozzie had prepared for the possibility of the boys stepping into their own roles by having his radio progeny age concurrently with them. In December 1948, while playing tennis with the Nelson boys, Bing Crosby's son Lindsay mentioned that he and his father were to guest star on an upcoming *The Adventures* episode. Rick and David promptly marched to their parents and demanded equal time.

But no matter how much they'd anticipated this moment, Ozzie and Harriet shared mixed feelings. "I remember Ozzie saying for years that he didn't want his sons to be child actors," said writer Paul West. "He was quite adamant about it." From a ratings standpoint, however, the novelty of a family playing itself on the air, a radio first, would surely pay off. In 1947 CBS foolishly moved the show from Sunday night to Friday night, when families were less likely to gather around the radio. Then the network lost the Nelsons to NBC, which returned them to their familiar spot but as part of a mortally weak lineup. Midway through its fifth season, *The Adventures of Ozzie and Harriet*'s C. E. Hooper rating, once 13, had dipped to 8.2.

Ozzie and Harriet also had more personal considerations in mind. They knew too well what happened to kids left undersupervised and adrift in Tinseltown. The final decision to let Rick and David play themselves was made more with an eye

24

to preserving the family than to saving the series. So the boys were told they could audition—but in the preview show, a warm-up staged for the studio audience only—though it's doubtful that stipulation was heard over their whoops of joy.

The night of the tryout, the show's writers and cast milled about wearing amused expressions, surprised that Ozzie would risk his future on two novices. "We knew David could handle it," said writer Bill Davenport, "but we weren't sure if Ricky was old enough."

At rehearsal, David stood between his parents, craning his neck to project into the box-shaped microphone. Rick was parked at a small table, his mike suspended from an extension rod. Mary Jane Croft, who played neighbor Clara Randolph as well as innumerable roles on other shows, recalled that when Rick piped his first line in a miniature voice, "Our mouths flew open and our eyes popped! We just couldn't believe how funny this skinny little thing was. The audience went crazy over him." Encouraged, Rick played to them like a show-biz veteran. "He had a wonderful confidence," said Croft, "strutting around, with his funny little straw hair sticking up. It was stunning."

Ozzie now led his own version of the Four Nelsons. Rick and David's first broadcast, "Invitation to Dinner," aired on February 20, 1949. Though its plot turned on David's quandary about whether to play basketball or attend a girl's party, Rick provoked the laughs and from that point on received the choice lines. His trademark "I don't mess around, boy!" coined by his Uncle Don and always delivered with cool aplomb, practically became a national catchphrase.

"Ricky was the one you went to when you wanted a laugh," said Davenport. "He didn't make any attempt to 'be funny,' but he was just such a cute little kid and had this totally different yet very believable personality, that he became the show's spark."

RICK: All my girlfriends are running after me like mad.
HARRIET: Is that so? And just how do you work that?

25

RICK: Easy. I introduced them to each other.

HARRIET: I don't get it.

RICK: I told ya: They're running after me, and boy, are they mad!

After just a few shows, Rick took to ad-libbing, which did not go over well with his persnickety director-father. During one of the cast's postshow conferences, Ozzie took him aside and said sharply, "Look, young man, there is no such thing as an eight-year-old comic!" Rick thought otherwise, taking off his shoes and socks and wiggling his toes for the studio audience's amusement. Other times the youngster drifted off and hummed, oblivious of his surroundings.

David delivered his lines with consummate professionalism, but as Davenport observed, "He never seemed comfortable performing. Being on the show was something he did for Ozzie. Ricky, as was later proven, was the more natural entertainer."

This was just one of many differences between the two brothers, who throughout their lives would have little in common besides their last name. The boys formed a composite of their father, the younger boy inheriting Ozzie's competitiveness and self-confidence, and the older boy his analytical mind.

In a remarkably true-to-life radio episode called "The Boys' Personalities," Harriet remarks to Ozzie, "Isn't that amazing, how two boys can be brothers, live under the same roof, and apparently be as different as night and day." Ben Gershman's plot synopsis accurately describes the Nelsons' real intrafamily relationships: "It's clear that Ozzie particularly admires Ricky for his aggressiveness and spirit . . . while Harriet seems to incline more to David's modesty and self-effacement." Ozzie truly did feel closer to Rick, who being second-born and physically slight reminded Ozzie of himself. Similarly, David and his mother shared a special bond in that both played subordinates on and off the show: Harriet to Ozzie, and David to Rick.

"Poor David," Ozzie says in "The Boys' Personalities," "I'm

afraid he's going to find himself left out of things if he doesn't show more enthusiasm."

Harriet counters protectively, "I don't see where David has any problem at all. It seems to me Ricky is the one who should be careful. There's such a thing as being too sure of yourself. I just hope he doesn't find out the hard way." Later, she privately chastens Rick, saying, "You know your father and I want you to have confidence in yourself, but occasionally you can go overboard. . . . You'll find later in life that it pays to be a little more reserved." Ironically, in his late teens Rick grew so reserved, it became a cause of concern to Harriet.

Ozzie, meanwhile, conducts a man-to-man talk with David:

OZZIE: You should try to display a little more self-confidence than you do; join in the spirit of things a little more. If you expect to get along in this world, you'll find you've got to have a little more drive. You've gotta have push.

DAVID: I thought you told me you had to have pull.

OZZIE: This is a different matter. . . . I'm afraid you're inclined to be a little too timid, and believe me, you're liable to get hurt later on in life if you don't heed my advice. . . . So try to show more enthusiasm about things. Get in the swing.

DAVID: I'll try, Pop.

OZZIE: Don't just say, "I'll *try*," say, "I'll *do* it." . . . Go into things with the confidence that you're the master. You have the upper hand. Can you do that?

DAVID: Okay, Pop, I can do it.

OZZIE: That's the way to talk! Say it again.

DAVID: I can do it.

OZZIE: That's it.

DAVID: At least, I *think* I can.

A typical father, Ozzie's character views his sons as reflections of himself. His concern over David's amiable nature, which he sees as an exploitable weakness, was a recurring theme on radio and, later, on television. Though Ozzie the actor spoke the lines, Ozzie the father wrote them. With the show anchored in reality, what effect did this have on David at such an impressionable age? And what did years of playing a passive character do to his self-esteem?

Soft-spoken and sincere, David later admitted with some bitterness that even in his teens he'd felt like "a little old man. I thought kids were looked upon with most favor if they opened doors, were polite, and said 'Yes sir.' It was nothing for me to bow down to people who I knew didn't deserve the courtesy." Perhaps he was unwittingly falling into his program "role."

Conversely, portraying such a boisterous child on the radio helped to draw Rick out of his shell. "All of a sudden he realized how funny he was," said David, "and for a while he became a miniature Jerry Lewis. But it was written for him. Rick's true nature was to be shy."

From the outset, the littlest Nelson was *The Adventures of Ozzie and Harriet*'s undisputed star, specially introduced as "the irrepressible Ricky" when the show went to television. In public fans would accost the Nelsons and exclaim, "David is a good boy, but Ricky is the cutest thing we've ever seen!" prompting Harriet to utter half-seriously, "It'll be a wonder if David doesn't murder Ricky in his sleep." If he felt any resentment, David kept it inside. Either that, or it escaped like steam from a kettle during the brothers' combative scenes together, explaining David's scathing delivery:

DAVID: You look to me like a little man who should really get ahead.
RICK: Thank you.
DAVID: The one you're using is cracked.

RICK: I'm getting pretty strong, boy.
DAVID: That's a laugh.
RICK: Oh yeah? Have you seen my muscles lately?
DAVID: What's the matter? Can't you find them either?

"It was explained to me that I was a straight man," said David, "and, lest my feelings get hurt, that the straight man is just as important as the comic." Whenever Rick's head swelled from being a pint-size celebrity, though, David wasted no time in cutting his little brother back down to size. Rick would brag, "I sure got a laugh out of that line," to which David would retort, "Yeah, but who set it up for you?"

The writers weren't instructed to distribute laughs more equitably, but Bill Davenport did sense that Ozzie and Harriet worried about the effect Rick's overshadowing David might have. Ozzie claimed that he and Harriet tried to compensate by showering their oldest son with attention and affection, perhaps overly so. At the same time, they monitored Rick for signs of a hyperactive ego, warning him, "Don't be a child actor."

Rick and David joining the cast wasn't the only significant development brewing. With two months left in the 1948–49 season, the Nelsons returned to CBS, which had vaulted past NBC to become the dominant network. Scheduled to precede Jack Benny's show, *The Adventures of Ozzie and Harriet* seemed assured a bright future.

Except that it was to be with the American Broadcasting Company. For five seasons Ozzie had tried securing a multiyear contract from Silver International, but each time the company renewed for just one year. Boldly, he ordered his agent from Music Corporation of America (MCA), David A. (Sonny) Werblin, to bypass sponsors and negotiate directly with the networks. In July 1949 ABC gave him the long-term commitment he was seeking: the first noncancellable, guaranteed ten-year contract in show-business history.

Additionally, the network met Ozzie's demand of a TV option. Not that he was enamored of the new medium, which after a fitfully slow two-decade start was finally in limited operation. On the contrary, Ozzie took a dim view of television's dubious artistic merit and doubted the public would ever embrace it— one of the few times his instincts proved wrong. Television was already beginning to supplant radio, with one thousand sets being installed in American homes daily. By the time Ozzie felt ready to move to TV two years later, the decision had all but been made for him.

Ozzie's approach was typically prudent: First he would test market his family's visual appeal in a film. There was good reason for caution. Of the four, only Harriet had established herself as a movie actress, and she'd let her motion-picture career lapse since the mid-1940s. Slight films that drew critical dismissals such as "any resemblance to a motion picture is purely unintentional" (1942's *Juke Box Jenny*) may have been why.

With over twenty years in show business, Ozzie increasingly demanded and received control over family projects. The feature-length *Here Come the Nelsons* was no exception. Ozzie wrote the screenplay with Don Nelson and Bill Davenport, and when Universal Pictures assigned the Nelsons to director Fred De Cordova, Ozzie sat right down with him to discuss details.

De Cordova had directed moderate-budget pictures for Warner Bros. and Universal, the best-remembered of which, *Bedtime for Bonzo,* starred a B-movie actor and registered Democrat named Ronald Reagan. De Cordova later found greater success in television, winning Emmy Awards for directing *The Jack Benny Program* and for producing *The Burns and Allen Show* and the *Tonight* show.

"Ozzie was very strong and firm," De Cordova recalled. Industry rumor had it that the Nelson family patriarch did not readily accept others' ideas, "but I found him not at all difficult. Some of the things I suggested, he liked; other things he wasn't crazy about.

"Oddly enough," De Cordova added, laughing, "we didn't do the ones he wasn't crazy about."

Rock Hudson, Sheldon Leonard, and Barbara Lawrence co-starred in *Here Come the Nelsons.* In this nonsensical romp, Ozzie plays a flack for the H. J. (as in H. J. Heinz, the radio show's sponsor) Bellows and Company Advertising Agency, racking his brain to devise a campaign for a women's girdle manufacturer.

30

Meanwhile, the town centennial celebration is underway. Ozzie invites a school chum's attractive kid sister to stay with the Nelsons, and Harriet extends the same courtesy to dashing Charles Jones, played by Hudson. Through a series of misunderstandings, insecure Ozzie turns jealous and desperately tries to prove he's still young. (This became a recurrent theme on the TV show.) When two robbers pilfer the fair's receipts, kidnap Rick, and escape into the mountains, Ozzie stops them by erecting a barricade of women's undergarments across a dusty road, saving the day as well as attaining publicity for his client. The end.

Rick was a natural onscreen, a wisecracking, skinny eleven-year-old with brush-cut hair and braces. He enjoyed cavorting for the camera and joined the adults afterward to eagerly watch the day's footage, or rushes. In contrast, David was nearly traumatized by how he looked on celluloid. Adolescence had afflicted him with a mild case of acne, an appealing crooked smile, a wide-bridged nose waiting for the rest of his face to fill out, and a husky build. Seeing himself only confirmed Rick's cruel taunts of "Fatty," and despite the fact that he grew into a handsome adult, "I never held myself in high regard after that," he said.

Studio expectations for *Here Come the Nelsons* were as modest as its budget, yet it fared surprisingly well at the box office. For the Nelsons, the venture was an unqualified success even before release, satisfying Ozzie that his family was indeed ready to leap to television. ABC reserved them an evening slot for the upcoming fall 1952 season.

"Hotpoint quality appliances proudly presents *The Adventures of Ozzie and Harriet,* starring the entire Nelson family: Ozzie, Harriet, David and Ricky . . ." At 8:00 P.M. on Friday, October 3, 1952, America was formally introduced to the newest neighbors on a video block already occupied by the Goldbergs, the Hansens of *Mama,* the Barbours of *One Man's Family,* and the Ricardos of *I Love Lucy.*

31

All but the latter had also relocated from the AM dial. Transplanting a program from one medium to another was like translating languages: The essence could easily be lost. Conservative to a fault, Ozzie made sure that the new TV show adhered strictly to the radio format, retaining the same homespun, wholesome quality. In fact, during its first two seasons, some scripts were mere rewrites of the old radio plays.

The premiere contained such charming scenes as David's first shave. Rick accompanies him to the bathroom and watches aghast, waiting for his older brother to slit an artery, but David completes the operation without spilling a drop of blood. As he towels off the excess lather, he exclaims brightly, "Next time I'll try it with a blade!" As intended, the scene elicits not convulsive laughter but soft chuckles and nods of recognition, a style of humor that would characterize the 434 episodes to follow.

Three

In its earliest days, television was seen not just as an exciting new form of communication but of transportation; a magic carpet that, like the airplane, would forever alter perceptions of distance and time. Through it, people witnessed global events as they happened without having to be where they happened.

Early programmers exploited this fascination by way of shows that transported audiences to the theater (*Philco TV Playhouse*), to sporting events (*Boxing From St. Nicholas Arena*), sightseeing (*America in View*), even back in time (*You Are There*). The irony, of course, is that while TV ostensibly broadened viewers' horizons by beaming the world into their homes, their lives became more insular and their homes their worlds.

Though he professed to disdain television, Ozzie understood that along with witnessing spectacle, audiences wanted to identify with the situations on screen and to see "themselves" and their daily lives depicted there. And that is what *The Adventures of Ozzie and Harriet* gave them, in weekly installments as predictable, warm, and unassuming as family newsletters.

"Ozzie and Harriet" has become an adjectival equivalent of "boring," the way "Mickey Mouse" is synonymous with "cheap." As suggested by the story line for "The Odd Bolt," an episode from the 1954–55 season ("Ozzie finds an odd bolt he's been saving and wonders why"), these were hardly adventures in the true sense. Situation was stressed over comedy, and laughs never strained for, derived instead from the natural interaction in a family facing everyday "problems."

The Nelsons experienced misunderstandings and mix-ups, the resolutions to which hinged on irony or coincidence. Or they magically resolved themselves, so that at show's end Ozzie could smilingly reassure everyone, "See? I told you there was nothing to worry about!"

No other domestic comedy of the 1950s and 1960s presented such a utopian concept of the home. *Make Room for Daddy,* starring Danny Thomas, cast wife and kids as sadistic tormentors, while *Leave It to Beaver,* written from a youngster's perspective, pitted Theodore Cleaver (Jerry Mathers) and his peers against authority in all its forms.

The family program most like *The Adventures* in its cozy portrayal of Middle America was *Father Knows Best,* starring Robert Young and Jane Wyatt as Jim and Margaret Anderson. Though set amid similar trappings, the Andersons experienced genuine conflicts and crises. Ozzie's family appears unflappable, but not Jim's. He is often melancholy, Margaret sentimental, and their three children—Betty, Bud, and Kathy—spoiled and selfish. This is not to say the Anderson family was any more real than the TV Nelsons, for many of *Father Knows Best*'s poignant resolutions were even more simplistic and implausible.

Claims that *The Adventures* mirrored typical family life suggest that such families existed, when clearly they did not: By the early 1950s over one-third of all marriages ended in divorce, children left home sooner, once-common extended families were quaint exceptions, and one in four mothers now worked outside the home. The show presented an ideal, by definition unachievable by most families. Viewers found comfort in it, perhaps not really wanting to see themselves and their lives portrayed after all, but their *idealized* selves and lives: contrast dimmed, brilliance heightened, and reception clear.

Ozzie never presumed to offer the secrets of domestic tranquility; he simply wanted to entertain. David recalled, "My father once told me, 'I just do the things I think are funny. If you want a message, call Western Union.'" TV critics presumed for him, however, holding up the Nelsons as an apotheosis. "The dream of what the American family should be" typified most comments.

Critical acclaim generally stressed the program's good old American values over its entertainment worth. With television so much a part of our lives today, it is hard to comprehend the power newspaper columnists and observers ascribed to it then. Many regarded television as the means by which all forms of societal corruption—from teenage rebellion to Communism—might enter and undermine the American psyche.

Consequently, many critics plainly believed that television producers had a moral, patriotic duty to fortify rather than to dilute traditional thought. Perhaps if enough viewers emulated the image (the fantasy) of family that shows such as *The Adventures* perpetuated, it could become reality. Instead of reflecting the American condition, TV could shape it, and life would imitate art.

So, whether they welcomed the responsibility or not, the Nelsons came to exemplify the sturdy, harmonious, all-American family, influencing a generation's ideas about nuclear unity. This, even though by the time the show premiered, Ozzie and Harriet had been glittering national celebrities—the bandleader and his songstress wife—for twenty years. Viewers' wholesale acceptance of the Nelsons' TV roles as reality bordered on desperate mass self-delusion. Years after the series' cancellation, strangers still approached them in public, confessing tearfully, "My family tried to be like yours, but we failed."

Connie Harper (who became Connie Harper Nelson, Rick's

aunt, by marrying Don Nelson in 1967) played "Miss Edwards" on the show, and in real life, as Ozzie's secretary, answered fan mail. "Some of the letters were pathetic," she remembered. "Boys wrote insisting that Ozzie and Harriet were their parents too and demanding their rightful place in the family. It was really sad."

Portraying America's favorite family turned into a twenty-four-hour-a-day job. "We would keep up the front of this totally problemless, happy-go-lucky group," David said after the series ended. "There might have been a tremendous battle in our home, but if someone from outside came in, it would be as if the director yelled, 'Roll 'em!' "

Ozzie, Harriet, David, and Rick not only endured the proverbial fishbowl existence, they were expected to be model fish. Today's public eagerly laps up and accepts the foibles of the rich and famous. But in the 1950s it tolerated nothing less than perfection. When Harriet innocently sipped a glass of sherry on an episode, a flood of audience protests followed. The TV Nelsons had the same worry, really, as millions of average families: "What will the neighbors think?"

A slavish media vastly diminished that concern. Except for the notorious blackmailing scandal sheets, the Fourth Estate then functioned as a Hollywood PR tool. Newspaper and magazine profiles typically polished the public facades of the stars, who reciprocated with "exclusive" carefully controlled interviews and photo opportunities.

The Nelsons habitually received such gushy press, you might compare bylines with show-ending credits. The most perpetrated myth about the family was its communal morning meals. As an ABC-TV spokesman told *Newsweek,* "They manage to eat breakfast together if it kills them." Had that been true, it just might have, since each kept drastically different hours.

But the Nelsons played along, Harriet earnestly telling *American Magazine* that she fixed breakfast in ten minutes flat every morning at seven-thirty. Seven thirty? At that hour, Ozzie, who wrote and revised the show's scripts until 4:00 A.M. most nights, would have staggered to the table half-asleep. In reality the four skipped breakfast, grabbed lunch on the set, and in the evening came home to a prepared dinner, served formally, jackets required.

There is nothing remarkable about the inevitable differences between the family America watched on TV and the one that resided at 1822 Camino Palmero. What is remarkable, and what gives *The Adventures* a unique vérité quality, are the many similarities between the two. Actor Skip Young, Rick and David's portly pal Wally Plumstead for ten seasons, said that performing opposite the Nelsons "wasn't like being in show business, it was like being in a family making home movies." Birthdays and anniversaries were celebrated both on and off camera, with "Ricky's Surprise Party" broadcast on May 8, 1957, his seventeenth birthday, and the 1954–55 season premiere, "The Wedding Anniversary," airing on Ozzie and Harriet's nineteenth.

Few programs have so completely reflected their originator's vision or recounted his personal past in such detail. Once Rick and David joined the radio cast in 1949, Ozzie no longer had their typical childhoods to draw on, so he turned to his memories of growing up in small-town New Jersey. *The Adventures of Ozzie and Harriet* actually should have been titled *The Adventures of George and Ethel,* with Rick and David as young Ozzie and Alfred. For a flashback scene in the series' second Christmas show, "The Miracle," Ozzie in fact played his father; Harriet, his mother; and the boys, Ozzie and his older brother.

Ozzie set his memories against a timeless backdrop. What year was this? Modern household appliances provided the only clues, for the television Nelsons led an appealingly hermetic existence unaffected by outside turmoil. Moreover, their suburban locale remained unnamed.

Almost eerily, the house erected on General Service Studio stage five exactly replicated 1822 Camino Palmero, astounding first-time visitors to the Nelson home. "It was bizarre," said

Bruce Belland, a cast member and leader of the Four Preps vocal quartet. "Even having never been there before, I could have told you where each room was. And the house was furnished precisely as the set was." The sole major deviation was the house itself. Each episode's opening camera shot tightly framed the family's expansive Colonial so it appeared half as large as life.

The Nelsons themselves were also scaled down for television, from the chronic overachievers they truly were to their bland TV personae. Of the four, Harriet's character was the most mysterious, glimpsed mainly in a knotty-pine kitchen.[1] Wearing a plain apron and a frumpy hairdo, the former glamour girl continually peeled apples, leaned through the serving window to pass plates of high-cholesterol nourishment, and hovered over the table, percolator in hand.

But Harriet seemed more maid than mother, going about her maternal duties with cool detachment. Other television keepers of the hearth, headed by *Father Knows Best*'s Margaret Anderson, *The Donna Reed Show*'s Donna Stone, and *Leave It to Beaver*'s June Cleaver (Barbara Billingsley), were certainly closer to domestic sainthood than Harriet.

Though Harriet played the typical fifties housewife, *The Adventures* depicted a more progressive concept of marriage than any of those sitcoms. Ozzie proudly pointed to the fact that he and Harriet were the first TV couple to sleep in a double bed, though you got the feeling that the two of them, in their comfy pajamas, always got *a good night's rest*. On *I Love Lucy* and *Make Room for Daddy* women were sweet, docile, manipulative creatures who plied their feminine wiles and sobbed dramatically at the snap of a purse in order to get what they were

---

[1] For the first four seasons, the Nelsons were virtual hostages in their Hotpoint-appointed kitchen because homage had to be paid the show's sponsor. Crass as it sounds, this was common practice at the time. Hotpoint's successors—Kodak, Coca-Cola, the American Dairy Association, Aunt Jemima—were likewise worked subliminally and not so subliminally into the scenes: the Nelsons wearing cameras around their necks like medallions; Ozzie pouring himself and next-door neighbor Thorny Thornbury (played by Don Defore) an endless stream of Coca-Cola; Rick and David guzzling enough milk to calcify their bones. Ozzie did, however, balk at forcing his family to subsist on an all-pancake diet.

after: usually an expensive dress, hat, or bauble. Harriet never stooped to such trickery, *The Adventures* suggesting that men and women could be equals.

Their television marriage may have flourished unencumbered by sexism, but at home Father truly did know best and rendered all vital decisions. From the day Harriet took a pay cut to join Ozzie's orchestra, she trusted him implicitly. "When I first started out with Ozzie, he was my boss. He still is my boss, and I wouldn't want it any other way," she said after twenty-two years of marriage.

Harriet once described herself as "a girl who wandered on stage by mistake and got tossed back and forth for the rest of her life by three men in an adagio act." Sally Hughes, another of Ozzie's secretaries and an actress on the show, pointed out, "Harriet was ambitious, but only for the good of the family."

Despite her star billing, Harriet's part was largely supportive. Ozzie worked the boys' interests into the scripts, not to mention his own banjo strumming and crooning, yet few episodes showcased Harriet's proven abilities as singer, dancer and, especially, comedienne. "She could do more with the raise of an eyebrow than the rest of us could do with a page of dialogue," praised actor Parley Baer, for seven seasons prissy, pedantic neighbor Herb Darby.

Typically, she downplayed her talent, sighing to a cast member one fall, "Every year I come on this show vowing to be a better actress, and I never am." There was little need for Harriet to apply herself, given the ample time she spent off camera, ostensibly consorting with her women's club or simply vanishing. John Guedel recalled kidding Ozzie about Harriet's limited role even on the radio show. "The plot would start, she would say, 'Ozzie, I'll be upstairs if you want me,' and she wouldn't come back down until the last page of the script. We used to say to him, 'Gotta get her in there more!' But Harriet didn't seem to care."

Referring back to when Harriet first ventured into motion pictures, Guedel observed, "She and Ginger Rogers had the same opportunities. Ginger chose career, Harriet chose Ozzie. She had a career, of course, but it was always associated with her husband. Over the long run, though, I imagine Harriet was happier than Ginger."

Many who know her believe that Harriet might have been happiest as a full-time homemaker, which she could only pretend to be on TV. Ivan Bonar, who played crusty Dean Hopkins, once asked her, "Well, Harriet, have you been up to anything exciting?" She answered with a chuckle, "Not unless you call Ajaxing bathtubs exciting." Rick's friends remember her constantly involved in some domestic activity, either making fudge, puttering in the garden, refurbishing antiques, doing laundry, or serving milk and cookies. "Just like on the show," they all add.

The widest discrepancy existed between Ozzie and his black-and-white alter ego. For one thing, on the series he never held a profession (so viewers could identify with his character more readily, he claimed), lending an air of mystery whenever he announced "Harriet, I'm home!"

Simply by maturing, Rick and, to a lesser degree, David would shape the program more than their parents. Their growth was the single greatest factor in the series' longevity, providing new situations for the same principals. During the first four seasons, however, *The Adventures* still expressed a parent's point of view, and, like the radio program, still starred its creator as the shaky pillar of the Nelson family.

Ozzie holds a unique place in the pantheon of 1950s–1960s American TV dads, neither stereotypical sage nor simpleton nor shah. Benevolent buffoon, perhaps. In a common scenario from a 1956–57 episode titled "The Borrowed Tuxedo," Ozzie expounds on taking care of other people's property, then, predictably, wears a borrowed tuxedo to a men's club dinner and falls into a sticky cake.

"You have to give Pop credit," Rick quips. "He'll do anything to prove a point."

40

Anytime their father loses face, the boys try to bolster his spirits, but blessed with the candor of youth only inflict further humiliation. When Ozzie worries aloud that his having to play the front end of a horse in a PTA pageant will embarrass his sons, Rick reassures him, "No, we won't be ashamed of ya, Pop."

"Of course not, Pop," adds David. "You'll be all covered up, won't ya?" As they shuffle out of the room, Ozzie's downcast expression deepens.

The most impetuous, incorrigible Nelson wasn't David or even the irrepressible Rick, it was Ozzie, whom the boys could manipulate into doing almost anything they wanted. Innocent and enthusiastic, his endearingly sensitive character stood out from other 1950s TV fathers. It's hard to imagine Danny (Thomas) Williams or Ricky Ricardo (Desi Arnaz) teetering atop a ladder with a candle to warm a nest of robin's eggs, as Ozzie does in "The Bird's Nest" (1953–54).

Offscreen, Ozzie didn't hold a single job, but twenty-one, including producer, director, cameraman, film editor, actor, drama coach, sound technician, and head writer. His colleagues on the set, who nicknamed him "The wizard that is Oz," once presented him with a framed scroll bearing eight different union cards.

In his fifties, the clean-living Ozzie maintained a rigorous fitness program that included jogging the one-and-a-half miles to the studio. He required only four hours' sleep a night and ate just one meal a day, consisting of steak and, his lone weakness, ultrarich Will Wright's ice cream.

The public knew Ozzie as an amiable Milquetoast, but as he forewarns Harriet in "The Hunter" (1953–54), "I'm basically not the mild, gentle creature you've believed me to be . . . There's a great deal of the savage beast lurking within me." Anyone who undertook business with him heartily agreed. A tenacious negotiator, Ozzie flattened opponents with his knowledge of the law. After going toe to toe with him, one harried network attorney returned to New York and shakily alerted his legal-department colleagues, "Don't mess with that Nelson. He'll knock your brains out."

In the early 1950s sponsors exercised total control over every one of ABC's television programs save for *The Adventures*. The fledgling network owned 40 percent of the series, in exchange for financing production costs. The remaining 60 percent, as well as full creative control, belonged to Ozzie, an arrangement virtually unheard of then. Thus the network was powerless to prevent Ozzie's naming himself joint producer and director and forming a production company, Stage Five Productions, midway through the second season.

Ozzie, a perfectionist, took five days to film episodes instead of the customary three, and refused to stint on film, directing up to twenty takes per scene. Unsatisfied with the brightly lit "flat" photography commonly used in early television, he paid Academy Award-winning cinematographer William C. Mellor $1,000 a week—$250 more than he was earning at MGM Studios—to shoot installments as if they were minifeature films. The program's superior production values paid off, literally: Whereas poor picture quality precluded syndication for most kinescoped 1950s programs, *The Adventures*, shot on 60 mm film, has been in reruns on independent and cable channels since 1967.

Excluding salaries, episodes cost $14,000 each in 1952 and between $55,000 and $80,000 in 1960, exorbitant figures for a half-hour sitcom. "Nothing is expensive if it shows up on the screen," Ozzie asserted, quoting movie mogul Cecil B. deMille. ABC bottom-liners didn't share that view and occasionally called from New York to complain. "But Ozzie usually got his way," said assistant director Dick Bremerkamp. Drawing eighteen million viewers weekly afforded Ozzie tremendous clout with the network, which from 1952 to 1957 placed only three programs in the A. C. Nielsen top twenty-five.[2]

[2] Surprisingly, despite its enormous cultural impact, *The Adventures of Ozzie and Harriet* attained only average ratings. This was largely due to the fact that during the 1950s ABC's national coverage lagged behind both CBS's and NBC's by 10 percent. The baby network didn't achieve parity until the Nelsons were off the air.

Within his own company, Ozzie was Boss. Anyone who overlooked that or fancied himself indispensable was effectively disposed of, as Don Defore learned. The accomplished stage and screen actor played the Nelsons' dapperly attired neighbor for *The Adventures'* first four seasons. Thorny Thornbury embodied every suburbanite's worst nightmare: the infernal nuisance from next door whose affable exterior conceals a con man's soul. A fellow fugitive from the workforce, Thorny regularly embezzled Ozzie's sodas, stuck him with the bill at the malt shop, and in general exploited his good nature. Defore was the only actor aside from the four Nelsons to ever receive star billing. His comical backyard scenes with Ozzie made up some of *The Adventures*'s early highlights.

But when Defore pressured Ozzie for a raise and more publicity following the 1955–56 season, Ozzie dropped the immensely popular Thorny from the show, angry that Defore failed to conduct business agent to agent. "I never should have said what I did to Ozzie," the actor lamented three decades later. "I was out of line." And temporarily out of work.

Skip Young offered this summation of Ozzie: "One of the greatest people in the world to work *with;* one of the toughest people in the world to work *for.*" Yet no matter what others thought of him, Ozzie always commanded respect. It's interesting that years after his death, men and women in their fifties and sixties still refer to him as "Mister Nelson." Those who didn't get along with him were mostly outsiders: network executives, casting agents, and the like. The actors and crew who worked for him daily pledged unanimous devotion, Young and Defore included.

"The years I spent on the show were the happiest of my life," Parley Baer said blissfully, a sentiment echoed by virtually all the show's actors. Working in such a stressless atmosphere, cast and crew became family, and members remained for so long, "When you came in season after season, it was rare to see anyone new in the studio," said Baer, best known as the voice of Deputy Chester Proudfoot on radio's *Gunsmoke*. That camaraderie, coupled with the leisurely pace, made *The Adven-*

tures of Ozzie and Harriet unusually enjoyable and problem-free for everyone—except Rick and David.

Originally Ozzie and Harriet incorporated the boys into *The Adventures* in order to remain close to them, yet in doing so they risked driving Rick and David away. Parent-child relationships are fragile enough even in the best of families. Any strain among the Nelsons was complicated by the fact that Rick and David related to Ozzie and Harriet on three levels: as children to parents, as actors playing children to actors playing their parents, and as employees to employers.

"It was a little tough on the kids," said writer Ben Gershman, noting that Ozzie didn't lower his rigorous standards even for his own sons. "He and Harriet were very strict. You couldn't monkey around, and you'd better know your lines." Harriet admitted in 1958, "When the boys were younger, it required some adjustment for them to get used to having Ozzie as boss and director during the day and their father at home."

Looking back, David said that it was vital to compartmentalize the real and fictional families, something not always easy for him. If wires crossed, sparks flew. Rick, however, reflected, "I don't think I ever had any trouble separating fantasy from reality. They were our parents first, and the relationship didn't change that much [when working together] on the show."

According to Charley Britt, a cast member and one of Rick's closest friends, Ozzie drew a clear line between his dual authority roles as father and director. "He never said, 'You do it that way because I'm your dad and I told you so.' I saw Rick and David take Ozzie to task sometimes over the way a scene is played, or certain dialogue. They argued professionally about a lot of things, but it didn't go outside the parameters of director-actor."

On the set Rick was known as "Mile-away Nelson," forever disappearing. He usually could be found on the lot either banging a piano in the family's private two-room bungalow; buying chocolate bars and sodas at the studio snack shack; or outside tossing a football and getting grass stains on his wardrobe. Rick loved riding the camera dolly, then later a bicycle around the set, and then, a motorcycle.

Containing Rick was the first hurdle; getting him to review his scripts was next. Before scenes, David repaired to a small room and studied conscientiously. His younger brother, however, passed the time with older actors such as Hal Smith, who later played the amiable drunkard Otis Campbell on *The Andy Griffith Show*. Smith incurred the crew's wrath for teaching Rick to blow saliva bubbles as part of a disgusting game they called Bombs Away.

The cast's seasoned actors were always impressed by Rick's ability to stop whatever he was doing, step right into a scene, and "be Ricky." But he could never memorize his lines. When he was eight and first acting on radio, Rick used to drift off and hum; as a teenager his mind still wandered. Yet no matter how many times Rick drew blanks—requiring as many as twenty takes of a single line—Ozzie rarely lost his temper, shouting encouragement like a third-base coach to a batter with men on base:

"Come on, Ricky, that's an easy line; you can get it!"

Inside, Ozzie was fuming, for Rick's flubs ate up time and money.

To compensate, Rick planted dialogue around the set with the deftness of a KGB wiretapper. "Hey, get out of that cookie jar! I don't want you spoiling your dinner!" Harriet continually scolded him on the show. It was either that or spoil the take: Inside the jar, scribbled on a slip of paper, was Rick's next line. Kitchen drawers and backs of doors were also popular hiding spots.

The Nelsons believed that work was work and home was home, confining family disagreements to prop master Jack Iannarelli's kitchen, which had soundproof double doors. He and crew members recall how well the four handled an enormously trying arrangement that would have unraveled many other theatrical families. Still, occasionally tension flared. The extraordinary number of hours that Rick and David spent with Ozzie and Harriet "in public" may have contributed to the boys' lack of expressiveness with their mother and father.

This is surprising given Ozzie's glowing memories of the George and Ethel Nelson household. In his 1973 autobiography, *Ozzie,* he wrote, "Ours was a hugging and kissing family with a great feeling of closeness and genuine affection." Brother Alfred and his wife, Kay, duplicated that with their brood of five sons, but Rick and David acted more aloof.

Jack Wagner, who played the waiter in the malt shop as well as numerous bit parts, recalled a small Camino Palmero Christmas gathering many years ago. "Ricky came walking into the room, and I remember Ozzie saying, 'Hi, Rick.' 'Oh, hi, Dad.' Like nothing out of the ordinary. I thought he'd been hiding in the kitchen or something. Later I learned that he'd been out of town for weeks and had just gotten back," said Wagner. "There wasn't any of that warm family affection. I don't know why."

Rick's cousin Rich Nelson suggested this lack of demonstrativeness was more Harriet's nature than Ozzie's. "She's just not a physically affectionate type of person," he explained.

Whatever the reason, it seems to have been the family way forever. "I used to watch Rick and Harriet," said a close friend from Rick's later years, "and it was like they had a professional relationship. They'd hug and kiss when they saw each other, but almost as if they were feigning affection for my benefit, like they thought they were supposed to 'be' Ricky and Harriet."

Even after their success, the Nelsons continued to live on quiet Camino Palmero. Ozzie and Harriet maintained as normal a home life as possible, not only for their sons but for themselves. "Home and family are important to Ozzie because he was raised in a stable, old-fashioned household," Harriet said in 1952. "They're important to me because I was brought up in a trunk."

Hollywood's life-style held little appeal for the Nelsons. The normally friendly Ozzie felt uncomfortable in large groups, preferring private get-togethers with family, colleagues, and close friends such as the Fred MacMurrays and the Andy Devines. The few parties he and Harriet threw were subdued, with more ice cream than liquor served.

As part of their effort to keep Rick and David unaffected, Ozzie and Harriet studiously downplayed their careers and status. Once the boys themselves became stars, they followed their parents' advice, "The best way to have people forget that you are a celebrity is to forget it yourself." Shy Rick was so modest about his fame, said friend Mary Jo Sheeley, "My sister Sharon and I once pulled up in front of his house the same time he did. Rick came over to the car and said he'd just gotten off work. Not thinking, Sharon asked, 'Oh? Where do you work?'

"Rick looked at her and laughed. 'I'm a box boy at Ralphs supermarket.' At times you just forgot who he was and what he did."

Joe Sutton, who lived two blocks away on Vista Street, said of the Nelson brothers, "They may have been stars, but not in their own house. They did what we did; we had chores to do, they had chores to do." Far from being objects of resentment or envy, Rick and David may have even been somewhat pitied. Other youngsters their age didn't have their playtime curtailed to accommodate work or lessons in swimming, tennis, tap dancing, skiing, karate, iceskating, music, and horseback riding. "They were working kids," Sutton emphasized.

So as to disrupt their lives as little as possible, Ozzie scheduled the filming of his sons' scenes around school and sports, usually on Saturdays. Complicating this tight schedule was a California law that prohibited child actors from working more than four hours a day. With such constraints, it was not unusual to shoot parts of four different episodes the same day, creating a nightmare for the script and wardrobe departments.[3]

---

[3] Through the 1953–54 season the Nelsons continued taping their radio series, which aired on ABC Friday nights at nine.

Despite all the maneuvering, work still infringed on school-work, which the boys grudgingly fit in at night and on Sundays. At the time of their TV premiere, David was a junior at Hollywood High School, legendary for alumni that include Lana Turner, Fay Wray, Carol Burnett, Mickey Rooney, and many more.

Rick had just enrolled in Bancroft Junior High School, where he made little impression, quite a feat considering his weekly television appearances. Librarian Esther Schuster, now retired, remembered him as "quiet and well behaved." But she saw very little of Rick, who disdained literature. Ozzie avidly devoured the classics and could finish a volume in one hour. Rick read mostly comics and *Motor Trend* magazine; hardcover books made him squeamish.

So did his classes. "I can remember as a little kid hating to get up and go to school," he said when he was thirty-five. "The smell of it, the lead pencils, the hair tonic, the whole thing." Once Rick had mastered his radio scripts, the fourth-grader-turned-celebrity casually informed Harriet, "I guess this means I don't have to go to school anymore." It never occurred to him that his acting career might end before puberty did.

Ozzie better understood the bleak future awaiting many, if not most, child stars, and consequently stressed education. He tested the boys' spelling and knowledge of U.S. geography at the dinner table, and at night read them passages from Charles Dickens and F. Scott Fitzgerald.

Both he and Harriet were active in Rick's and David's schools and extracurricular activities, regularly attending PTA meetings. "They were very devoted, concerned parents," said Schuster. "Ozzie used to help the students work the audio-visual equipment." One pictures Ozzie unable to resist directing the children, advising, "You know, if I were centering that illustration on the opaque projector, I might, uh, try it *this* way . . ."

Rick followed David to Hollywood High and left his mark on the institution by sharing with classmate Bruce Belland the distinction of flunking typing class. Said Belland, a senior during

Rick's freshman year, "He was introverted, so I'd do these outrageous things to make him laugh, and then we'd both get in trouble."

Rick's schoolmates, supposedly accustomed to celebrities, made it difficult for him to get from class to class, "It was like making an appearance," he recalled. In his junior year Rick dropped out to study privately with Professor Randolph Van Scoyk, a bookish-looking man who'd worked in other capacities for motion-picture studios: contract writer, assistant director, talent scout, and storyman.

As required by law for actors under seventeen, Rick received a minimum three hours a day of instruction at General Service Studio. Many former child actors have criticized their studio-sponsored educations, claiming they were left disadvantaged once their show-business days were over. "It was pretty much a sham," contended Billy Gray, Bud Anderson on *Father Knows Best*, "fifteen minutes here, half an hour there. There was no continuity."

Rick's curriculum was oriented toward English and political science—classic preparation for law school—with no math or science. "Ozzie arranged it so that we had a full morning together every day," said Van Scoyk, who also taught David. "There was never any problem getting Ricky's time." Or his attention. Despite his distaste for academics, Rick was cooperative and always well mannered. "Ozzie and Harriet saw to that."

Still, both brothers barely stayed ahead in their studies. "Because we had so little free time," said David, "on weekends we'd try cramming everything into two days of partying. We'd be so exhausted by the end, our grades suffered as a result."

By normal standards Ozzie and Harriet were very good parents. And by show-business standards, with children casually farmed out to maids, nannies, and boarding schools, they were exceptional. Harriet was especially determined the boys not be raised "by remote control," as she called it, and so even though they could afford a full household staff, the Nelsons retained only a housekeeper.

Despite their conservative political bent, Ozzie and Harriet could be surprisingly liberal when it came to youthful self-expression, illustrated in a scene from "The Late Christmas" (1952–53). Rick trots downstairs on his way out of the house, dressed in an outrageous ensemble of polka-dot tie, wildly patterned hat, and baggy, cuffed pants. Had he been young Rusty Williams of the abrasive *Make Room for Daddy,* his fascist father would have executed an exaggerated double take before wagging a finger and shouting, "You get upstairs and change outta that clown costume, young man, before I rip it off-a your back!" *Father Knows Best*'s Jim Anderson would have taken son Bud aside and patiently explained the importance of conforming to community standards.

Harriet merely glanced up and smiled. Had the scene been for real, she probably would have done the same. Ozzie also possessed a sensitivity rare to adults, that of reflecting honestly on his own youth whenever guiding and disciplining the boys. His philosophy is contained in "Rick's Old Printing Press," a 1964–65 installment: "Most people don't take the trouble to understand kids," he tells neighbor Joe Randolph (Lyle Talbot). "But if you're reasonable with them and respect their point of view, they'll be reasonable with you."

Ozzie's tolerance had its limits when it came to the length of his youngest son's thick dark brown hair. In Rick's early teens it looked as if he combed it in a wind tunnel: parted on the left, lashed down with brilliantine on the right, and swept up in front, with random strands sprouting like TV antennae. On the show, David had a number of insulting descriptions for Rick's hair style, among them "porcupine special" and "melon head."

"It was a real point of contention between Ricky and his father," said Sally Hughes, who as Ozzie's secretary had the unpleasant task of driving the reluctant young victim to the barber shop. "He'd climb silently into the car and sit there like this"—she folded her arms in front of her and imitated Rick's sulk—"the whole way." Ozzie never issued his edicts imperiously, often phrasing them as questions that to the uninitiated sounded nonthreatening. Rick understood, though, that "Um, son, don't you think it's time you got your hair trimmed?" meant "Get a haircut *now*."

"There was no talking back," said Hughes. Rick never dared protest like he did on an episode called "Individuality" (1954–55): "I have to keep it this way . . . Otherwise people would think I'm David!"

Depending on which generation you speak to, Ozzie is described as either strict or tyrannical. Don Defore, himself a father of five, had nothing but admiration for how the elder Nelson kept his boys in line "without dogmatic, harsh discipline. Ozzie did a great job raising the two guys; extremely unusual for a Hollywood family." At home Rick and David addressed their parents with the same filial piety as on the show: "Yes sir," "No sir"; "Yes ma'am," "No ma'am."

Frequently sounded out for advice on parenting, Ozzie told a newspaper in 1958, "I don't think a father or mother deserves a child's respect merely by virtue of being a parent. What we've tried to do is earn the boys' respect." Without question, they succeeded. "Those boys respected their parents the way kids are supposed to respect their parents, and maybe don't anymore," said friend Sharon Sheeley.

She and others who knew Rick and David suggested the brothers may sometimes have feared Ozzie. Not that he was physically abusive; in fact, few can recall hearing him raise his voice. And to be fair, adolescents as a rule tend to feel persecuted by most adults, often viewing them as more ogreish than they really are. But "Ozzie ruled with an iron hand," said Lorrie Collins, one of Rick's first serious loves. "He was an extremely domineering, intimidating person and expected an awful lot from Ricky and David. They didn't want to let him down."

One way David tried to please his father was by participating in sports. Like his dad, he played quarterback and running back, wearing numbers 15 and 70 for the Hollywood High B and varsity teams. David, broader and more muscular than Ozzie, stood five foot ten and weighed 170 pounds by the time he was sixteen. He may have even been a better player.

"But I don't think his heart was really in it," observed writer Bill Davenport. "David idolized his dad and just naturally followed in his footsteps." In "The Football Hero" (1955–56), Harriet says accusingly to Ozzie, "I think [Rick's] out there [playing football] just to please you." In real life the line actually applied to David.

Rick also pushed himself in athletics. A gifted baseball and football player, he was one of the few pesky kid brothers permitted to join David and his friends on the ballfield. "Rick was the pip-squeak," neighbor Joe Sutton recalled, "a feisty little guy who never backed down from a challenge."

Blessed with remarkable coordination, Rick was the fifth-ranked tennis player in the California junior boys division. He and doubles partner Allen Fox reached the 1956 National Indoor Junior Championship semifinals. "Rick could compete with anyone in the country," said Fox, now tennis coach at Pepperdine University in Malibu, California. A three-time member of the U.S. Davis Cup team, Fox believes that had Rick committed himself fully to the sport, "he'd have been one hell of a player."

Though several credits short, Rick officially graduated from Hollywood High School in June 1958 with a B average. David, meanwhile, had studied cinema at the University of Southern California but quit in his junior year. He recalled, "After a big talk with my father—and this was a *big* talk, because he was really procollege—I finally convinced him that a degree wasn't going to do me much good."

Rick, too, saw little reason for college when he was already in the 93-percent income-tax bracket. At thirteen he was making over $100,000 annually and by his sixteenth birthday had amassed a personal fortune of $500,000. Rick found financial matters as boring as school, replying indifferently to reporters' ceaseless inquiries about his money, "I don't handle it, and I don't care about it."

Ozzie and Harriet managed it for him, conferring once a year with family attorney Donald Kelley—the real Donald Kelley, not the imperious TV-show character (played by Joe Flynn, later Captain Wallace B. Binghampton on *McHale's Navy*) in whose law firm David worked. Both boys' earnings went into trust funds supervised by the Los Angeles Superior Court and payable on their twenty-first birthdays. When they reached that age, Rick and David reinvested the estimated $250,000 in other trusts maturing when they turned thirty, thirty-five, and so on.

Subject to court approval, other monies were invested on their behalf, though Rick was hard-pressed to spell out the details. "I think David and I own part of a place called Santa Claus Village, near San Francisco," he feebly explained to gossip columnist Hedda Hopper. "Then I think there's a place near Palm Springs. It's an apartment house." After a pause, the shy teenager added, "I actually don't know; they didn't explain it to me."

"They," his parents, were legally entitled to 50 percent of Rick's and David's salaries but put their half into additional trust funds for the boys. With a joint yearly income topping $300,000, Ozzie and Harriet were rich, and had been for most of their adult lives. However, to his sons Ozzie always underplayed the extent of the family fortune, perhaps recalling Horatio Alger's cautionary words that "to be born to wealth removes all the incentives to action and checks the spirit of enterprise."

While not about to denounce capitalism, Ozzie wasn't bound ethically by the bottom line, believing, "You shouldn't work for money itself as a goal, but for the enjoyment you get out of doing your best; the money will follow." His influence on Rick is clear. In 1959 the teenager told a reporter, "If you

53

worry about just money, you'll never be successful, you know?" he said. "I've never thought about it. To me there's something much more important, and that's personal satisfaction."

Throughout Rick's life, money would remain an abstract concept because he rarely carried any. At fourteen he scraped by on fifty cents a week; four years later his parents raised his allowance to fifty dollars. On *The Adventures,* the boys go to Ozzie for pocket money—only their father is perpetually strapped for cash and borrows sheepishly from Harriet, as might be expected of a man with no discernible source of income. Offscreen, Ozzie was more freespending than Harriet. Whenever Rick asked his mother for movie money, she'd say, "How much is it?" "One dollar." And she'd give him one dollar. At least Ozzie would come across with ten.

Rick often found himself short at week's end. He and Sharon Sheeley wanted to see a movie one night, but digging their hands into their pockets found only lint. So they resourcefully collected empty bottles, loaded up Rick's car, and cashed them in. When the store clerk dumped the bottles out back, where Rick was hiding, he regathered them, brought them around to the front, and cashed them in again.

Another time, Sharon's younger sister accompanied Rick, David, and David's date to the drive-in. "When we got there, we realized none of us had any money," Mary Jo recalled. "So we backed the car in through the exit gate." The picture they'd snuck into, an Irwin Allen adventure titled *The Big Circus,* starred Victor Mature, Red Buttons—and featured one David Nelson. David too was always low on funds. While in high school he nearly took an afternoon job at a supermarket for fifteen dollars a week, though his weekly TV salary was $1,500.

In his late teens, Rick increasingly expressed dissatisfaction with his financial arrangement. One day a friend named Robin Luke, also a young singer, remarked enviously about how much Rick was making. "Yeah," he grumbled, "but I won't ever get to *see* it." Rick never learned to handle money, and despite Ozzie's and Harriet's efforts to the contrary, his cavalier indifference was much like that of any other child born into wealth. Two decades later his being shielded from financial responsibility would haunt him.

With a national outcry over increased juvenile delinquency, the public, the network, and Ozzie expected Rick and David to serve as positive role models. David recalled, "My father would say to us, 'Listen, you guys, there's a morals clause in our contract with ABC that could be applied if either of you gets into any major trouble.'"

Both brothers did their best to faithfully uphold the Nelson reputation. When Rick was twenty-three, and David, twenty-six, *TV Guide* marveled, "The nation has watched them grow to manhood as examples of clean-cut respectability. No breath of scandal or minor scrape has touched either of them." One reason why, said David, was that "Rick and I really didn't have that much free time to get into trouble.

"Sure," he conceded, "we'd have loved to toss beer cans onto the street like everyone else, but we felt a responsibility to behave in a manner compatible to what we were on the air. And I honestly believe there was nothing wrong with that." Their obligation wasn't only to their family but to the extended family on the set. As Ozzie frequently reminded them, "You'll be putting forty adults and their families out of work."

Rick gave Ozzie more cause for concern than his older brother. At cliquish Hollywood High David belonged to the Elksters, a fraternity of about a dozen conservative, sports-minded teenagers. When Rick pledged to the Elksters a few years later, they turned him down, claiming he was too wild. In retaliation he joined the Rooks, more a gang than a club, its members' reputations as sullied as the Elksters' were sterling.

Rooks sported sideburns, leather, and heavy boots. Anxious to fit in, Rick lubricated his hair till it practically dripped oil like a leaky transmission, tattooed his hands, wrist, and shoulder with India ink and a sewing needle, and accompanied the Rooks on their nighttime cruises, harassing, and beating up random victims along Hollywood Boulevard. Another group pastime, stealing road barriers by the Hollywood Bowl, landed Rick in jail twice. Both times Ozzie had to bail him out. Fortunately, said David, "In those days, if anybody got into trouble, the studios tried like hell to keep it quiet."

Some Rooks graduated to armed robbery. And prison. Rick did not participate in those crime sprees but admitted he came perilously close to being corrupted. "I was always a greaser at heart," he once said. Only fear of his father's wrath kept him relatively in line during his youth. Unlike David, Rick was naturally rebellious and insecure, and his urgent desire for acceptance sometimes overrode his sense of family duty.

Rick didn't need a gang to get into trouble. One night when he was eighteen, he and Sharon Sheeley went to visit a friend at the Park Sunset Hotel. Rick parked in back despite a sign's posted warning, "Tenant Parking Only." Returning to the lot several hours later, they spotted a policeman waiting by Rick's brand-new customized bronze 1958 Plymouth Fury. "I told you we were going to get into trouble," Sharon hissed at him.

"Just do what I tell you," he whispered back, as the officer approached and asked accusingly, "Is this your car?"

Pretending to be distracted, Rick replied, "Uh, no sir. We're looking for ours."

The policeman walked a few steps away, and Rick murmured to his companion, "When I yell 'Now!' jump in the passenger seat and don't say a word . . .

"Now!"

As Sharon leaped into the Fury, Rick spun around and sucker-punched the cop, scrambled in, and sped off, tires screeching. They raced along Sunset Boulevard, back to Camino Palmero. "You assaulted a policeman!" Sharon shouted in astonishment.

"Better to assault a policeman," Rick answered, "than to be assaulted by my dad."

Rick made a quick left from Vista Street onto his own, then jammed on the brake. There in front of his house sat a black-

and-white police car. America's most famous teenager had been recognized. "Shit!" he blurted, while Sharon glared at him as if to say "Now what?"

After some thought, Rick led her around to the back door. Tiptoeing into the kitchen, they wedged themselves behind the refrigerator and listened as Ozzie calmly responded to the officer's charges.

". . . striking a policeman? That doesn't sound like Rick. I'll have a talk with him when he gets home. . ."

From behind the refrigerator: "Shit."

". . . good night, and thanks . . . you fellows on the force do a terrific job . . ." After seeing the policemen out, Ozzie closed the front door, marched into the kitchen and barked, "Rick? Sharon? You can come out now." Rick never revealed to her his punishment, but assumedly it was swift and severe.

Normally Rick didn't seek trouble, it sought him. Being a celebrity, and by his late teens every adolescent girl's fantasy, he was sometimes the object of male envy and harassment. Larry Geller attended Fairfax High School, a football rival of Hollywood High's. After classes, he said, many of the students there congregated at a North Fairfax Avenue delicatessen. "One afternoon Ricky showed up because he liked some girl that went to our school," recalled Geller, later Elvis Presley's hair stylist and confidante. "The place started buzzing: 'Ricky Nelson's here! Ricky Nelson's here!'"

Not everyone welcomed his presence. One hoodish teen muttered, "Who the hell does he think he is? I'm gonna get him."

"I went up to Ricky and told him, 'Hey, man, there's this guy here, and there's gonna be a problem,'" Geller said.

Rick looked perplexed. "A problem? I can't have that."

Another teenager came up to him, offering support and, if necessary, his fists.

"No, that's all right," Rick said quietly. "I think I should just get out of here."

The agitator spoke up. "You don't have to go." Then, squinting, as if sizing Rick up, he added, "You're not a chicken-shit, are ya?"

"No, man, I'm not a chicken-shit," Rick retorted.

Just then the ally charged the tough, who after fending off a few weak jabs lifted and heaved him through the front window with a resounding crash. Shards of glass and splattered blood covered the sidewalk, while startled passersby helped the injured boy to his feet. Rick saw none of this, having bolted for the door as soon as the first punch was thrown.

Avoiding a conflict wasn't like Rick, six foot one by his eighteenth birthday and a student of karate. Outside a Laguna Beach hamburger drive-in where he, Sharon Sheeley, and Glen Larson, a member of the Four Preps, stopped, he once took on three assailants. Rick had just switched off the ignition in the parking lot, when a trio from Sharon's high-school football team sauntered over and began testing the car's suspension, rocking it back and forth. Then they all sat on the hood, arms folded, smirking.

Calmly, Rick warned, "Don't sit on the car."

More smirks. "Oh yeah? What are you gonna do about it, *pretty boy?*" And they bounced up and down on the front end some more.

Rick's hand was on the door handle in a flash. "Are you with me?" he called to Larson, hunkered down in the back seat and not anxious to be deputized.

"No way, Red Ryder. You're on your own."

With that, Rick stepped out and, combining karate kicks and right hooks, leveled all three. Surveying the damage, he then said coolly, *"I told you not to jump on my car."*

Cars were one of Rick's passions, the other being girls. The two are so closely linked in California culture that licenses and contraceptives should probably be issued together. Rick, however, experienced back-seat pleasures before ever getting behind the wheel.

The newspaper promo for a November 1957 *Adventure* pictured fetching blond actress Rosemary Ace, who, according to the caption, "gets Rick Nelson's first TV kiss tonight." But "Ricky's Big Night," as the episode was titled, actually took place about four years before. Sexually precocious, Rick told friends two stories of losing his virginity. In one, he was thirteen, and his partner was the eager teenage maid for a neighboring household. In the other, he was summer-vacationing overseas with his family.

On the eve of the Nelsons' departure from London, Rick, David, and a friend from the States went cruising the city's notorious East End for prostitutes. The nervous fourteen-year-old kept declining women's offers until finally his disgusted mates left him in the car, hiked to a nearby pub, and returned with a plump blond hooker. Before Rick could blurt "No thanks," she had his sweaty hand in hers and was pulling him out of his seat. The two disappeared down a dark alley, Rick wearing a derby and twirling a cane like Charlie Chaplin, and trying to get his bony arm over the woman's broad shoulders. David thought he'd never see his little brother again.

The next day the Nelsons were chauffeured to Southampton for their voyage home. Worried that his mother somehow knew where he'd been and what he'd done, Rick guiltily averted his eyes the entire trip. When he returned to London in 1972 and 1985 to sing at the Royal Albert Hall, Rick spent half the night after the shows searching for that alley. As if conducting a guided tour of a historic landmark, he announced to his companions, "This is where I became a man!"

Teenage Rick rendezvoused with hookers other times, often while on weeklong tennis tours. After tournaments, the bored young players "went out drinking and partying," said partner Allen Fox, "whatever we could do." One night entailed several of them piling into a Champaign, Illinois, brothel, where each paid to spend time with a black prostitute. Except for sixteen-year-old Rick, all the other boys were virgins.

Looking back, Fox believes "Ricky went along to be one of

the boys," and probably reluctantly. Had the whorehouse been raided, the team members arrested, and their names released to the papers, "Ricky would have been hurt the most out of all of us. He wasn't looking out for himself too well."

The same could be said of Rick's youthful disregard of speed limits. For his sixteenth birthday Ozzie and Harriet gave Rick a beautiful metallic green Porsche.

At three in the morning the Saturday before Christmas 1956, the car skidded out of control on slick Sunset Boulevard, flipping three times before finally coming to a rest utterly demolished. Passenger Forrest Stewart walked away from the accident uninjured, but Rick had to be hospitalized with a bumped head and a cracked vertebra. "I wasn't speeding or anything," Rick solemnly swore to *Photoplay* magazine, which regularly covered the Nelson brothers' exploits. Unless the Beverly Hills limit had been raised to eighty miles an hour.

Indicative of the kind of parents Ozzie and Harriet were, Rick received no lectures or I-told-you-so's. "I guess they figured if I hadn't learned by then, I never would," said Rick. However, the next time he pulled into the General Service Studio lot, it was in the replacement car they'd wisely selected for him: a sedate blue Plymouth.

Four

A t sixteen, Rick was America's most celebrated teenager. A TV star. An adolescent sex symbol. On his way to becoming a millionaire. Yet despite all he'd accomplished at such a young age, for Rick life truly didn't begin until he discovered rock & roll.

Since early childhood, Rick had used music as an escape. When he was five, he would come home from school, dial in a classical station on his parents' Victrola console radio, and curl up beside a living room heat duct. Lost in reverie, warmth, and music, he'd lie there for hours. Subsequent interests included Dixieland, modern jazz, rhythm & blues, and country & western, all components of the form that would alter his destiny.

A musical mongrel, rock & roll existed long before its 1951 christening, allegedly by Alan Freed, a white disc jockey on

Cleveland radio station WJW. But how long before? The two-and-four backbeat that inspired Freed's coinage powered 1940s black rhythm & blues recordings, or "race records," in music-industry cant. The familiar I-IV-V chord pattern dated back to pre–World War I New Orleans blues. And the imploring, impassioned vocals hailed from country & western, blues, and gospel, the roots of each traceable to previous centuries, to Deep South plantations and levees, to Great Britain, and to Africa.

Such genealogy was superfluous to Rick and the millions of other teenagers who came of age in the mid-1950s. They were instantly, utterly, consumed by rock & roll, which seemed spanking new and, most important, uniquely theirs. As one sympathetic elder, pediatrician Dr. Benjamin Spock, observed, "We keep our adolescents in school and colleges, where they go on learning about the techniques of our civilization, with little opportunity to feel they are full-fledged members of it."

Rock & roll united this age group, giving it a subculture and a strident communal voice. Grown-ups, previously ambivalent, perhaps distrustful, toward teens, grew irrationally fearful. *Cosmopolitan* magazine asked parents, "Are You Afraid of Your Teenager?" The answer for many was yes.

Without the spark of youthful restlessness, rock & roll might never have ignited, but invariably it was blamed for everything from juvenile delinquency to premarital pregnancy; irrefutable evidence of a generation going to the dogs. Even in the wake of failed McCarthyism, paranoia and conspiracy theories lingered, and establishment backlash to rock & roll verged on the hysterical. Southern segregationists charged that the National Association for the Advancement of Colored People (NAACP) was infiltrating white America with this "immoral" music and demanded it be banned at once. Others branded rock & roll what else but a Communist-inspired scourge.

The U.S. news media set out on a concerted campaign to discredit rock & roll, especially savaging teenage favorite Elvis Presley. In 1956 he made an easy target: a twenty-one-year-old southern truck driver, divinely handsome, incomparably successful, and, to his detriment, exceedingly polite. Reporters nationwide gleefully sharpened their pencils.

Ultimately, the vicious antirock crusade failed to whittle teenagers' enthusiasm. If anything they rallied in more fervent support of maligned heroes such as Presley, who counted among his ardent fans sixteen-year-old Rick Nelson.

Inexplicably, Rick felt a kinship with Elvis and other singers from the poor rural South whose records he heard on the radio: Carl Perkins, Johnny Cash, Roy Orbison, Jerry Lee Lewis, Billy Riley. All initially recorded for Sun Records, the laboratory responsible for the musical hybrid known as rockabilly.

Housed in a converted radiator shop at 706 Union Avenue, Memphis, Tennessee, Sun was started in 1950 by an entrepreneurial ex-disc jockey from Alabama named Sam Phillips. At first it functioned solely as a recording studio, Memphis Recording Service. But by 1953 when Elvis Presley recorded a ten-inch acetate of two Ink Spots numbers there, it was Sun Records. A year later the blue-eyed singer's "That's All Right (Mama)" created a regional stir. Phillips had long quested for a white performer with what he called "the Negro sound and the Negro feel," certain he could make a billion dollars. He found that singer in Presley, but settled for $35,000 when he sold Elvis's contract to RCA Records in December 1955.

What a steal, thought Phillips, and it was—for RCA. The next year alone Presley racked up four number-one hits and earned an estimated $1 million, streaking down the road to stardom in a guady Cadillac. There is no overstating Elvis's lasting impact on popular music and popular culture, no such thing as hyperbole. The most illustrious star of the twentieth century? The most influential? The ultimate American success story? Yes. Yes. Yes.

The same month Elvis left Phillips's label, another West Tennessean lugged his guitar and amplifier to the corner of Union and Marshall and inside recorded a song he'd just written, "Blue Suede Shoes." Released on January 1, 1956, Sun single number

63

234 launched two careers: that of Carl Perkins and, indirectly, that of Rick Nelson, for whom "Blue Suede Shoes" was an epiphany. He later called it the first truly rock & roll record he ever heard.

Rick revered Presley but felt his influence mainly stylistically. When his friend Sharon Sheeley mentioned that Elvis dyed his hair black, Rick, then seventeen, immediately had her do the same to his dark brown locks. David deflated his brother's ego by telling him, "You look more like Danny Thomas than Elvis Presley." Harriet had a fit, not over her son's appearance but the mess in the bathroom. "My God, you kids," she yelled, brandishing a ruined towel, "look what you've done!"

Musically, Carl Perkins moved Rick more than any other artist. "I wanted to sound like him as much as I could," Rick said many times. The son of an indigent sharecropper, Perkins briefly rivaled Presley, but plain looks and ragged luck worked against him. With "Blue Suede Shoes" ascending the pop-music charts, the singer-guitarist, his manager, and his band were en route to New York for appearances on the Perry Como and Ed Sullivan shows when their car crashed near Dover, Delaware, in the early morning hours of March 22, 1956.

Perkins fractured his shoulder and broke four ribs, and couldn't work for six months, irreparably damaging his momentum. Convalescing at home, he practically fell out of bed while watching Presley announce, "I wanna do my new record," and belt out "Blue Suede Shoes" on *The Milton Berle Show.*

By coincidence, *The Perry Como Show* rebooked Perkins for the same fall show as Ozzie and Harriet Nelson. Before the broadcast, he lounged in his dressing room with drummer W. S. Holland and his guitar-playing brothers Jay and Clayton, when Harriet stuck her head in, wanting to know which of the four was Carl.

"I am," he said, then exclaimed, "Why, you're Mrs. Nelson!"

"That's right. Carl, do you have a song called"—she thought for a moment—" 'Stopping the Blues'?"

With southern politesse, Perkins gently corrected her. "Why, no ma'am: *'Boppin'* the Blues.'" It was his second single, issued over the summer.

"That's the one! Ricky is driving me insane singing that song. He loves it, and he loves you."

When Rick finally met his idol in 1985, he laughed as Perkins recounted the story. "That sounds like Mom," he said, shaking his head. "*'Stopping* the Blues.' That's how much she knew about rockabilly."

Word of a new Perkins or Johnny Cash 45 sent Rick scurrying to Wallich's Music City at the corner of Sunset Boulevard and Vine Street. Fittingly, Rick's Hollywood star, awarded in 1975, was placed in front of the store, which has since closed. Singles cost eighty-nine cents in the late 1950s, and Rick spent many times that amount snatching up every Sun record he could find. Just gazing at the golden yellow label that promised music as bold as the block-letter SUN logo filled him with excitement.

Why did rockabilly stir Rick's teenage soul? What made this "blues with a country beat" combust were its performers, among the most colorful rock & roll has ever seen. Presley, Lewis, Gene Vincent, and lesser-knowns Billy Riley, Johnny Horton, Johnny and Dorsey Burnette, the Collins Kids—their distinctive personalities reverberate through the sparse instrumentation.

All but a few were recording novices; thus their rollicking performances boil over with nervous excitement. Tempos are hellbent, vocals giddy. On "That's All Right (Mama)," Presley sounds so keyed up, voice quavering throughout, your leg twitches sympathetically just listening to him.

It makes perfect sense that rockabilly, with its ingenuous, instinctual style, captivated Rick, always averse to the precision of acting. Rock & roll was immediate, stressing emotion over perfection. "He liked the honesty in the lyrics," said girlfriend Lorrie Collins, a singer-guitarist and one-half of the Collins Kids with her younger brother, Larry. "That's what Rick wanted to be: an artist who could sing a song about the way life really was."

Rick kept his desire to rock & roll secret for two years. He'd test his voice in the bathroom and the Los Angeles Tennis Club showers, to simulate that gloriously echoing Sun Records sound. But his tennis teammates were unimpressed and razzed him mercilessly. "No one thought he was any good at all," Allen Fox remembered. "It was quite a shock to us that he did so well later on."

Rick was as naturally inclined musically as he was athletically. At eight he took up the clarinet, later tooting it in the Bancroft Junior High School band. Next he received a drum set, which he practiced in a small upstairs space muffled with blankets, until Ozzie and Harriet banished him outside to the soundproof poolhouse.

David, meanwhile, had been forced into taking piano lessons. "A real drag," he called them. "I had maybe three, and that was it; from then on I didn't have anything to do with music." But he did teach fourteen-year-old Rick his first rudimentary guitar chords on Ozzie's "pregnant ukulele," a four-string tenor guitar.

"We'd go in the bathroom," David recalled, "and play Johnny Cash records and sing along." Until Rick began studying with famed flamenco guitarist Vincente Gomez at eighteen, he could play a regular guitar only by removing the bottom two strings.

Rick's intentions to record turned serious for the same reason that has motivated thousands of careers: He wanted to impress a girl. Her name was Arlene, a bronze beauty, and the desire of every male at Hollywood High. That she was an older woman of seventeen only heightened Rick's infatuation, as did her distinct lack of interest in him, which remained unchanged after several dates.

Their last evening out together, Rick was returning Arlene to her San Fernando Valley home, speeding up twisting Laurel Canyon Boulevard in his Porsche. Conversation having expired somewhere around Mulholland Drive, he turned on the radio in desperation, filling the car with a robust voice bawling, "Blue moon of Kentucky, keep on a-shinin' . . ."

Arlene sprang to life. "Ooooo, Elvis! He's the absolute end!" she cried, hiking the volume until The King seemed to be riding between them. Arlene recited a litany of Presley's attributes: how gorgeous he was, what a dreamy voice he had, and—

"Aw, he's not so much," Rick blurted. Before he could stop himself, he added, "*I'm* making a record too, y'know." Arlene responded with a disbelieving laugh. It was a lie, of course, the kind corruptive hormones will teenage boys to tell teenage girls. As Arlene continued snickering, Rick thought, *Now I have to make a record, just one, so I can hand it to her and say, "Now laugh."*

Not long after, Rick briefly imitated Presley on an episode of *The Adventures.* The brothers are on their way to a masquerade party, David descending the stairs exotically costumed as Yul Brynner in *The King and I,* followed by Rick with pasted-on sideburns, striped wide-lapel jacket, string tie, gaucho hat, and guitar. Campily swiveling his narrow hips, the sixteen-year-old leers into the camera while mumbling a snatch of "Love Me Tender" and hits a chord. When Dick Bremerkamp yelled "Cut!" the crew erupted in wild applause.

"Everybody just went crazy," said Sally Hughes, struck by how Rick, normally reserved and expressionless, grinned shyly, his blue eyes gleaming. She noted, "It was the first time I ever saw him seem pleased with himself."

So pleased, that the next day he announced to his father, "Pop, I'd like to make a record. Can you help me?" From Rick's serious tone, Ozzie knew this was no youthful whim. And having been a musician—and a pop star—himself, he treated it accordingly.

Rick had by now converted Ozzie to rock & roll. "I wish you'd listen to some of this stuff with an open mind," he'd say. "A lot of it is really good." Ozzie later admitted, "At first Harriet and I took a dim view of it." But he was broad-minded enough to recognize that dance music has traditionally drawn adult ire, and that "Be-Bop-A-Lula" and "Tutti Frutti" were no sillier than his era's "Mairzy Doats" and "A-Tisket A-Tasket."

Ozzie rose to the defense of teenagers and their music, telling *Look* magazine, "Anyone who connects rock & roll with juvenile delinquency is out of his mind or doesn't know anything about it," and the *New York Times,* "For the most part, I've found that it has simplified chords and a good beat."

Still, he also found much of it unmelodic and repetitious, and occasionally poked fun at the country's newest fad on the show. In "The Banjo Player" (1956–57), while Rick gathers his drums for a rehearsal, Ozzie asks, "You guys have any special arrangements at all?"

"No, we just rock & roll."

"Well, I mean, you can't do that all night. What do you do for a change of pace?"

"We stop playing."

Ozzie ultimately agreed to help Rick, but proceeded with characteristic caution. First he wanted to test his son's ability to perform minus the security of an ensemble. At Skip Young's suggestion he contacted George Stuart, director of Knott's Berry Farm's Birdcage Theatre in Buena Vista, California, and quietly reserved a spot for Rick during the vaudeville segment of its old-time melodramas.

As the play progressed, Rick paced nervously backstage. "He couldn't wait to get on and was driving us crazy!" Stuart recalled. "Every now and then he'd stop and *plink* a chord on his guitar, so finally we had to send him out back," because he was distracting the actors. When it came time to introduce Rick, Stuart simply announced, "And now we have on guitar, a young gentleman . . . Ricky Nelson." No mention of his famous parents sitting in the audience or their television series.

Thus, in the tradition of his father and Uncle Alfred, Rick staged his public musical debut in the olio. Stuart's recollection is that he sang "western-type music, no rock." But what sounded like western numbers to him were probably comparatively quiet, solo renditions of rockabilly. "The response was very good," said Stuart. "His mother and father wanted to see how he'd handle an audience that didn't know who he was, and they found out he could handle it real well."

Well enough for Ozzie to film Rick singing his then favorite song, Antoine "Fats" Domino's "I'm Walkin'," supported by an ad hoc group of musicians from the orchestra that supplied background music for the TV series. In early 1957 the Nelsons' MCA agents played the audio portion for record labels, twenty-two of which either flatly rejected it or made insultingly low offers. Then the tape crossed Barney Kessel's desk at Verve Records.

Owned by producer Norman Granz, Verve was one of approximately fifteen hundred independent U.S. recording companies. Today goliath corporate-owned labels dominate a centralized record industry in which independents stand little chance. But in 1956 "indies" accounted for more than one-third of the $300 million in retail record sales, with the rest going to the Big Four: RCA Victor, Columbia, Decca, and Capitol.

Independent labels such as Dot, Gee, and Specialty had profitably tapped into the burgeoning teenager record market with Pat Boone, Frankie Lymon and the Teenagers, and Little Richard, respectively. Though Verve recorded jazz acts, it sought to share in the riches rock & roll could generate and hired the thirty-three-year-old Kessel as pop-music A&R (artists and repertoire) chief. Catch us a hit act, he was told, and just weeks into the job he landed a big one.

Kessel was a famed jazz guitarist in his own right and, in the early 1940s, a Nelson orchestra sideman on radio. While not bowled over by Rick's demonstration tape, "It didn't take a genius," he said, "to figure out that if you work with someone already known and accepted, you don't have to spend as much time and energy breaking him to the public. Ricky was a cute kid on a successful TV show, and I figured that if he could learn to sing, even if he didn't know a note, it was worth trying."

Granz and Ozzie shook hands on a one-record deal with a

second-single option, and Kessel set to work with Rick. Up at Verve's offices the two rummaged through prospective songs, Kessel strumming them on his guitar, and Rick singing along. After lengthy trial-and-error they settled on a trio of tunes including "I'm Walkin'," a loping rhythm & blues number built around a simple, repetitive bass line.

White pop acts routinely pilfered R&B material previously recorded by black artists unable to reach as broad an audience due to the limited number of radio stations programmed to black tastes. Though many white forgeries, or "covers," slavishly copied the black originals, they almost always paled in comparison. Arrangements were tidier; lyrics, expurgated when necessary; and vocals gratingly earnest rather than playfully salacious. Inadvertently, these records seemed to point up the vast cultural differences between the two races.

Fats Domino had been victimized once already: In 1955 singer Pat Boone, whose skin tone extended to his trademark white buckskin shoes, enjoyed the first of six number-one hits with a painfully emasculated "Ain't That a Shame," stalling the New Orleans pianist's own version at number ten. However, Fats had co-written the song with trumpeter Dave Bartholomew, and so Boone's plunderage helped subsidize the glittering diamond rings that adorned his stubby fingers.

Verve Records archives show that the recording date took place at Master Recorders on March 26, 1957. Kessel produced, though session leaders customarily went uncredited then. Also in the control room was Abe "Bunny" Robyn, who'd previously sound-engineered recordings by Domino, Little Richard, and Chuck Berry.

"I despised rock & roll," the classically trained Robyn admitted, "but at the same time I understood it." In 1955 he'd built the functional, no-frills Master Recorders, where over the next few years Rick would spend many late hours.

Producer Kessel had assembled the backing musicians. At the drums sat Earl Palmer, whose New Orleans-bred parade snare-drum beat propelled the original "I'm Walkin'," as well as Little Richard's delirious "Tutti Frutti," and Lloyd Price's "Lawdy Miss Clawdy," to name a few; on saxophone, Plas Johnson, also a transplanted Louisianan and a mainstay on records featuring Domino, Bobby Day (he tweeted the piccolo on "Rockin' Robin"), and many others; and on guitar, future Country Music Hall of Famer Merle Travis.[1]

Naturally shy, Rick understandably felt intimidated by the older, experienced pros. Consequently, recording his voice "required a lot of takes," said Kessel. "It was difficult to get him to project into the microphone." For better or worse, today's sophisticated recording technology makes it possible for anyone to impersonate a professional singer. Through multitracking, feeble voices are electronically enhanced, and engineers deftly "punch in" vocal lines word by word if necessary, a godsend for the forgetful or tone-deaf.

No such options existed in 1957, when only a single monophonic track, or band of recorded sound, was available. Thus Rick sang both live with the instrumentalists and later alone, overdubbing onto a second tape machine while listening to the completed backing track and his practice, or reference, vocal over headphones. Robyn then synchronously fed the two separate recordings of voice and music into a third tape recorder, yielding the master recording from which the records were pressed.

Two lumbering generic doo-wop ballads, "A Teenager's Romance" and "You're My One and Only Love," were completed that day, as well as "I'm Walkin'." Comparing Rick's version

[1] Determining who played bass and piano is a guessing game. Although the American Federation of Musicians retains recording-session contracts back to 1945, it is nigh impossible to locate them for a particular early rock & roll recording because labels or session leaders were then listed under *client*, rather than the artist. For instance, the contract for Rick's "I'm Walkin' " session (apparently missing from the Los Angeles local's files) would name Verve Records, which purchased the studio time, or perhaps Barney Kessel as "artist."

It is truly a tragedy that so much rock & roll history was left unrecorded, leaving present-day chroniclers to depend on studio musicians' sketchy datebooks and faded memories. To the best of Kessel's recollection, George "Jud" DeNaut played bass—a belief Palmer seconds but DeNaut denies—and Gene Garf was on piano. However, Garf himself, who has played on thousands of recordings, believes he did not become Rick's accompanist until later that year.

71

to the original, Earl Palmer said, "We intentionally kept the feel as close as we could get it; that was the whole idea. Ricky's record was a little cleaner and a little more precise than Fats's because he used musicians who were more used to studio work.

"I was somewhat shocked that Ricky was going to sing that kind of song," the drummer admitted, "but he did an awfully good job on it." Listening to the playbacks, his voice enfolded in echo, the sixteen-year-old smiled to himself. "He felt good about it," said Kessel. "I think everybody was pleased."

According to popular-music lore, Rick begged his father to let him sing on TV, when actually the opposite was true. Ozzie constructed an April 10, 1957, episode around him, "Ricky the Drummer," in which Rick gets to sing with one of his favorite bands at a local dance. Ozzie suggests to the maestro, "How about Rick singing a rhythm & blues tune?" and history is about to be made.

Aware that much of his adult viewership considered rock & roll anathema, Ozzie shrewdly camouflaged the sinful music, referring to "I'm Walkin'" as *rhythm & blues*, less sinister than *rock & roll*. He also outfitted Rick in an oversized tuxedo, so that it hangs on his thin shoulders like a flashy zoot suit, and had his son front a Big Band, though the soundtrack the musicians mime playing to is pure rock & roll.

Compared to Presley, Rick comes across subdued; he tucks his chin into his chest and sings intently, looking curiously serious. But in the context of *The Adventures of Ozzie and Harriet* it is positively lascivious. As the song proceeds, he limbers up, and the kids in the crowd strain forward, shoulders swaying to the backbeat. By the second verse a pretty brunette claps her hands to her cheeks and sighs. Rick closes his eyes, snaps his fingers, and during the guitar solo shakes a leg, which sends the girls whimpering and brings a sly smile to his lips.

To lessen the impact, or perhaps to make the preceding minute and a half appear like a fleeting lapse in good taste, Rick's family immediately join him on the bandstand for a cheery barbershop-quartet ditty, "My Gal Sal." The show closes with

Ozzie's most brilliant stroke of all, as Rick and a curvaceous partner energetically Lindy to a blaring Big Band version of "My Gal Sal" bordering on swing and rock. This was Ozzie's subtle demonstration of the two styles' similarities, intended for rock & roll partisans and critics alike.

As anticipated, letters expressing outrage over the Nelsons' endorsement of rock & roll poured in, and sponsor Kodak registered its disapproval. But Ozzie stood his ground, answering detractors through a scripted editorial in a subsequent episode:

RICK: Hey, Mom?

HARRIET: Yes, dear?

RICK: What's your honest opinion of rock & roll?

HARRIET: Well, I'm not a good one to ask. Your father and I have been pretty well brainwashed by now, trying to at least stay in the same room with it.

RICK: I know you like some of it.

HARRIET: Well, I have to admit, there's a lot of excitement there. I guess it's a musical expression of the modern teenager's enthusiasm, or something. I'm not going to knock it, I'll tell you that much.

RICK: I think teenagers like to feel that they're just people with normal, average reactions. And rhythm & blues records usually tell a story or express an emotion.

HARRIET: Oh, I agree.

And with that she gave Rick the downbeat for "A Teenager's Romance."

Two weeks after "Ricky the Drummer" aired on ninety-three stations nationwide, Verve Records issued "I'm Walkin'" to uproarious demand. In Cleveland alone, 58,000 copies flew out of record shops the day of release, and by Rick's seventeenth birthday in May, sales eclipsed half a million. "I'm Walkin'" reached number four on the trade publication *Billboard*'s Best

Sellers in Stores chart, the same position attained earlier by Fats Domino's original.

Its flip side, on which Rick sounds the eternal adolescent cry "Our parents don't understand us," scaled even higher. "A Teenager's Romance" got to number two behind Pat Boone's saccharine "Love Letters in the Sand," a song Ozzie Nelson and His Orchestra had introduced in 1931.

Hearing his record played on the radio might have been the greatest thrill of Rick's life. When the chattering disc jockey announced his name, with no ". . . starring the entire Nelson family, Ozzie, Harriet, David and . . ." preceding it, Rick shook his head in ecstatic disbelief. For the first time he'd received recognition solely on his own, doing something neither his parents nor brother could do. He relished the feeling.

Rick's ultimate triumph, though, was the phone call from Arlene. Yes, *that* Arlene, still tan and beautiful, only now interested in Rick, whose music she'd heard on the air. A friend drove her from the Valley to 1822 Camino Palmero.

"Why don't you ever call me?" she demanded.

"Well, you know, I've been busy recording," Rick replied, sending her off with a noncommittal "Maybe I'll give you a call sometime—if I get the chance." Rick didn't see Arlene again until she materialized backstage at one of his concerts in the 1970s.

With the television series on summer hiatus, Rick went on his first road trip, playing four state and county fairs. He was accompanied by the Four Preps, who had been responsible for his first live public rock & roll performance that spring. A white vocal quartet in the style of the Four Aces ("Love Is a Many Splendored Thing") and the Four Lads ("Standing on the Corner"), Bruce Belland, Glen Larson, Ed Cobb, and Marv Ingram were all Hollywood High School graduates. After financing several independent singles, they signed with Capitol Records in 1956 and broke nationally with a moderate hit, "Dreamy Eyes."

The Preps, all several years older than Rick, also portrayed crewcut college fraternity brothers on *The Adventures*. Between scenes they'd disappear into Ozzie's bungalow, now decorated with an Elvis Presley poster and cluttered with musical instruments, and harmonize to the Fats Domino songs Rick plucked on his tenor guitar.

One afternoon Rick accompanied the group to an assembly at Hamilton High School. Though undecided whether or not to join them on stage, he brought along his guitar and fidgeted in the wings while the Preps went into their act. Finally, after thirty minutes of self-debate, Rick signaled he was ready, and Belland, the frontman, announced with a broad grin, "We've got a surprise for you: Ricky Nelson!"

Shrill girls' cries swept across the auditorium the moment he stepped on stage, multiplying in volume as Rick sang "I'm Walkin'," still weeks away from release. "Ordinarily at these assemblies, the kids were allowed to be responsive," said Belland, but he'd never witnessed anything like this. "They were all out of their seats and rushing the stage, screaming. You couldn't hear much of the music." He described the scene as chaos. "I don't think anybody was prepared for the reaction."

Least of all Rick. Whenever nervous, he tended to laugh awkwardly. During an instrumental break Rick turned toward the quartet, convulsing with laughter as if to say, Isn't this crazy?! But also: Isn't this incredible?! A short time later the sixteen-year-old reflected, "From that moment on, I knew that making records and singing before a live audience was the beginning of a new world for me. I'd been in show business nine years, but I'd never felt like [that] before."

After "A Teenager's Romance" and "Blue Moon of Kentucky" they hastened from the auditorium as hordes of girls tore at Rick's clothes. It took a wedge of beefy Hamilton High football players to escort him and the others through the hysterical teenage throng and to their car.

On the ride back to the studio, Rick kept repeating, "Man, can you *believe* that? Did you *see* that?" laughing every other word. Normally the Preps would have resented being upstaged, but bringing Rick to the assembly "made us enormous heroes," said Belland, who still tours as the Four Preps with Cobb and two other members. "We're no fools."

The day's commotion would seem tame compared to the pandemonium Rick incited at the Ohio and Minnesota state fairs that summer. While waiting to deplane in Columbus, Ohio, he saw a crush of three thousand straining against a heavy-gauge chain-link fence. *There must be some big politician on this plane,* he thought. As soon as Rick stepped off the aircraft, the fence toppled, and local police had to move into action restraining the crowd.

In Minneapolis Rick played to approximately twenty-five thousand fans from a stage erected a zip code away in the center of an enormous racetrack. To make themselves as visible as possible, the Four Preps donned glittery silver lamé jackets with black lapels, but, joked Belland, "We could have stood there naked with our hair on fire, and no one would have noticed us." All eyes were on Rick, smartly outfitted in a crisp cream-color jacket, a white-polka-dotted burgundy shirt and a white tie, and holding a guitar with his name tooled on its leather cover.

As he surveyed the crowd, Rick's legs trembled uncontrollably. *What am I doing here?* he asked himself. *This is ridiculous.* "I felt like I either had a lot of guts or I was incredibly stupid," he recalled. "But as it went on, I really started to enjoy it."

His repertoire limited, Rick performed outside favorites such as the Everly Brothers' "Bye Bye Love" and Elvis's "Loving You," tongue-in-cheekily introducing it as "a song by an up-and-coming young talent." The Four Preps additionally stretched the show with two sets of their own, opening and closing for the star.

Though in a world of his own, Rick never fully escaped his family. For these early tours Maury Foladare, the Nelsons' press agent since 1939, came along to oversee everything from his young charge's stage introduction to his personal safety. Like a ringleader plotting a bank heist, Foladare drilled his explicit instructions on how to evade fans after the show: Before the final note reached the grandstand, Rick and the others were to dash down a flight of stairs, through a tunnel, up another flight of stairs, and into the getaway vehicle. Preservation of life, limb, and locks depended on it.

But still glowing from the feverish response, Rick dawdled in the tunnel to give autographs, pose for pictures, and answer high-school newspaper reporters' questions. He glanced up from the piece of paper he was signing to see a shrieking mob of approximately eight thousand surging toward them. He and the Preps took off, Rick gripping his guitar's neck and laughing hysterically, looking back over his shoulder and laughing some more. They dove inside a police car and sped away just as the fans burst through a metal gate, shouting, "Where's Ricky? Where's Ricky?"

Once out of danger, everyone laughed, a bit shaken. Belland leaned back and whistled in relief. "That's when it hit me," he recalled. "I thought to myself, *My God, this guy is a legitimate superstar.*"

Five

In Ozzie's eyes, Rick was a legitimate superstar deserving of a larger record company than Verve, which had underestimated demand for "I'm Walkin' " and shipped it late to stores. The jazz label, unaccustomed to such prodigious sales, was also slow to account and release artist royalties (then averaging 4 percent of gross sales). When Norman Granz threatened not to pay unless Rick recorded a full album for Verve, Ozzie yanked his son off the label.

"You can't do that, we've got a deal!" Granz cried.

"Not in writing, we don't," retorted the former law student. Indeed, Verve had no paper proof, although Barney Kessel, privy to the original negotiations, contends that was only because "Ozzie kept delaying signing the contract. MCA [the Nelsons' representatives] said, 'You have our word on it,' but they never signed it. They let us carry the ball and put Ricky in a position where he was more marketable. Then Ozzie played a waiting game, trying to get the best deal possible." Kessel added sourly, "Very unethical."

Hearing that Rick had left Verve, other record companies came courting, including those that had rejected him only months earlier. Eventually father and son fell for Imperial Records: Ozzie, because of the control he reckoned he could exert over a locally quartered independent company; Rick, because of the glossy black-and-white photo of his idol Fats Domino adorning a wall at its Hollywood Boulevard office. In early summer he signed a five-year deal guaranteeing $1,000 per week against 4 ½-percent royalties and full approval over song selection, production, artwork, advertising, and publicity. For a 1950s rock artist, such autonomy was enviably rare.

Ozzie immediately sued Verve for $43,185 and a royalty audit, instigating a countersuit by the label that charged Rick with reneging on a verbally promised one-year contract. While waiting for a court date, Verve took immediate revenge by putting out its lone track of Rick's "You're My One and Only Love." The flip side, "Honey Rock," was a bright, beat-heavy instrumental that contained not even a sneeze from Rick Nelson. "We kind of implied he played drums on it," admitted Kessel, "but he didn't. He wasn't on it."

Verve showed great ingenuity in conserving its limited Rick resources, packaging the two singles (one and a half?) as a four-song EP (extended play) and as part of an album, *Teen Time,* padded with four unknowns. Ozzie eventually prevailed against the company, winning a $31,964 settlement in February 1959.

When it came to business savvy, Imperial Records president Lewis R. Chudd was Ozzie's equal. The former NBC radio executive founded the label in 1945 for $10,000, initially building it on Latin music. Four years later, while scouting talent in New Orleans, Chudd discovered twenty-year-old Fats Domino and entered the rhythm & blues field.

Chudd's strength wasn't music ("I don't think he knew an

A-flat from a G," said Bunny Robyn), it was marketing. He saturated stores with product, one time commandeering a Greyhound bus and delivering discs to retailers himself when a truckers' strike threatened his operation, worth $7.5 million at the time of Rick's signing.

Chudd assigned his valuable new acquisition to Jimmie Haskell, Imperial's staff arranger and A&R man. Congenial and soft-spoken, Haskell was the polar opposite of Chudd, whom he describes as "abrupt, rude, very difficult to work for, but good for me, because he forced me to be on my toes." Ordered to supervise Rick Nelson in the studio, Haskell asked, "What does that mean?"

"Go in and make hit records," his boss replied gruffly.

It turned out to be nearly that simple. With 750,000 advance orders, Rick's first Imperial single, "Be-Bop Baby," backed with "Have I Told You Lately That I Love You?" ascended to number three and sold well over a million copies.

Both sides received invaluable exposure on *The Adventures of Ozzie and Harriet,* now watched devoutly by an estimated 10 million teenagers each Wednesday at 9:00 P.M. For a point of comparison, consider that in an average day 100,000 young people between twelve and seventeen view the video-music cable channel MTV, according to A. C. Nielsen. To lure the younger demographic, ABC's newspaper promo for the 1957–58 premiere duly noted, "Ricky launches the new season by singing his latest hit recordings, 'Be-Bop Baby' and 'Have I Told You Lately That I Love You?' at a dance given by David's fraternity."

It is hard to say which benefited more, the TV show from Rick's singing, or vice-versa, but just as Rick and David had revived the radio program in 1949, Rick the Rock Idol singlehandedly gave *The Adventures* a new sheen and delivered a wider audience. Rick figured more prominently in story lines and performed every few episodes under the pretexts of serenading starry-eyed dates or, usually, entertaining at teen functions.

He didn't really sing, but mouthed the words while following a TelePrompTer. Even with the camera fixed on his face one couldn't tell the difference until the fadeout. Then Rick's upper lip curled into a sheepish smile, while the girl dancers—referred to as "screamers" and "head bobbers"—squealed, applauded, and bounced up and down.

When between singles, Rick performed tracks from his number-one debut album, *Ricky*, an intriguing grab bag of styles that demonstrates the teen rock & roller's atypically catholic musical taste. The inclusion of Carl Perkins ("Boppin' the Blues" and "Your True Love") and Jerry Lee Lewis ("Whole Lotta Shakin' Goin On") comes as no surprise, but Rick's affection for rhythm & blues is represented by Little Walter's gritty "If You Can't Rock Me," transformed into a spirited rockabilly shuffle. "Have I Told You Lately That I Love You?" a warm country & western love song, dates from the Great Depression. And *Ricky* concludes with a gift to Harriet, the delicious Cole Porter standard "True Love." Future albums would also contain one or two of his mother's favorites.

To Rick's mounting dissatisfaction, he still recorded with session musicians, among them drummer Earl Palmer; bassists Jud DeNaut, Bill Pitman, and LeRoy Vinnegar; guitarists Joe Maphis and Howard Roberts; pianist Gene Garf; and background singers the Jack Halloran Quartet. Most were jazz schooled and openly contemptuous of rock & roll, with the notable exceptions of Palmer and Maphis. Since relocating to Los Angeles earlier that year, Palmer fast became the dean of West Coast rock session drummers, and country star Maphis was a favorite of Rick's from KTTV's *Town Hall Party*, a televised Saturday-night barn dance that featured the Collins Kids. But Palmer and Maphis were a generation older; he wanted bandmates more his own age.

Rick had decided to form a permanent group after playing the Ohio and Minnesota state fairs, where promoters provided amateur accompanists. Rick described them as Salvation Army bands, no exaggeration, say the Four Preps' Bruce Belland

81

and Glen Larson. "It was like a one-armed World War I drummer, an accordion player, and the music teacher from the local school. Rick used to go *crazy*."

In Lew Chudd's office one day that fall, Rick pricked up his ears at the muffled sound of one of his favorite songs, "Red Hot." He traced it to an office at the end of the hall and listened to a rehearsal in progress. What he heard, fingers slapping bass strings and mesmerizingly expressive guitar playing, impressed him so much that he slipped inside.

Two youths looked up at Rick from their instruments. The one caressing the hulking upright bass, dark-haired and handsome, introduced himself as James Kirkland. The jug-eared one with the electric guitar was also named James—James Burton. Both were accompanying country singer Bob Luman, a fellow Imperial artist.

Kirkland hailed from Atlanta, Texas, and Burton from Shreveport, Louisiana, where they and Luman regularly appeared on the popular KWKH Saturday-night radio program *Louisiana Hayride,* that region's answer to WSM Nashville's famous *Grand Old Opry.*

"Rick listened to us play for about three hours," recalled Burton, who the next day received a telegram from Ozzie requesting that he and Kirkland come to General Service Studio. *Bring your instruments,* it instructed, for a jam. Ozzie liked what he heard and contracted them on the spot to support Rick, but on the television show only. While Rick continued hunting for compatible musicians, Burton played rhythm guitar on his fourth release of 1957, "Stood Up," which would have topped the charts had it dislodged Danny and the Juniors' "At the Hop" from number one.

Just after New Year's Ozzie asked Burton if he was interested in becoming a member of Rick's band. The eighteen-year-old eagerly accepted. Ozzie then surprised him with another offer. "James," he said, "Harriet and I know what it's like to be away from home, and we'd like you to be our guest here for as long as you want." Rick gained both a bandmate and a roommate, as Burton resided at 1822 Camino Palmero for nearly two years. "It was just like living with my own family," he said.

James Kirkland joined next. After signing his contract, the bassist and Burton went to the Hollywood Knickerbocker Hotel for lunch with some old friends: Scotty Moore, Bill Black, and D. J. Fontana, Elvis Presley's guitarist, bassist, and drummer.

"Guess what," Kirkland announced excitedly, "we're working for Ricky Nelson!"

Smiles froze, and Burton remembered noticing, "They all had funny looks on their faces." Finally, someone broke the strange silence with halfhearted congratulations.

"That's great, man."

"Yeah, man, really great."

Moore, Black, and Fontana, it turned out, had secretly auditioned for Rick themselves. Unhappy with their salaries, all three were planning to defect from Presley to Rick. (Moore and Black did eventually quit, in 1958, though the guitarist rejoined two years later.) "Once Elvis started making movies, we were in Hollywood for weeks on end," said Scotty Moore, "and Rick and his friends hung out with us at the Knickerbocker. The idea of going to work for him evolved from that."

Without Presley's knowledge, the trio and Rick rehearsed in Master Recorders, "but nothing ever came of it," said Moore. "It may have had to do with money." Actually, money was not a factor. As Rick told a friend, "Things didn't work out; it wasn't what I wanted soundwise." In other words, he'd rejected Elvis's band.

Rick completed his group with Richie Frost, whom he'd met when the drummer mimed playing to a prerecorded track for a musical scene on *The Adventures*. A veteran of the burlesque circuit, Frost had stroked rim shots behind a then-unknown emcee and comic, Lenny Bruce. Though ten years older than the other three, with a receding hairline, Frost fit in well. He was kindredly quiet and cooperative, if slightly eccentric: One summer, frustrated by the California sun constantly scorching his lawn brown, he painted it green.

Since Frost and pianist Gene Garf were the only band members that read music, arranger Jimmie Haskell sometimes relied on hand signals to conduct Rick, Burton, and Kirkland, resembling a traffic cop at a bustling intersection. Other times he raised hand-scrawled signs: "A," "E," "B-flat."

Evidenced by its very first recording, the group's youthful enthusiasm more than compensated for its lack of formal training. "Believe What You Say" clacks along like a fast-flying train, performed with the cohesiveness only a *band* can achieve. Whereas many early rock & roll records derived their personality solely from the singer's style, Rick's were now distinguished doubly by his voice and the taut rhythm section.

Just listen to the opening bars of "Believe What You Say": to the way Burton's metallic scraping, Kirkland's percussive slapping, and Rick's vigorously strummed acoustic rhythm guitar lock in precisely with Frost's *chicka-chicka-chicka-chicka* played on a closed hi-hat. The four instruments meld into one, insistently motoring the song forward and setting up Rick's vocal entrance.

Burton soon starts to vent steam, teasingly tossing off two measures of terse soloing to announce the second verse. It's just a matter of time before the guitarist erupts, and you can hear the anticipation in Rick's voice. On "Be-Bop Baby" and "Stood Up" he sounded self-conscious, but here, thrilled to be surrounded by musicians his age—*rock & rollers*—he's exuberant and unrestrained.

When Rick shouts gleefully, "Well let's take it now!" Burton explodes on cue with a blaze of brilliant notes. The sixteen bars that follow are as exciting as any ever recorded, Garf hammering triplets against the beat, Frost splashing cymbals, swinging madly, and Burton wringing his Fender Telecaster's neck before a tumbling chordal pattern, intuitively accented by the drums, begins the descent back to the song. A number-four hit in spring 1958, "Believe What You Say" remained one of

Rick's perennial favorites and a staple of his live shows throughout his career.

For the next few years the salaried band members conformed
their schedules to Rick's, which meant keeping nocturnal hours.
He preferred recording vocals at two, three in the morning,
when "the voice is looser," he claimed, so the musicians didn't
even file into Master Recorders until about eight-thirty. Despite
Rick's already having put in a full day's work, ten hours could
pass in the dimly lit studio, and he would still be going strong.

"It was murder," remembered Bunny Robyn. "I'd fall asleep
on the goddamn mixing board." Tape editor Frank McKelvey,
music editor on *The Adventures of Ozzie and Harriet,* had to poke
him in the ribs and call out, "Hey, another take." Since songs
weren't spliced together as liberally as they are in contemporary
recording—with take thirty-two's verse edited to take eight's
bridge, and so forth—as many as one hundred run-throughs
were sometimes needed to get it right.

In rock & roll's early days, record company A&R men usually
dictated song selection and arrangements. Today they would
be called producers, then a nonexistent term. As hours of studio
outtakes substantiate, Rick essentially ran his own sessions. He
granted his young band creative latitude, but knew when to
take charge, albeit tactfully. "Richie, why don't you try that
shuffle on the cymbal?" he'd suggest. Or, "Uh, James, I think
that lick kinda steps on my vocal here."

Rick alone chose nearly all his material from demo acetates
submitted by songwriters. In an era of largely insipid pop tunes,
the words were extremely important to him. (And to image-
conscious Ozzie, who forbid even remotely suggestive lyrics
or titles.) Rick once explained his criteria: "If it's not sincere,
it's not too good . . . I hate to hear lingo . . . I like a song
that tells a story." Jimmie Haskell remembered, "He'd listen
to a song and say, 'That's good, that's good.' Then perhaps
we'd get to the bridge, and he'd look up and say, 'I wouldn't
say something like that.' " Off came the needle, and another
acetate began spinning on the turntable.

Haskell, greatly involved in Rick's recordings, helped to interpret his ideas musically. But Rick mainly relied on an anonymous executive producer who helped pioneer the rock & roll sound: Ozzie Nelson.

The former orchestra leader was, literally, a founding father of rock & roll. "You might not think rock was Ozzie's style, but *music* was his style," said Haskell. "He had good ears and a sense of what was right." Partial to emphatic rhythm sections, Ozzie boosted bass and drums in the final mix, knowing those high- and low-frequency instruments typically washed out when broadcast on television. "At the time, most producers cut the bass and drums," said Earl Palmer, naturally sensitive to such matters. "They didn't understand that in rock & roll they should be prominent. Ozzie did."

With daily rushes to review after filming *The Adventures,* Ozzie rarely made it to the recording studio before 10:00 P.M., his arrival inciting a frenzied effort to hide all traces of nicotine and beer. "Uh-oh," Rick would whisper, panicked, "I'd better put this cigarette away; I hear Dad coming down the hall." It wasn't for several years that Ozzie learned his son habitually sneaked tobacco at sessions, believing it made him sing better. Much to Ozzie's annoyance, but fortunately for Rick, Master Recorders' new owner, Bill Putnam, always locked the street door.

"I'd tell him it was because the neighborhood was bad, which it wasn't." Indeed, the lethal knishes sold at the nearby Jewish delicatessen posed the greatest danger at North Fairfax and Melrose. While Putnam stalled for time, Rick and the others "scuffled around, pitching in to get the place cleaned up. It was stupid to think we were concealing anything, of course," Putnam added. "Ozzie would walk into a smoke-filled room reeking of beer."

A&R men and engineers weren't terribly glad to see him. "Ozzie was murder on a record date," remembered Charles Bud Dant, West Coast A&R director of Rick's third label, Decca Records. "We'd get the instrumental track on tape, and he'd play it back over and over, even though everyone agreed it was fine. Then Ozzie would make us do an overdub he'd thought of, or redo the track. It was," Dant complained, "a pain in the ass." Haskell would have to tiptoe behind Richie Frost's drum kit and nudge the drummer, fast asleep on the floor, with his foot.

Opening an eye, he'd ask, "One more?"

"Yep, one more."

For additional musicians drawing union scale, Ozzie's presence usually ensured them a bigger paycheck. On Rick's early recording dates, Jud DeNaut and Earl Palmer deliberately engaged the loquacious Ozzie in conversation, with DeNaut laying the trap:

"Hey, Earl, tell us about the time you saw Ozzie's band in New Orleans." Palmer then recounted how as a boy he bussed tables at the Roosevelt Hotel, where the Nelson orchestra played the Blue Room.

His memory stirred, Ozzie waxed nostalgic. "Oh, yes, those were nice days. New Orleans, such a great city . . ." According to the drummer, "He'd go on for another half an hour," pushing the session into overtime and earning the musicians time and a half.

There's no question that Ozzie relived his musical past through Rick. "The first time I worked with him," recalled Jimmie Haskell, "we were talking about instrumentation, and he said, 'Jimmie, in this spot I was thinking of getting the sound of a rhythm banjo.'" Knowing Rick would sooner incorporate a sousaphone section than a banjo, Haskell countered, "That's good, but you know what? We can also get that sound with an electric guitar."

"Ozzie listened politely," the arranger continued, "and said, 'Uh, Jimmie, well, I was thinking of maybe a *banjo* at that point . . .'" Haskell laughed. "He wanted to play on Rick's record." Whenever his father suggested wedding banjo or, worse, ukulele to rock & roll, Rick reacted with stony silence. Apparently Ozzie took the hint, in the end never getting either instrument recorded. He did, however, play piano on "Someday," a tune on Rick's second album, and tenor guitar on the 1961 hit "Hello Mary Lou."

Over his son's objections, Ozzie picked Rick's first number-one single. The song was "Poor Little Fool," composed in a state of despair by sixteen-year-old Sharon Sheeley, a pretty, willowy brunette then dating Don Everly of the Everly Brothers. While Sharon was in San Francisco to see them perform, Don's younger brother Phil sidled up to her and confided, "You're a nice girl, so I'm gonna tell you something I never told the rest of 'em: He's married."

On the long bus ride home to Newport Beach, California, through tears she scribbled her heartbreak on an envelope: *I used to play around with hearts, they'd hasten at my call. And when I met that little boy, I knew that I would fall. Poor little fool.* Sharon submitted the piece to her high-school English teacher, who returned it to her etched with a red *F.* The poem's meandering journey seemed destined to end inside a dresser drawer.

One night she shared it with her younger sister. "Why don't you put a tune to it?" Mary Jo suggested. Though Sharon didn't play an instrument, melodies echoed in her head all the time. She plucked a suitably plaintive theme and now had a song but no singer, a situation she plotted to rectify with the help of Rick Nelson.

It was common knowledge among local teens that Rick and his family weekended in nearby Laguna Beach. Borrowing her mother's car, Sharon spent an entire Saturday parked on the city's main street, checking out every vehicle that went by. No luck. A week later she came back, anxiously tapping her fingers on the dashboard, then sitting up with a start. "There they were," she recalled, "just like a fantasy": Ozzie, Harriet, and Rick in one car, followed by David in his. She trailed the Nelsons to a guarded security gate, watched them pull into a cul-de-sac, and vowed to return the following Saturday.

Which she did, Mary Jo accompanying her to glimpse the famous family's two-bedroom home. Luckily, the guard was off-duty, enabling them to drive on through. When Sharon pulled in front of the Nelson residence, perched on a jagged twenty-foot cliff, she deliberately stalled the engine.

"Sharon, what are you doing?!"

At that moment, seventeen-year-old Rick ambled out the front door, casually flipping a football.

"I swear, Sharon, I'll never speak to you again." This time the voice came from the backseat, Mary Jo having dived there in embarrassment.

"Ya havin' trouble?" He was standing outside the car now, all six-feet-one of him, and Mary Jo, frozen in awe, thought to herself, *My God, this guy has the most gorgeous eyes I've ever seen.*

Rick made small talk from under the hood, gallantly tinkering with the motor, although Sharon remains convinced he didn't have a clue what he was doing. Then she "just happened" to interject that she and Mary Jo had recently met Elvis Presley. Rick's eyes widened.

"You met Elvis?"

He pressed her for details, no longer a star in his own right, just another fan of The King. "What was he like? What did he say to you?" When Rick invited her inside for a Coke, Sharon suppressed a squeal, and as they started down the walk he called to Mary Jo, still undercover in back, "You wanna come in and have a Coke too?" In his bedroom Rick played them his two current favorite records, Eddie Cochran's "Sittin' in the Balcony" and Jerry Lee Lewis's "Great Balls of Fire," and talked passionately about music for hours. Rick and Sharon became close platonic friends over several months, by which time she'd concocted her scheme to get him to record "Poor Little Fool."

"I told Rick that a friend of my father's was a very successful songwriter and that he'd written a song Elvis was going to record." *Was* going to record. Weeks earlier, in March 1958, the Army had drafted Presley; a government plot, outraged teenagers theorized, to rid the country of the rock & roll menace.

"Do you think your father's friend would let me hear it?" Rick asked.

"Gee, I don't know . . ." As Sharon had hoped, her reluctance only made him more intent on cutting "Poor Little Fool." Finally she "relented," playing him a demo tape recorded with a guitarist, and breathlessly awaited his verdict. She had to mask her mortification when Rick said, "I don't like it at all." *Still*, he reasoned, *if it's good enough for Elvis* . . .

Rick ultimately recorded "Poor Little Fool," buried it on side two of *Ricky Nelson*, due out that summer, and promptly forgot about it. Then an odd thing happened: A Cleveland disc jockey began playing the song off an EP released in advance of the album. (In the late 1950s LPs were commonly sliced into four-song sections and served on seven- or ten-inch platters called EPs, a format that despite attempts to revive it has never found lasting favor with consumers.)

After airplay spread to Detroit, midwestern distributors inundated Imperial Records with demands for shipments of Rick's now-hitbound title. Failing to convince Rick that the song should be issued as a 45, Lew Chudd set to work on Ozzie. Sharon Sheeley joined the Nelsons for dinner the night Rick's father told him, "Son, Lew Chudd and I had a meeting today, and 'Poor Little Fool' is your next single."

"It broke his heart," she said. "He begged Ozzie not to." Besides abhoring the song, Rick protested because sales of the EP were then streaking toward the one-million mark. The availability of "Poor Little Fool" as a single surely would cut into future EP sales. Rick lost this battle but spitefully withheld approval of the sleeve artwork and refused to perform the song on the TV show.

Basically a passive person, Rick habitually avoided confronting authority figures—particularly his intimidating father. But when it came to music, not even Ozzie could sway Rick from his convictions, which sometimes undermined his professional best interests. In this instance he never did sing "Poor Little Fool" on *The Adventures*, despite its selling over two million copies.

And in Rick's passive-aggressive way, even once he realized his obligation to sing "Poor Little Fool" in concert, he never bothered to learn the last two verses, scribbling the lyrics on a piece of paper and taping it to his guitar. Because he perspired profusely on stage, this created a problem at one show. When it came time to sing the lines, "I looked down," Rick told Sharon afterward, "and the words were rolling off the guitar!" Thinking fast, he raised his hands in the air Mitch Miller style and exhorted the crowd, "Everybody sing!" Fortunately, they knew the lyrics.

Almost comically, while Rick feuded with his father and Chudd and the single shot up the charts, its composer was mad at *him*. It wasn't until Sharon first heard Rick's recording while sitting in a Hollywood coffee shop that she angrily discovered he'd halved the tempo. Just then, David Nelson spotted her and came over to offer congratulations. "You can tell your brother thanks a lot," Sharon snapped. "He *ruined* my song."

Hardly. On August 4, 1958, "Poor Little Fool" topped *Billboard* magazine's newly instituted Hot 100 singles chart, and suddenly every record producer wanted to get his hands on a Sheeley tune. As for Rick, in addition to a number-one record, he claimed three of the nation's top ten EPs, and two of the top twenty-five albums.

"Move over, private Presley," UPI columnist Vernon Scott declared, "young Ricky Nelson's moving in to commandeer your rock 'n' roll brigade." Disarmingly humble, Rick never would have advanced such a conceit. But during 1958 and 1959, while Elvis served in West Germany, he legitimately vied with Presley for chart domination, outscoring him twelve to eleven in Top Twenty hits.

"Ricky Nelson: The Teen-agers' Top Throb," proclaimed *Life* magazine, one of many periodicals to splash his picture on its cover. Each week Rick received two dozen requests for guest appearances on other television shows, all declined by Ozzie, and fifteen thousand fan letters, all handled by Connie Harper Nelson, a staff of five, and a special department at the Hollywood post office.

"Most of them were from little girls between eleven and fourteen," said Connie, adding, "Not a single letter went unanswered." By 1960 the Ricky Nelson International Fan Club boasted nine thousand chapters worldwide, with memberships ranging from a dozen to fifteen thousand each.

In addition to threatening Presley's superiority in terms of hit records, fan clubs, and media coverage, Rick appropriated Elvis's vocal group, the Jordanaires. Since forming in 1948, the quartet's silvery voices have graced more secular and sacred recordings than probably any other background singers. Gordon Stoker, Neal Matthews, Hoyt Hawkins, and Hugh Jarrett originally sang spirituals, later teamed up with gospel and country acts, then in 1956 began a fourteen-year association with Presley.

The Jordanaires met Rick while in Hollywood to film Elvis's second movie, *Loving You,* in early 1957. Through Skip Young, who happened to be a cast member, Rick learned that Presley's musicians were staying at the Knickerbocker Hotel. First-tenor Stoker remembered answering the door to the Jordanaires' suite, and a shy boy extending his hand and saying, "Hi, I'm Rick Nelson!"

"I know."

"You know who I am?!"

"Sure," Stoker said, laughing, "I watch you on TV all the time."

Rick, still not fully aware of the extent of his family's fame, appeared shocked. "You know," he mused naively, "we took a trip back east last year, and we ran into a lot of people that knew who we were . . ."

"From then on," Stoker reflected, "Rick and the Jordanaires became very close friends. He said, 'I may get to cut a record one day, and I want you guys to work with me,' which was the same thing Elvis had said to us when we met for the first time at the 1954 Memphis Cotton Carnival." Sure enough, a year later Ozzie arranged for the quartet to overdub some album tracks, "Poor Little Fool" among them.

Through the mid-1960s, the Jordanaires sang on most of Rick's hits when they were in Hollywood on a Presley movie shoot. "That way," explained second-tenor Neal Matthews, "our expenses were already paid. It was one of Ozzie's shrewd business moves." During the Jordanaires' stays at the Knickerbocker, Rick visited them constantly. "He was always asking us questions about Elvis," recalled Matthews.

Presumably, Rick wanted to know what Presley thought about the Jordanaires working with his most formidable competitor. According to Ray Walker, who replaced Jarrett in April 1958, just in time to append his bottomless bass voice to "Poor Little Fool," "We had a handshake agreement with Elvis that we wouldn't put our name on the label of Rick's records."

In the summer of 1958 Rick undertook his first full-scale tour. Commanding an average $5,000 nightly, he headlined bills that seemed better suited to one of his parents' vaudeville shows than to a 1950s rock & roll concert: A typical odd assemblage included a trapeze artist, a female vocalist, a juggler, and a sorry comic-singer who climaxed his act by playing two trumpets at once. But once Rick and his trio (he rarely toured with a pianist) hit the stage, context was restored.

It took the young star a while to adapt to his predominately female audiences' hysterical outbursts, which at first he found both confusing and downright embarrassing. In Long Beach, California, he came out, "and the audience went wild, applauding and screaming," recalled Jimmie Haskell, there to see Rick perform for the first time. "Rick didn't even smile or wave at them." He just stood there center-stage waiting for the tumult to die down so that he could sing. When five minutes passed without a drop in the decibel level, he shrugged, turned to James Burton, and counted off the first song. The din continued throughout the entire thirty-five-minute set.

"Some of the musicians from the opening acts used to ask me how I could stand the noise," said Richie Frost, who battered his drums until his hands swelled in order to overcome the din. Fans beyond the first several rows could discern only clattering cymbals and whining lead guitar, and as for Rick's voice, it simply couldn't be heard. His cousin George, a bodyguard on the three-week tour, recalled, "I used to stand backstage and wonder, *Why does he even bother opening his mouth?*" Despite the uproar around him, Rick nuzzled the microphone and sang in his warm, understated style.

The girls didn't much care that they couldn't hear Rick, they'd come to *see* him. When he was fourteen he'd gone from cute to awkward-looking, his face narrow and bony. Now at eighteen he had matured into an impossibly handsome youth, with smoldering blue eyes, luxurious lashes that he accentuated with a touch of mascara, hair molded into a slight pompadour, and a remarkable pair of lips: thin on top, full and sensuous on bottom. The hint of a smile sent entire sections into fits of ecstasy.

Francine Falik, a fan from Texas, attended her first Rick Nelson concert at age eleven. "Ricky had a gentle, romantic way about him," she recalled. "He'd close his eyes when he sang [Rick claimed it helped him to hear himself better], and I'd just flip. He was all I talked about. My friends teased me, but he was so gorgeous!"

Though resplendent in an emerald green suit, gold shirt, and white tie, Rick remained a reluctant sex symbol. Presley claimed likewise but played up to expectations, leering suggestively and pumping his hips. If it was deliberate self-parody, as he later claimed, the joke was lost on most of the audience and certainly on grown-ups.

Presley came across overtly sexual; Rick, covertly so. "Elvis never appealed to me," said Falik, expressing the common sentiment of Nelson fans. "He was always greasy and didn't have that clean-cut look." Perhaps the best description of Rick came from a sobbing teenager outside his Wichita hotel room: "It's like he was Elvis and my brother at the same time." In short, girls wanted to lose their virginity to Presley, but Rick was the man they wanted to lose their virginity to and then marry (or vice-versa).

Critics have generally considered Rick's act and image a spruced-up, parentally sanctioned version of Elvis's, implying it was contrived. Granted, Ozzie would not tolerate Rick doing anything to besmirch the Nelson reputation. When Rick bought a flamboyant, painfully tight suit for an appearance on Dick Clark's *American Bandstand,* his father forbade him to wear it. "Then I won't do the show," Rick shot back. Along with Presley he was one of the few major rock & rollers never to lip-sync on what became the longest-running pop-music program in TV history.

Another reason Rick didn't thrust his pelvis or don black leather: His audience simply wouldn't have bought it. To them he was and would always be the well-mannered Boy Next Door they had grown up with. In that sense, Rick's years of TV exposure worked against his music career. Performers with private pasts can reinvent themselves for the public, in some instances over and over. But Rick was bound by the television show and the Nelson image.

"Rick knew the sound he wanted to get, but he didn't know what sort of attitude he was supposed to have," David Nelson explained. "All he was seeing was Jerry Lee Lewis breaking pianos and Elvis Presley snarling and bumping and grinding, and he knew he couldn't do that. For lack of anything else, he decided to do a slight impression of Elvis and yet try to be himself."

While Rick sang, bodyguards Jack Ellena and Paul Cameron, both former professional football players, hustled out from the wings to intervene every time women rushed the stage. In Vancouver, British Columbia, the onslaught of young girls was so unrelenting that the two finally stationed themselves in front of Rick and pushed invaders back into the crowd as gently as possible. The fans' fervor could be dangerous: In Dallas two frenzied girls toppled from the balcony but miraculously escaped serious injury.

Off stage, the formidable task of shielding Rick from the public continued, falling mainly on tour manager Maury Foladare. It is unlikely his experience as Bing Crosby's publicist prepared the older man for the logistical nightmare of shepherding 1958's biggest teenage star and his entourage from city to city. While the band enjoyed itself, Foladare, in his conservative suit and tie, snapped at negligent airline reservations clerks, ensured that everyone had his daily meal money, and probably wished Rick would find a new career, and soon.

Having seen Rick nearly get shredded by rabid fans the previous year, for this tour Foladare employed the two bodyguards, plus Jack Iannarelli, the forty-nine-year-old property master from *The Adventures,* and Rick's cousin George. Despite precautions, Rick still faced occasional danger.

One of the most frightening incidents occurred outside the Vancouver arena. "We drove into the empty parking lot and were climbing out of the limousine," recalled Richie Frost, "when this crowd of screaming teenagers came running around the corner." The drummer, still sitting in back, wisely locked all doors and stayed put. But the rest of the entourage broke for the stage door, thirty feet away.

The mob overtook them before they made it, knocking the slight, bald Foladare to the ground. Hands were everywhere, grabbing, grasping. "Rick jumped on my back," said Ellena, a 230-pounder, "and we plowed through and got inside," though not before fans had snatched Rick's tie, shoes, sports jacket, and several clumps of hair. Frost, watching from the limo, remembered spotting Rick in the middle of the maelstrom, "taking it all calmly. He was strong."

And a little lonely, confined to his opulent hotel suite because venturing out posed too much of a problem. Iannarelli once engineered a rare visit to a city zoo, disguising Rick in a long overcoat, a floppy hat, and glasses, but the kids recognized him anyway. "What am I supposed to do," he complained afterward, "wear an armored suit?"

Unable to sightsee, Rick slept until early afternoon, then breakfasted on his favorite food, hamburgers, accompanied by Cokes and chocolate malts. The Hamburger Kid, Iannarelli called him. Rick spurned salads ("It's like eating grass") and especially vegetables. At home, the family's antique dining table contained a drawer into which young Ricky had spooned his greens when his parents weren't looking.

Whiffle-ball games, tag-team wrestling, and general horseplay were ways of passing time in hotels, but mostly Rick, Burton, and Kirkland jammed on guitars, purely for enjoyment's sake. George Nelson, who sometimes joined them, remembers being struck by their innocence. "Here were these three kids," he said, "not at all concerned that they had to go on in front of a huge audience in a few hours. They were only interested in playing among themselves and having a good time."

Outside, guards posted at stairwell entrances and elevators did their best to ward off the roving packs of girls. Fans hid in maids' carts, under the sheets and towels; scaled fire escapes; somehow snuck into Rick's shower stall; and phoned his hotel posing as cousins, aunts—even as Ozzie and Harriet. When Rick went to retrieve his messages one time, the switchboard operator told him about a repeat caller who kept insisting she was his mother. Why, she even handed the phone to a man claiming to be his father! Moments later an urgent telegram arrived from home. *Please call us immediately*, it read. *The operator won't believe we're your parents.*

Not all girls were content with an autograph or a peck on the cheek. Some flung their damp panties on stage, "which always gave us a laugh," said Frost. And others brazenly offered their bodies to anyone with access to Rick.

Due to the threat of paternity suits and bogus rape charges, Ozzie ordered that all pleas for a private audience with his son be denied, no matter how innocent. "Some of those girls were pretty sharp," said Iannarelli. Having worked at MGM Pictures for many years, he knew how scam artists exploited their children to extort money from male celebrities: Mother waited down the hall while daughter charmed her way into the star's room, then once inside ripped her own clothes and cried rape, with Mother, naturally, playing witness.

If the teen star wanted sex, to protect Rick and anyone with him, his handlers set him up with prostitutes. In Detroit Iannarelli queried a friendly policeman, "Don't you have any whores in this town?"

"Sure. How many you want?"

"Get me three or four."

"He sent over a bunch," recalled Iannarelli, "and we had a ball. Ricky would go hog wild. He'd say, 'How about this!'" Touring musicians inevitably fooled around, Iannarelli reasoned, "so why fool around with jailbait?"

"I had to laugh at some of the things that went on," said George Nelson, then twenty-one. He remembered thinking, *If Ozzie knew, he'd die.* Probably not. A former traveling musician, Ozzie knew enough to overlook his son's escapades, as long as they never became public.

The Sunday before Labor Day 1958, Rick played to 44,221 at the Atlantic City Steel Pier, breaking the previous attendance record of 41,000 set in 1950 by Frank Sinatra. From the late nineteenth century until 1975, the popular entertainment complex featured first-run films, children's productions, and top-name talent. At the end of the promenade, facing the Atlantic Ocean, stood a water circus, its principal attraction a diving horse.

Ozzie and Harriet had played the Steel Pier in the 1930s, when it was owned by George Hamid, Sr. Two decades later his son, George Jr., booked Rick for two days there at the then extravagant fee of $5,000 per. Not long before, Hamid Jr. had turned down another "new-style" act, this one demanding $4,000 per. "You've got to be kidding," he told the William Morris Agency. "I don't think this country is ready to buy a guy with a crazy first name like Elvis." Hamid wasn't about to pass up a similar opportunity again.

By dawn on August 31, four hours before the Steel Pier opened, a two-mile line of well-behaved teenagers had formed along the boardwalk, all the way up near the Absecon Lighthouse. They filled the 2,800 seats in the Music Hall Theatre within fifteen minutes, waiting patiently for nearly two hours until the vaudeville portion of the show began at one o'clock.

The kids tolerated the first couple of novelty acts, but Henny Youngman's fermented one-liners proved too much to bear:

". . . My wife went to the beauty parlor and stayed four hours. And that was just for the estimate!"

"Get off!" "Ricky-y-y!"

". . . Take my wife—please!"

"YOU take her!" With that, the crowd began a rhythmic chant: "We want Ricky! We want Ricky!"

Hamid prudently cut short Youngman's act and introduced Rick. Bedlam erupted, flashing instant cameras illuminating the darkened theater like lightning. Standing backstage, Hamid calculated Rick would have to play twenty shows in the Music Hall Theatre to accommodate the additional forty thousand or so youngsters milling about outside, so he decided to move him to the larger Marine Ballroom, which handled eleven thousand standees.

The problem was, how to transport Rick to the pier's end without instigating a riot? Someone happened to spy a striking, brown-haired, blue-eyed fifteen-year-old who closely resembled Rick loitering in the wings. A year later Fabian Forte himself became a teen singing idol, but for now he was pressed into service as a decoy. Fabian went out the back door, into a limo, and was driven away, with hundreds of Rick's fans in pursuit. The bodyguards and musicians then formed a flying wedge in front of the real Rick Nelson and with arms locked sprinted to the ballroom.

It was suffocatingly hot inside, bodies packed so tightly together that fainting girls were literally held upright in place. Security guards tossed ammonia capsules to the throng and collected the inert female forms passed up onto the stage, for the only unobstructed exit was through the rear door. "Once the kids saw that," said Hamid, "they all started 'fainting,' figuring they were going to get backstage."

Early in the tour the chaos had unnerved Rick, but by its end he admitted, "Now I like it when it gets really wild." However, his exhilaration over everything happening to him was tempered by the awareness that fame is ephemeral. Hamid remembered a cryptic comment the teenager made while sitting in his suite at Del Webb's Claridge Casino Hotel.

"Rick looked up at me and said, almost sadly, 'I guess when I'm twenty-one, I'll be a twenty-one-year-old has-been.'" Though at the height of his career, he knew how fickle the public could be.

Six

Once Rick returned home from the road, depression inevitably set in. For weeks he'd been the object of adulation, waited on, addressed servilely as Mister Nelson. Now Harriet nagged him to pick up his clothes, and Rick thought, *Doesn't she realize she's talking to* Mister *Nelson?* With David ensconced in his own Hollywood Hills bachelor digs, the eighteen-year-old now occupied both their bedrooms, sleeping in whichever one was less messy. Framed gold records hung on the walls, which Rick had wood-paneled to make his room resemble a hotel suite. Only there did he feel truly at home.

Like a soldier back from war, Rick felt disconnected, convinced that no one could appreciate what he'd experienced. For the first time, this included his own family. How could he explain the bite marks from overzealous fans? Being implored to spit on album jackets or clothing held forth by sobbing teenagers? Having girls lie down in front of his limousine, begging to be run over?

Rick struck up friendships with other young musicians because they *understood*: the Four Preps, now well established on their own, Johnny and Dorsey Burnette, Baker Knight, Robin Luke, Gene Vincent, Lorrie Collins, the Everly Brothers, Eddie Cochran. David, pursuing a film career on the side, palled around mostly with theatrical types, the brothers' social circles rarely intersecting.

When Rick wasn't working, he hung out with Sharon Sheeley in her spacious new Hollywood duplex, purchased with earnings from "Poor Little Fool" and a subsequent staff writing job at Liberty Records. Sister Mary Jo, their mother, and a friend named Dotty Harmony lived there too, and musicians visited all the time. "We'd set up these big, clumsy amplifiers," said Mary Jo, "and they'd jam all night."

Rick especially admired Sharon's fiancé, Eddie Cochran, who for many rock historians embodied early rock & roll at its raucous, spirited best. He and manager Jerry Capehart co-wrote rhythm-charged songs that treated teenage oppression with playful humor instead of overwrought anguish ("Summertime Blues"), and the boyishly handsome Cochran sang them with a conspiratorial grin and a wink.

Despite his pivotal role in rock's development, Cochran found broad commercial success only in England. That is where his life ended on April 17, 1960. At the conclusion of a triumphant tour, he, co-headliner Gene Vincent, Sharon, and a British theatrical agent were taxiing to London Airport for the flight home when a tire blew, sending the vehicle careening into a lamppost. Sharon, given just a fifty-fifty chance of survival, spent two months in the hospital; Cochran, only twenty-one, died of head injuries.

"Rick adored Eddie," Sharon said, and wanted him to play guitar on one of his records. At their informal nighttime jams, they and whoever else dropped by previewed newly written songs, spun favorite 45s, but mostly sat around talking and laughing. "There were never any drugs or drinking," said room-mate Dotty Harmony, a blond dancer who dated both David Nelson and Elvis Presley. Because Hollywood was much safer then, with doors routinely left unlocked at night, "We never knew who'd be on our floor when we woke up," she said. "Maybe Troy Donahue." Or maybe a would-be psychopathic killer.

One blistering August afternoon, Sharon, Mary Jo, and Dotty left their downstairs door ajar in hope of catching a breeze. They, the Burnettes, Cochran, Rick, and several others sat scattered around the upstairs living room, guitars out. Cochran was singing his new single, "Somethin' Else," which Sharon and his brother Bob had written. When a glassy-eyed stranger entered and took a seat as if he belonged there, no one paid him any mind, assuming he was somebody's friend.

Suddenly he announced, "I came here to *kill* one of you," and brandished a knife.

Before he could use it, brawny Dorsey Burnette wrapped him in a bear hug. The former heavyweight boxer turned singer had once sparred with Sonny Liston and never lost a fight. "Dorsey picked this kid up and pitched him down three flights of stairs," Sharon recalled. While tumbling to the bottom, the intruder accidentally jabbed a vein with his own knife, staining the walls and carpet crimson. Then he dashed out the door.

A gangly seventeen-year-old named Kim Fowley observed the scene. Son of actor Douglas Fowley (Doc Holliday on TV's *The Life and Legend of Wyatt Earp*), he later became a barnacle on the Los Angeles music scene as performer, songwriter, label owner, producer, and gadfly. But Sharon remembered him this way: "a dorky, pesky creep nobody wanted to talk to." Fowley immediately called the local newspapers from a nearby pay phone, breathless with scandalous details: ". . . a rock & roll stabbing! . . . at Sharon Sheeley's! . . . *Ricky Nelson!*"

Everyone's first thought was to get Rick out of the apartment in case the police showed up. As he trotted down a staircase to exit out a back door, he grumbled, "Times like these, I wish my name were Pete Smith!" Harmony, on her hands and knees with a rag and cleanser, desperately tried scrubbing away the incriminating bloodstains that led right to the Sheeleys' front door.

When the police arrived, she explained politely that there couldn't have been any trouble at the apartment. Why, she'd been taking care of these two poor flu-ridden girls all day, gesturing at Sharon and Mary Jo, who, in nightgowns, sniffled and sneezed dramatically. Cochran and Johnny Burnette, hiding in the bathroom, could barely contain their laughter.

Once the officers apologized and left, Sharon and Harmony cruised up and down Fountain Avenue until they spotted Fowley's Volkswagen, pounded on his apartment door, and confronted him. At six foot five, Fowley towered above Harmony. "So I stood on a chair," she said, "and punched him." Then she ordered him to retract his story, which Fowley sheepishly did.

As Rick's fame escalated, there were other times when he yearned for the anonymity of a "Pete Smith." His cousins from Tenafly remember Rick always asking them what growing up conventionally was like, genuinely curious because his life was turning increasingly bizarre.

Previously unbothered by curiosity-seekers, the Nelsons were now besieged. Fans made off with Rick's hubcaps and rang the doorbell every ten minutes, as late as 3:00 A.M. Instead of their idol, they often encountered his fuming father. After Rick's death, a woman confessed in the *San Francisco Chronicle* that she'd once kept a month-long vigil parked in front of 1822 Camino Palmero. "I have the unique distinction," she wrote, "of actually inciting the benign Mr. Ozzie Nelson to profanity. I got Ozzie Nelson to use the *s*-word." Exasperated, the Nelsons took refuge behind an electric gate and a wrought-iron fence.

Rick coped with stardom by erecting his own barriers, withdrawing into himself. Always shy, he grew so remote that he made others nervous, responding to the most innocent questions with monosyllabic yups and nopes. The same teenager who could command an audience of twenty thousand admitted, "I'm kind of scared being with a lot of people I don't know." Music had become his main emotional outlet. "It's the best way I know to relate to people," he said years later.

Friends and relations offer varying explanations for Rick's abrupt personality change (which was mirrored on *The Adventures of Ozzie and Harriet,* his character going from irrepressible to repressed). "He had trouble expressing his feelings," said Connie Nelson, "and was afraid to communicate. He wanted to, but he didn't have the ability to let it out."

Perhaps now Rick couldn't or wouldn't compete in a family of imposing personalities. Everyone deferred to Ozzie, needless to say, but offscreen Harriet too was strong and determined, and David, sharp-witted and more extroverted as he matured.

Or maybe Rick, whose life had been public property since age eight, needed to reserve a private place within himself. He'd crawl home after twenty-hour days and fall asleep in the bathtub, not waking until the water turned cold.

Singer Robin Luke, a close friend, believed Rick retreated into a protective shell because "he felt everybody wanted a piece of him, either physically, financially, or figuratively," an opinion borne out by a story Skip Young related. Shortly after "I'm Walkin'" and "A Teenager's Romance," the actor found Rick moping dejectedly outside a party.

"I don't have a friend in the world," Rick said with all the weariness a seventeen-year-old can muster.

"That's not true; why do you say that?" Young asked.

"Well, I can't believe that all these people like me for myself and not because I have a hit record."

Young replied, "They acted the same way toward you when you didn't have a hit record—when you 'only' had a hit television show—so what's the difference?"

Sheltered throughout his life, Rick was naively trusting, even as an adult. Still, in moments of insecurity he questioned others' motives, a feeling Robin Luke well understood. "When you're

105

an entertainer, there are people around you who clearly have your best interests at heart," he said. But the constant demands of sycophants, businessmen, well-meaning fans "cause you to become very defensive and sour. It took me a while to get 'normal' again." Luke was just sixteen when his first single, "Susie Darlin'," sold over two million copies in 1958.

"There were many times when Rick wanted to escape the pressures of the entertainment business," he recalled. On rare days off the two slipped away to friends' secluded homes to play tennis, make music, talk about cars and girls, and compare pimples. Yes, blemishes blotched Rick's masterpiece of a face during adolescence, requiring heavy pancake makeup and skillful photo retouching. "We used to eat junk food," said Luke, mildly afflicted himself at the time, "then joke about our acne: 'Wonder how they're gonna get rid of *this* one?'"

Acting like a typical teenager, if only on occasion, was essential to Rick, who suffered the age-old anxiety: Do I fit in? "We didn't feel we were normal," said girlfriend Lorrie Collins. "Rick and I talked about it a lot.

"People are mesmerized by you, yet in your own mind you're not that wonderful. I think that disturbed Rick," explained Collins, a regular on TV's *Town Hall Party* at age eleven and a recording artist at thirteen. Marianne Gaba, Rick's steady in 1957, added, "He was amazed that he became such a big success; I don't know if deep down he believed he was worthy of it." Though Rick's confidence grew over time, he never completely shook his self-consciousness about his Hollywood upbringing and remained acutely aware that cynics questioned his dedication to rock & roll, his "authenticity."

Sadly, he was right. Incongruous as it may seem that the seventeenth-ranked recording artist since 1955[1] could be underappreciated, Rick's role in spreading the rock & roll gospel and his consummate musicality remain glaringly overlooked.

[1] Joel Whitburn's Record Research ranks Rick number seventeen on its list of Top 200 Artists, based on an artist's total weeks on the *Billboard* magazine Hot 100. As of 1990 Rick is preceded only by Elvis Presley, the Beatles, James Brown, Stevie Wonder,

This might not have been the case had he come from penury rather than privilege. Pork and beans fueling Great Art? Time-worn, romantic, it remains one of the more ludicrous arguments bandied about by pop-music critics (which is really saying something), the most influential of whom, incidentally, are college-educated middle- and upper-middle-class white men. In truth, relatively few white rock & roll musicians endured financial hardship. In his thirties, trying to rejuvenate his career commercially, Rick politely made that point whenever journalists criticized him for "lacking the experience of poverty and struggle," as one wrote in 1973.

Any correlation between Rick's Tinseltown roots and his music's legitimacy was wholly irrelevant to, among millions, John Fogerty. Now a soloist, from 1968 to 1972 the band he led, Creedence Clearwater Revival, released hit singles as prolifically as Rick in his prime. While growing up in comfortably suburban El Cerrito, California, Fogerty regularly watched *The Adventures of Ozzie and Harriet*'s musical segments, pretending to play along on a broomstick "guitar."

"I've always considered Rick equal to the Sun Records artists," said Fogerty, also a passionate Carl Perkins and Elvis Presley fan. "Maybe he came from Hollywood, but the sound was strictly Memphis."

The first phase of Rick's career can be labeled the Rockabilly Years, 1957–1959, and certainly "Stood Up," "My Babe," "Waitin' in School," "Believe What You Say," "It's Late," and "Just a Little Too Much" rank among the genre's finest recordings. The latter four, all Top Twenty hits, were written by Johnny and Dorsey Burnette, two of rockabilly's foremost composer-musicians, though their songs were mainly hits for other performers. Rick gave them and several highly successful songwriters their big breaks.

The hell-raising brothers were born and reared dirt-poor

Pat Boone, Marvin Gaye, Aretha Franklin, the Rolling Stones, Neil Diamond, Fats Domino, Elton John, Ray Charles, the Beach Boys, Paul McCartney, the Supremes, and Chicago.

in Memphis. Elvis Presley lived on nearby Alabama Street, and his path crossed the Burnettes' time and again: at L. C. Humes High School and at Crown Electric Company. Before forming the Rock 'n Roll Trio with Dorsey and guitarist Paul Burlison, Johnny led a band that included two-thirds of Presley's future backing group, Scotty Moore and Bill Black.

The night Elvis first appeared on *The Ed Sullivan Show* in 1956, the brothers performed as finalists on Ted Mack's *Original Amateur Hour,* and not long afterward landed on Coral Records. However, the Burnettes soon discovered their management was bilking them of thousands of dollars. Disgusted, Dorsey quit and moved to Los Angeles at the behest of a producer there who urged him to make hillbilly records. "But I'm not a hillbilly," he protested. "I don't sing that way," shrill and nasal.

"Then we'll put a clothespin on your nose," the producer told him. Too proud to return to Memphis defeated, Dorsey stayed with some friends and got a regular job. His younger brother Johnny joined him six months later, in summer 1957. By night they sang in clubs, and by day they pitched songs, barging in on publishing and record executives.

To get a song called "Waitin' in School" to Rick, the brothers used a characteristically direct approach. One afternoon Johnny waited in front of Rick's house until the seventeen-year-old returned home, then sang him "Waitin' in School" right there in the driveway. Rick liked it so much that he recorded and released it immediately as the flip side to "Stood Up."

Johnny and Dorsey placed many more tunes with Rick, five on 1959's *Songs by Ricky* alone. They essentially owed their livelihoods to him. In exchange, Ozzie insisted on publishing the Burnettes' material under one of two companies established for Rick, Hilliard Music Co. and Eric Music, Inc. This then common practice is believed to have originated in the 1920s with Al Jolson, who in addition sometimes demanded a coauthor's credit on songs he recorded, when in fact he contributed neither a note nor a word.

The publishers' and artists' somewhat valid argument was

that composers benefited from having stars sing their songs. Eager to get a foot in the door and faced with ruthless competition, many novice songwriters signed away their rights, unaware that the lion's share of record profits derive from publishing, not performing, and that a hit tune might produce a lifetime's income.

"Johnny and Dorsey were ignorant country boys as far as the publishing business was concerned," said Johnny's widow, Thurley. "Everything they wrote belonged to somebody else." Since Johnny's death at age thirty in a freak 1964 boating accident, and Dorsey's succumbing to a heart attack in 1979 at age forty-six, royalties from Rick's records have helped sustain their families.

"For years, all the Burnette kids' Christmases depended on the Nelson check," said Thurley. "Depending on how big it was, was how big Christmas was that year." Between her and sister-in-law Alberta, the two have nine children, including singer Rocky Burnette (1980's hit "Tired of Toein' the Line") and guitarist Billy Burnette, currently a member of Fleetwood Mac.

"When the Nelson name is mentioned around this house, we all genuflect," joked Thurley, who has had to battle other publishers for back monies. According to Alberta, "Ozzie never, ever missed a payment. Everything was straight up. There was nobody like him in this town, I'll tell you. And every time Rick did a talk show, he'd mention the Burnettes and give them plugs."

Both Johnny and Dorsey (who Rick occasionally mixed up) were insightful songwriters, expressing suburban teenage woes with wit and insight. "Waitin' in School," inspired lyrically by Chuck Berry's "School Day," vividly evokes the frustration of clock-watching followed by the Pavlovian surge of energy at the final bell's ring.

And 1959's bouncy "It's Late," modeled after the Everly Brothers' "Wake Up Little Susie," encapsules those maddening times during adolescence when parents, circumstances, *every-*

thing, conspire against you: *It's late, we're 'bout to run outta gas/ It's late, we gotta get home fast/Can't speed, we're in a slow-down zone/Baby, look at that clock, why can't it be wrong?* Rick sings with appropriate fatalism, and the Jordanaires compound his anguish by echoing each grim thought like a guilty conscience.

Today's rock-oldies radio stations tend to neglect Rick's rough-hewn rockabilly in favor of his quieter, pop-oriented material, creating the false impression that he was primarily a balladeer. Admittedly, his voice's velvety texture worked wonders on hit ballads such as "Lonesome Town," "Sweeter Than You," "Never Be Anyone Else but You" and "I Wanna Be Loved," all composed by Baker Knight.

Most of Knight's compositions brought out Rick's romanticism, but his first, "Lonesome Town," was bleak and despairing; the forlorn twenty-four-year-old's cynical impressions of Hollywood, *a place that lovers go/to cry their troubles away.* He'd moved there from Birmingham, Alabama, to seek his fortune in songwriting, but six months had passed without a sale. When Sharon Sheeley brought Rick by Knight's room at the Park Sunset Hotel in fall 1958 to hear some songs, he was down to thirty-seven cents.

"A couple of days later," he remembered, "I got a call saying that Rick liked two of them, and would I take a two-thousand-dollar advance?" Within weeks both "Lonesome Town" and its feverish flip side, "I Got a Feeling," occupied the Top Ten. Knight went on to write for Frank Sinatra, Dean Martin, and Elvis Presley, who recorded his dramatic ballad "The Wonder of You."

"Lonesome Town" began as a calypso number, with a percolating conga-drum rhythm and a piano countermelody. Then one of the Jordanaires suggested using just guitar, confounding Jimmie Haskell because, he said, "Back then it was almost unthinkable to put out a record that didn't have rhythm on it." The final take, performed live, involved only fingerpicked acoustic guitar, haunting backing vocals, and Rick's mournful lead, mixed prominently to heighten the sense of solitude, as if he were singing from a stark, neon-lit room at the Heartbreak Hotel.

Criticisms of Rick's voice rarely take into account his age at the time of these recordings. Elvis Presley, Carl Perkins, and Jerry Lee Lewis were all in their early twenties when they cut their debut albums. Physically and stylistically developed, they'd already discovered their limitations by playing at local dances, talent shows, and radio jamborees.

Rick's trial-and-error period was documented on his first two albums, which contain their share of embarrassments. His versions of Lewis's "Whole Lotta Shakin' Goin' On" and Presley's "There's Good Rockin' Tonight" were clearly beyond his range then, his voice colorless and thin. A short time later, however, on "Lonesome Town" and "Never Be Anyone Else but You," Rick was revealing a rich, resonant bottom end and a three-and-a-half octave range.

Granted, Rick could not compete with Presley, one of popular music's truly magnificent voices. "But he had a way of expressing himself with a lot of feel and soul," said Jordanaire Neal Matthews. Even in his teens, Rick convincingly conveyed adult emotions, as on his rendition of the country-blues "Tryin' to Get to You," which Elvis included on his first LP. The contrast between their styles and personae was never more evident.

Presley's version trembles with carnal longing and anticipation, his voice breaking on the chorus (*I kept travelin' night and day/runnin' all the way, baby/tryin' to get to you*) and suggesting throughout, Now that I'm here, how 'bout some lovin'? Rick's is low-keyed and in a lower key, his voice warm and intimate, as if murmuring to a lover while they bask in passion's afterglow. Rick secretly wished he'd been endowed with Ray Charles's gravelly texture, saying, "I always wanted to sound like somebody else, but I always sounded like me." Yet it was his voice's naked quality that made it so distinctly personal.

Any analysis of Rick's music has to cite the band, of which

111

he was an integral member as well as the obvious focal point. Having grown up in a family that worked as a team, and having worked with a TV-show cast that fancied itself a family, Rick thrived on the camaraderie, the interplay—and the security— of an ensemble.

"He got more of a kick playing with a band," said Jimmie Haskell, "than he did singing." His group, never christened in the manner of Buddy Holly's Crickets or Gene Vincent's Blue Caps, was the best of its time. "We were tight," said guitarist James Burton. "I don't think we ever dropped a note. Everything was so precise and so well rehearsed . . . It was *happening*."

Burton is universally regarded by critics and peers as one of rock & roll's premiere innovators on guitar. No one admired his extraordinary talent more than Rick, who felt confident enough to share the spotlight. He set the self-taught Burton loose on freewheeling, incandescent solos that were revolutionary for a time when most guitar breaks merely restated melody lines.

Few bandleaders were so generous, a fact Burton appreciates to this day. "Rick and I had such a good feeling together musically," he said. "We knew exactly what we wanted to do and how to do it." The guitar work on tracks such as "Believe What You Say" and "Milk Cow Blues" influenced scores of future greats, including George Harrison, a friend of Rick's in the 1970s. "In the early days of the Beatles," Harrison told him, "we used to copy your songs lick by lick, chord by chord."

Rick shares his greatest contributions to rock & roll with Ozzie. A quarter-century before MTV, both recognized television's awesome marketing power. And, not to be overlooked, the concept of inserting lip-synced performances into a sitcom's plot provided the basis of several TV shows. On the mid-1960s comedy *The Monkees*, a quartet modeled after the Beatles mugged for the cameras and plugged its records, generating phenomenal sales. A few years later, another series launched a fabricated act not even made up of real people: the cartoon Archies, whose number-one "Sugar, Sugar" was the biggest-selling record of 1969.

Furthermore, Rick's performing rock & roll in the context of his family's safe and acceptable TV program lent the music respectability. That he did so without diluting its vitality ultimately should stamp him as much a subversive as any of his more menacing-looking peers. As has often been said, Rick *smuggled* rock & roll into America's living rooms.

Finally, consider the incalculable impact Rick's discovery of rock & roll had on the ten million teenagers who watched *The Adventures* weekly. Bill Haley and Elvis Presley may have introduced rock to the young white masses, but each defied mainstream adolescent identification: Haley, because he was too "old," a balding, spit-curled thirty-year-old by the time of 1955's "Rock Around the Clock"; and Presley because he was too beautiful, too extreme, too enigmatic, seeming to have ascended from anonymity to deity overnight.

In contrast, the first wave of Baby Boomers had grown up with Rick. And just like them, he'd fallen under the spell of the same first-generation rock & roll stars. Though "I'm Walkin'" followed Elvis's first national hit, "Heartbreak Hotel," by just one year, Rick has to be considered part of the second wave; he holds the distinction of having been both Presley's contemporary and disciple.

"Rick did something that was probably every kid's dream," said singer/songwriter Eric Andersen, "to pick up a guitar and rock the kids at the party." For Andersen and countless others, the Nelson series was an oasis, "the one TV show people like me could relate to and look forward to, because we knew we'd hear some rock & roll." Andersen, later a close friend of Rick's, gravitated toward folk music and has been recording contemplative, evocative albums since 1965.

"Rick rocked in a more visceral way than anybody else, in the sense that it hit him and he responded immediately, just like every kid who watched TV did. There are only a handful

113

of great, pure rockers—Elvis Presley, Buddy Holly, the Beatles, the Rolling Stones—and Rick definitely ranked right up there with them."

It stung Rick, then, that some 1970s and 1980s critics casually dismissed his early music as trifling. "An inspired fake," the *Village Voice*'s Robert Christgau called him. When the 1976 edition of the *Rolling Stone Illustrated History of Rock & Roll* relegated Rick to the "Teen Idols" chapter instead of "Rockabilly," "it stung him more than all the negative reviews he ever received put together," said his friend and manager at the time, Greg McDonald.

In "Teen Idols," essayist Greg Shaw actually praised Rick's records as "exceptionally tough and exciting" and went on to practically apologize for his placement in the book. "In truth," Shaw wrote, "Nelson can more closely be compared with an urban rockabilly like Eddie Cochran than with the run-of-the-mill teen idols of his day." But Rick was crushed to find his picture surrounded by those of Fabian, Bobby Rydell, and Pat Boone.

"What *Rolling Stone* did was unfair," said John Fogerty. "You can't talk about Rick and Fabian in the same breath, yet the tragedy is that some people do." Fogerty's theory as to why? "The curse, really, was that Rick was so good-looking. I think it's almost as simple as that."

Certainly Rick served as the model for many 1950s teen idols, who derived their popularity more from aspiration and bone structure than from inspiration and song structure. Fabian, born Fabiano Forte in South Philadelphia, was manufactured—exploited, he later contended bitterly—in Rick's image by impresario Bob Marcucci, allegedly the inspiration for the 1980 film *The Idolmaker*. Singing was not Fabian's forte, but in 1959 the magnetic teenager fired off six records into the Top Forty and had newspaper columnists asking, "Is Fabian a Threat to Rick?"

The music business's cynical beliefs that a) rock & roll was merely artless pabulum mass-produced to satiate adolescent demand and, b) it could therefore catapult any sullenly handsome youth to stardom by recording him in an echo chamber

114

and then greasing the proper disc jockeys, was disproved by some spectacular failures. In 1959 RCA Records invested $100,000 in a fifteen-year-old from New Jersey named Johnny Restivo, who clung briefly to the bottom rung of the Hot 100 before plunging into oblivion. The same year Columbia Records poured $70,000 into a handsome North Carolinian, Billy "Crash" Craddock. He lived up to his nickname, spending just one week on the chart and then vanishing until 1974, when he belatedly scored his first hit, "Rub It In."

In the wake of Rick's success, record labels also descended on television soundstages. Decca Records signed George Burns and Gracie Allen's adoptive son, Ronnie, a regular on their long-running sitcom. Once company executives heard him sing live on *The Perry Como Show*, however, "They offered me fifteen-hundred dollars to get *out* of the contract," said Burns. Not surprisingly, promoters also approached David Nelson. He spurned all offers, admitting candidly, "I don't think I sing well enough to inflict my voice on the public."

By definition, until the mid-1960s all rock & roll singers were teen idols, since primarily teenagers bought their records. Today the late-1950s teen-idol era connotes shallow, derivative pap and performers with little or no lasting value. That historians didn't always draw distinctions between Rick and what he called "the shiny-tooth guys" was an injustice that troubled him for many years. In a 1972 *New York Times* interview, he acknowledged, "A lot of people try to equate me with guys like Frankie Avalon and Fabian . . . but in the old days I sold a lot of records over a period of time, and you can't sustain that by being just another pretty face."

Later in life, Rick accepted his place in rock & roll, gratified by the knowledge he had earned the respect of his peers. "That was more important to him than the public's or critics' opinions of his music," asserted Lorrie Collins. He did have to earn it, because as Collins well remembered, many of the country and rockabilly musicians Rick admired were initially skeptical or resentful of him. "They thought he was the little rich kid whose daddy was backing him up with all the money in the world."

115

Johnny Cash, for example, "took Rick very lightly in the beginning. But as time went on, he realized there was some talent there and that Rick was totally dedicated to his music." Collins introduced Rick to Cash in 1957 at Hollywood's Roosevelt Hotel. "Meeting Rick was a thrill for Johnny; he was intimidated by his background. Yet Rick couldn't believe that Johnny Cash would invite him into his room and take the time to talk to him.

"Even though he was probably a bigger star than most of the musicians he met," said Collins, "he had this very respectful quality of admiring their talents. That was one of the things I liked about him the most. He never took himself so seriously." Sharon Sheeley added, "Rick would meet a Jerry Lee Lewis and be in awe, like any fan, just purely and honestly in awe." Sharon accompanied Rick the memorable night he visited the "Killer," recently wed to his thirteen-year-old second cousin Myra Gale Brown, at Lewis's Knickerbocker Hotel suite.

"Neither Ricky nor I had met Jerry Lee before, so we're like two wide-eyed teenagers," she recalled. "We walk into his suite, sit down, and there are wall-to-wall people, all very drunk. It was not at all like we'd expected. About a half-hour later Jerry Lee barges out, grabs Ricky's hand, and practically pumps his arm out of the socket. 'Love yer records, boy, love yer records! And who's this pretty li'l girl? Nice ta meet ya!'

"Next Jerry Lee says, 'Come over here, boy!' and Ricky takes my hand. 'You're going to come with me, *aren't you?*' 'You bet.' We're both nervous now. We go over, and Jerry Lee pours each of us a big, stiff drink. Since we didn't drink, we just looked. Then he says, 'You'll 'scuse me for a minute, won't ya, boy?'

"And Jerry Lee turns his back to us and pisses against the wall!

"Ricky looks at me. 'Sharon, we're out of here.' "

As they drove away, Rick quipped, "Boy, that really was Great Balls of Fire, wasn't it?"

Seven

Rick may have been nervous about meeting Jerry Lee Lewis and Johnny Cash, but he was positively petrified as he walked into Elvis Presley's luxurious hotel suite in October 1957.

Presley had recently cited Rick as one of his favorite newcomers. Nonetheless the seventeen-year-old worried aloud about a frosty reception. What if Elvis considered him a pale imitator? Did he take the trumped-up press reports of a Presley-Nelson rivalry seriously? Rick almost backed out several times.

Following a Presley concert at the Hollywood Pan-Pacific Auditorium, Rick and his date Marianne Gaba were whisked to the Beverly Wilshire Hotel for a private party. The moment Elvis spotted Rick across the crowded room, he made his way through the pack of celebrities, politely shook Gaba's hand, then grabbed Rick in a bear hug.

"Ricky Nelson!" he exclaimed, lifting him off the ground.

"Man, I just love your new record, 'Be-Bop Baby.' You know what my favorite part is? . . ." For the next half-hour Presley rambled on about music and about how he rarely missed *The Adventures of Ozzie and Harriet,* reciting entire scenes verbatim. Rick mostly stood there speechless.

As Rick and Gaba rode the elevator down to the lobby, she held up her hand. "God, I'm never going to wash this again," she said.

"Neither am I," agreed Rick, reverentially examining his own.

From then until Presley's death in 1977, he and Rick maintained a casual friendship, though according to Jordanaire Gordon Stoker, "Elvis didn't like Rick much at first because Rick would just sit there and stare at him. Lord, in those days you had to pump a conversation out of the boy. But Elvis liked his records and kind of felt for Rick, and he kindly encouraged him."

Rick and Presley were closest during the early 1960s when, following his Army discharge, Elvis resumed his Hollywood filmmaking schedule of two or three pictures annually. Rumors that the two stars competed hotly against each other were false. Except when it came to football.

What began as a friendly contest between their two teams evolved into a Sunday-afternoon tradition attended by assorted starlets and celebrities such as Johnny Rivers, Trini Lopez, and Pat Boone, the latter frequently bringing his family. Rick issued the initial challenge to Presley, an enthusiastic player who thought nothing of renting a Memphis high-school stadium for games with friends when back home at Graceland. Elvis's team included muscular cousins cum bodyguards Red and Sonny West; Alan Fortas, nephew of the Supreme Court justice; top aide Joe Esposito; and 270-pound gofer Lamar Fike.

Rick, in turn, enlisted every college and professional player he could find and conducted strategy sessions beforehand. On game day the Bel Air park's lot overflowed with limousines and Cadillacs. To one spectator, it looked like a convening of Cosa Nostra bosses. Elvis's squad came clad in numbered uniforms, Rick's in T-shirts and jeans. The two captains, both receivers, faced off in the middle of the field, legs spread apart, hands on their hips, eyes narrowed.

"You ready to play?" Elvis drawled.

"We're ready," said Rick.

Though they followed touch-football rules, "It was a serious game," Rick remembered. "People were flying through the air." Rick's team handily won the first five-hour match and most of those that followed.

Afterward both entourages usually repaired to Presley's rented oriental-style Bel Air home, previously owned by Prince Aly Khan and Rita Hayworth. There they played pool, pinball, and board games, drank Pepsi's and ate the host's famous fried peanut-butter-and-banana sandwiches. Rick and Elvis sometimes snuck away to play guitars and talk. The five years between them became less of a barrier as they grew older, and notwithstanding their enormously different backgrounds, the two shared much in common.

Both were shy men who'd achieved early stardom, forever altering their lives. They were vigilantly protected, not only from the public but from adult responsibilities, Presley by his notorious "Memphis Mafia" retinue, and Rick by his father. But having lived with fame all his life, Rick suffered less than Elvis. Actress Joan Staley, a former *Playboy* Playmate, appeared in several episodes of *The Adventures* and in Presley's 1964 film *Roustabout.* "Rick had a lot less confusion in his life and a lot stronger roots," she said. "He didn't need to be surrounded by an entourage all the time and was an easier person to be with."

For most of his adulthood, Elvis lacked a firm family foundation. His only sibling, twin Jesse Garon, had been stillborn; his beloved mother, Gladys, passed away when he was twenty-three; and his ne'er-do-well father, Vernon, whom he provided for, was hardly a source of sound support. To compensate, Presley invented a portable reality in which he felt relatively secure. One suspects that he watched *The Adventures of Ozzie*

119

and Harriet as much for its reassuring family depiction as for its rock & roll. "How's your Mama and Daddy?" he always asked Rick. "How's David?"

When not swapping rock-star stories and talking about favorite songs, the two discussed film acting. Rick was more selective than the prolific Elvis, whose pictures turned into vehicles for marketing soundtrack albums. A naturally dynamic screen presence, Presley hated most of his movies and envied Rick for his work in several quality films.

At twelve Rick starred with Ethel Barrymore, Leslie Caron, and Farley Granger in "Mademoiselle: A Fantasy," one of three segments in MGM's *The Story of Three Loves.* The trade magazine *Variety,* while lamenting the lightweight script, noted, "Ricky Nelson scores as the child."

A late riser, it took three alarm clocks to awaken him at nine when shooting *The Adventures.* For *The Story of Three Loves* he had to get up every morning at six. "Never again, boy," Rick said afterward. "The money isn't worth it!" But it was by the time of his next picture, the 1959 Technicolor western *Rio Bravo.* Just eighteen and one year into his singing career, Rick was in such demand that Ozzie hiked his movie fee to $150,000.

Rio Bravo was maverick director-producer Howard Hawks's rebuttal to *High Noon.* That 1952 film starred Gary Cooper as a marshal who fails to rally his apathetic townspeople behind him when threatened by a band of outlaws. Hawks and actor John Wayne both sneered at the notion of a true professional seeking help from amateurs, so in *Rio Bravo* they reversed the premise.

Wayne's laconic sheriff, John T. Chance, puts murderer Joe Burdette (Claude Akins) behind bars, provoking his wealthy brother Nathan Burdette (John Russell) to have his henchmen seal off the Texas border town. While Wayne tensely awaits the U.S. Marshal's arrival, they repeatedly try springing Akins from jail. Rick's character, a taciturn young cowhand known only as Colorado, pulls in with a wagon train. After his boss, played by Ward Bond, is gunned down by one of Burdette's men, Rick volunteers to help capture the killer.

The sheriff has just two deputies by his side—Walter Brennan's cackling, irascible Stumpy and Dean Martin's broken alcoholic, Dude—and is clearly outnumbered. But he stubbornly refuses Rick's aid, until the quick-drawing Colorado saves his life. In the film's climactic shootout, Wayne and his ragtag posse emerge victorious against the Burdette gang, enabling Martin to regain his dignity, and Wayne to develop trust.

Though many critics dismissed *Rio Bravo* as merely another epic western, it is now regarded as a genre classic. Oscar-nominated director and film aficionado Peter Bogdanovich calls it "beautifully made, Hawks's most completely realized picture. It seems like a simple comedy-drama western, but there's an awful lot going on beneath the surface." Adhering to a pet Hawks theme, *Rio Bravo* examines camaraderie among rugged men and women.

During the four-week shoot in Arizona the sixty-two-year-old Hawks helped Rick develop his inscrutable character, suggesting he run an index finger along the bridge of his nose whenever he was supposed to be thinking. (He'd given Montgomery Clift the same gesture for the 1948 classic *Red River*.) The leathery six-foot-four Wayne also worked patiently with the teenager.

Rick nearly quit the film, though, over the two western tunes he was to sing, "My Rifle, My Pony and Me" and "Cindy," in a jailhouse scene with Martin, Brennan, and Wayne. He hated the songs and had a showdown with the music director, Dmitri Tiompkin. Rick wanted to perform "Restless Kid," which Johnny Cash had written for him. At a Hollywood party, he'd mentioned to Cash that he was looking for a song for his new movie and ran down the story line. Next morning the sheet music to "Restless Kid" was stuffed in his mailbox. But Tiompkin, backed by Ozzie, ultimately prevailed, and the song wound up only on the *Ricky Sings Again* album.

Based on Rick's *Rio Bravo* performance, American motion-picture exhibitors voted him the number-one performer in its 1959 Stars of Tomorrow poll. His next film, the World War II farce *The Wackiest Ship in the Army,* shot in Hawaii in 1960, costarred him opposite Jack Lemmon. In real life Rick's asthma exempted him from military service, but here he plays first officer Ensign Tommy Hanson aboard the decrepit USS *Echo,* sent on a secret mission against the Japanese. Columbia Pictures tried capitalizing on Rick's rock & roll popularity—recommending that theaters blare his music over their sound systems and sponsor Rick Nelson look-alike contests—but the movie was only a middling success.

Including *Here Come the Nelsons,* Rick's first four releases had all been filmed during the *The Adventures'* summer hiatuses. Sometime after *The Wackiest Ship in the Army* he was offered the lead in United Artists' screen version of the Lillian Hellman drama *Toys in the Attic.* The problem was that if Rick took the challenging role of Julian Berniers, a shiftless New Orleanian living with two spinster sisters, he would have to leave the family series temporarily.

Though a clause in Ozzie's ABC contract stipulated either or both boys could quit at any time, the network allegedly threatened to cancel the show if Rick took a sabbatical. Were network executives bluffing? Probably not. George Burns's network gave him a solo series after Gracie Allen's 1958 retirement on the condition that their son Ronnie join the cast. And other television formats, such as quiz shows, also now catered to the increasingly powerful adolescent market.

"Are Teen-Agers Taking Over TV?" a leading newspaper asked. The answer was a mumbled *Yeah.* Kids between ages thirteen and nineteen comprised 60 percent of the total television audience. Naturally then, the network was anxious about the effect Rick's absence would surely have on one of its few competitive series.

After discussing the matter with Ozzie, Rick eventually turned down the film role, which went to Dean Martin. However, for a brief time the young man entered General Service Studio with a deeper realization that he could put his family and all their employees out of work. The pressure and tension were excruciating. Actress Patricia Reed, then dating Rick, remembered his father telling dinner guest Fred MacMurray, "Rick had to let go of the part for the family's sake."

The potentially explosive situation was quickly diffused. But ABC's apparent willingness to drop the series humbled Ozzie. His show's survival now rested mainly on his youngest son's shoulders.[1] A movie magazine's cover blurb, "Is Ozzie Jealous of Ricky?" while hyperbolic, probably contained a shred of truth.

Ozzie justifiably felt slighted within his profession. He'd built a television empire, masterminding every creative facet. Former associates freely label him a genius. Yet most of Hollywood viewed Ozzie as an anomaly; an enviably prosperous one-trick pony and a perennial outsider. Ironically, the show's most unique elements—Ozzie's writing about and directing his family, the natural quality of the dialogue, the seemingly effortless acting—led others to underestimate his abilities. "The industry's conception was that the show directed itself," said David. "To a certain extent, after so many years, it did."

Ozzie felt frustrated, wanting to be more than just *The Adventures*, whereas his son had transcended the program while still in his teens, through rock & roll. What's more, Rick had achieved stardom exclusive of the family, which Ozzie was never able to do. For Rick, this generated conflicting feelings of satisfaction with his success and uneasiness over outshining his father. "I think Rick also felt an amount of guilt," said Lorrie Collins, "about being so in love with music."

Acting on the series was his job; he never felt emotionally connected to it. Back when Rick was seven, Ozzie used to run radio-show scripts past him, to make sure youngsters could understand the gags. "Oh, I understand it okay, Pop," Rick once said, "but it's *your* program. Why don't you do what you want with it?"

[1] Inexplicably, in June 1960 it was announced that from then on the show would be called *The Adventures of the Nelson Family*. Yet when the series returned for a ninth season in the fall, it retained its familiar title.

Singing, however, meant everything to Rick, bringing him the same self-fulfillment that the TV show brought Ozzie. He'd originally envisioned music as his private realm, a place he could reveal his true self, free from paternal rule. But like many devoted fathers, Ozzie couldn't let go of his son. A painful transition for most parents and children, the normal problems of a child growing up and away were multiplied in the Nelson household, where familial and professional ties overlapped. Inevitably, in his early twenties Rick began bridling at Ozzie's continued involvement in his recording career.

"He expressed resentment all the time," said friend Robin Luke. "Ozzie was pushy with both Rick and David, but especially with Rick. He took hold of his career and made him do things that otherwise Rick would not have done"—brassy old-time numbers like "Yes Sir, That's My Baby," and soggy string-arranged ballads such as "Young Emotions," a Top Twenty hit in 1960.

Rick particularly disliked the song "Teenage Idol," feeling the self-pitying lyrics made him sound egotistical: *Some people call me a teenage idol/Some people say they envy me/I guess they've got no way of knowing/How lonesome I can be.* "But Ozzie insisted he record it," said Jimmie Haskell. The record went to number five in 1962.

Ozzie thwarted the release of "Gloomy Sunday," which Richie Frost called "the best thing Rick ever recorded." The few outsiders to hear this powerful 1959 performance of an elegiac Depression Era blues number agree. Rick discovered the song in a listening booth at Wallich's Music City, where he would sample everything from avant-garde jazz, to Spike Jones, to the early ambient recordings of Martin Denny.

Covered by Billie Holiday and Paul Robeson, among others, "Gloomy Sunday" is an ominous three-minute suicide note.[2] Rick's heavy voice, accompanied only by acoustic guitar, conveys calm despair, as if his mind were made up. Ozzie, concerned

[2] In the 1930s "Gloomy Sunday" was actually promoted and advertised as "the suicide song" and purportedly spurred several suicides. In a bizarre coincidence, one of its two composers later killed himself.

about its possible effect on Rick's impressionable audience, prohibited Imperial Records from issuing it.

David clashed more virulently with his father. From the time he was fourteen, he wanted to be a radio producer, then a television and film director. It seemed logical that David gain experience by directing occasional episodes of *The Adventures*, but in hindsight he'd have been better off apprenticing on another program.

By the time of David's directorial debut, the series was in its eleventh season, and Ozzie understandably resisted tampering with a proven formula. Having appeared in several well-received films, David tried to initiate more character development, a concept his father flatly rejected. When Ozzie directed, if a line didn't sound right, he voiced it himself and had the performer mimic him. Method? Motivation? To Ozzie's mind, a paycheck was motivation enough.

The few times a year David sat in the director's chair, Ozzie could not help meddling. Finally Harriet implored her husband to stay home. "David had a hell of a time," crew member Jack Iannarelli said sympathetically. "He'd get upset and say, 'Dad, do you want me to direct, or do you want me to go back to college?'" More than once, when no one was around, David put his fist through a wall in frustration.

Some psychological studies on driven people suggest that dynamic fathers tend to produce noncompetitive children. This certainly was not true of Ozzie, whose sons went to extremes in asserting their independence.

In his teens, David secretly raced midget cars under the pseudonym "Mike Sullivan." One time his car flew into the railing, but he escaped injury and switched to racing motorcycles instead. A few years later, to prep for his role as Tommy Gordon in the adventure film *The Big Circus* he became a trapeze "catcher": the acrobat who hangs upside down above the net and catches his partner, the "flyer."

125

Filmed in 1958, *The Big Circus* cast many authentic big-top acts, including Del and Babs Graham of the Flying Viennas aerial troupe. David, exhilarated by the experience, worked out with the couple at their tented trapeze rigging in Thousand Oaks, California. When the Flying Viennas' catcher left, David took his place. Later that year he volunteered Rick to perform with him, though at 170 pounds the younger brother outweighed the average flyer by roughly forty pounds.

The two took their acrobatic act to fairs and arenas, once dazzling eighty thousand spectators at a charity football game at the Los Angeles Memorial Coliseum. David suspended himself from the catcher's bar while Rick swung back and forth, hurtled through the air, somersaulted, clasped hands with his brother, then regrasped the bar, swung again, and vaulted himself back onto the pedestal board. Even with a net thirty-two feet below, both risked serious injury.

Rick raced cars as well, nearly burning to death in a demolition derby while on location for *Rio Bravo*. His vehicle caught fire, and he could not undo his safety belt. Flames lapped at the gas tank as several bystanders struggled to yank him free. During his month in Arizona Rick also became interested in bullfighting, so he read up on the spectacle, went out and fought a bull; horseback riding, so he practiced after work on his quarter horse, Tinker Toy, a birthday present from Ozzie and Harriet; and karate, so he studied until he earned a black belt. As soon as Rick mastered something, he lost interest, but not before Ozzie had based a TV episode on it.

"When you do anything requiring skill and courage," Rick once explained, "you first learn how to do it, then you work hard at it, then you study the odds, and after you know the odds, you dismiss them." Dennis Larden, one of his backing musicians during the 1970s, observed, "Rick had no sense of his own vulnerability. He didn't ask, Can this be done? He just did it. Something popped into his mind, he visualized it, and made it happen. He was Zen in a very natural, uneducated way."

126

Why were both brothers compelled to flirt with danger and possibly court death? David toured America and Europe with the Flying Viennas on and off for five years, to work before a live audience, he claimed. But it was also a way to escape the pressures of the family television show and to be on his own. David literally ran away from home and joined the circus.

Following the fiery car accident, Rick told friends he'd entered the demolition derby to show the crowd he wasn't afraid. Afraid of what? they asked. He didn't answer. Sharon Sheeley speculated, "Rick always lived on the edge because he desperately wanted to prove that he was more than Ozzie and Harriet's kid." His only fear, in effect, was of not being able to step outside his father's considerable shadow.

Rick approached his twenty-first birthday acutely aware that his musical career had cooled. Between fall 1957 and summer 1959 he'd charted ten consecutive Top Ten hits; in his era, only Elvis Presley and Pat Boone did better. But Rick's next four singles, "I Wanna Be Loved," "Young Emotions," "I'm Not Afraid," and "You Are the Only One," fell short. And, in an inglorious career first, the latter two failed to penetrate the Top Twenty, despite "You Are the Only One" receiving three plugs in five weeks on *The Adventures*.

Meanwhile, a gleeful media was preparing rock & roll for burial. "Rock 'n' Roll Decline Seen," the Associated Press reported. Radio station KAVI in Rocky Ford, Colorado, announced it would now play only "good family music," demonstrating its resolve by smashing a rock & roll platter on the air every ten minutes. Of course, industry "experts" had been predicting rock's demise since it began. The patient, however, continued to linger, though judging from some of the top records of 1960—Mark Dinning's "Teen Angel," Brian Hyland's "Itsy Bitsy Teenie Bikini," Bobby Rydell's "Volare"—just barely.

Someone took the hint, for Rick's album that year, *More*

127

Songs by Ricky, was conspicuously short on rockabilly and long on glitz. Ozzie and Lew Chudd obviously hoped to recast him as Bobby Darin, whose 1959 Big-Band-style rendering of Bertolt Brecht and Kurt Weill's "Mack the Knife" won a Grammy Award for Record of the Year.

Elvis Presley also appeared to be aiming for wider appeal, snapping fingers alongside Frank Sinatra on television two months after his Army release. The title of his album *Something for Everyone* indicated his future direction. Unlike Elvis, Rick regained his artistic bearings for a while, redemption coming in the form of a song called "Travelin' Man." How he came to record it was as much an accident as "Poor Little Fool" had been.

In 1960 Rick revamped his band, with saxist Plas Johnson's brother Ray unseating Gene Garf on piano and James Burton's boyhood friend Joe Osborn replacing James Kirkland on bass. Every day the mail brought demos of songs for Rick's consideration. When the pile was about to topple, someone in the band or Rick himself sifted through the acetates and reel-to-reel tapes. One day Osborn got elected and sat in Lew Chudd's Imperial Records office preparing for a tedious afternoon.

The office next door belonged to soul singer Sam Cooke's manager, J. W. Alexander. Through the wall Osborn heard a sparkling melody set to a gently tugging rhythm. He knocked on the door and asked if he could hear the song again. "You can have it," Alexander grunted, retrieving the tape from a wastebasket and tossing it to him. "Travelin' Man" became Rick's biggest record, selling over 6 million copies and hitting number one in twenty-two countries, including the United States in June 1961.

"It's actually a fairly mediocre song," writer Jerry Fuller chuckled. He dashed off "Travelin' Man," about an itinerant Romeo with an international harem, while sitting in a park and leafing through a world atlas. "I'd pick a city or country, then find out what they called the girls there." Ergo, from Alaska, *my cute little Eskimo; my China doll down in old Hong Kong;*

and, from Hawaii, my *pretty Polynesian baby*. "At the time," Fuller explained, "I didn't know they were called *wahines*."

The chorus's first line, *Oh, my sweet Fräulein down in Ber-lin town. . .* , posed a serious problem for Ozzie. In keeping with Fuller's demo, Rick accented the first syllable of *Berlin* instead of the second, causing his stickler father to cringe every time he heard it and leading to an argument.

"Rick, it's not *Ber*-lin town, it's Ber*lin*. And Ber*lin*'s not a town, it's a city!"

"Well, that's the way Jerry Fuller wrote it."

"Yes, but Rick, long after you're gone," Ozzie warned, "people will play 'Travelin' Man' and wonder why you called Ber*lin* *Ber*-lin town!" You need only listen to the record to learn the debate's outcome.

Ozzie set aside his disgruntlement to create one of the first conceptual rock videos, superimposing Rick over background travelogue footage of the song's various locales. Shot in black-and-white, it's a far cry from today's million-dollar three-minute spectacles. The flip side of "Travelin' Man," "Hello Mary Lou," written by twenty-year-old Gene Pitney, also received a modest video treatment and went to number nine. Its cantering drum-and-cowbell intro is one of the most instantly recognizable in rock & roll.

"One of the greatest double-sided records of all time," John Fogerty called the pairing that rekindled Rick's popularity. However, this second career phase, the Pop Years, 1960–66 (which began with 1960's "Young Emotions"), was less daring and satisfying than the rockabilly period. A-sides were almost exclusively pop ballads arranged more meticulously than before and with guitarist James Burton sounding far too restrained. When Rick returned to performing his early repertoire in the late 1970s, he included little material from these years.

Paradoxically, while pop success frees artists financially, it often enslaves them creatively. Internal and external pressures mount to repeat the winning formula, and as evidenced by "Travelin' Man" 's calculated follow-up, Rick proved vulnerable.

"A Wonder Like You," another Jerry Fuller composition, reprises the same "rockalypso" flavor and travelogue theme: *I've seen the pretty dancing girls of Siam/the happy Polynesian people too (wahines,* Jerry, *wahines*). It rose to number eleven on the Hot 100. Blueprinting songs became something of a Fuller trademark in the 1960s, his lecherous 1968 smashes for Gary Puckett and the Union Gap, "Young Girl" and "Lady Willpower," containing melodically interchangeable verses.

Fuller also penned Rick's "Young World" (number five, 1962) and "It's Up to You" (number six, 1963), submitting demos featuring his soulful lead vocals, and Dave Burgess and Glen Campbell on guitars and harmonies. Rick liked the blend of their voices so much that he hired the trio to sing backup.[3] Burgess had a varied history: lead guitarist for the Champs, whose 1958 "Tequila" stands as rock's first number-one instrumental; co-owner of the label for which Fuller recorded, Challenge Records; and author of Rick's "Everlovin'," the Top Twenty flip side to "A Wonder Like You." While on a Dick Clark Caravan of Stars tour, he and Fuller discovered Campbell leading his group the Western Wranglers at an Albuquerque club called the Hitching Post and talked the six-foot, blue-eyed musician into moving to Hollywood.

Rick, increasingly fascinated with recording technology, decided he wanted to supervise instrumental tracks from the control booth, so Campbell replaced him on acoustic rhythm guitar. The Arkansas-born singer-guitarist exuded the same easy manner and rustic humor that would make him a hit with TV viewers in the late 1960s and early 1970s. He and Fuller, also a country boy, enlivened the atmosphere at United Recorders' studio B, where Rick now recorded.

"Glen and Jerry would face each other at the microphone," recalled Jimmie Haskell. "One would start singing, and the other would start laughing:

[3] In 1962 Campbell, Fuller, and Burgess cut two rare 45s with Rick, who sang bass vocals: "Scratchin'," under the nom de disc the Fleas, and "Desire," as the Trophies. Radio stations had begun to air the latter when somehow word leaked that Rick was part of the "group." Imperial's Lew Chudd exploded, and Challenge Records, fearing a lawsuit, pulled the record off the market, rendering the potential hit a collector's item.

130

" 'About your breath!'

" 'What?'

" 'Smells like the hind end of a *hawg*!'

"This," said Haskell, "would go down on tape."

According to Fuller, "It used to take us all night to get the backgrounds done, because Glen kept cracking us up." The songwriter is convinced that Rick, who footed the bill for recording costs, let the three of them eat up the clock because "he knew that none of us was on easy street." At the time, Campbell and his wife, Billie, lived on beans, ham hocks, corn bread, and milk.

Rick took to Campbell right away, envying his extroverted personality, though according to Burgess, "Glen used to ride Rick real hard: 'C'mon, Rick, tell us a joke! Be funny!' " Rick got even one night. After Campbell had shared a filthy joke, Rick glanced at the control room and said to him, "Glen, tell us that joke again." Campbell obliged. Over the studio intercom came Harriet Nelson's voice:

"That's *really nice*, Glen."

"We didn't know she was there," said Fuller. "Glen was so embarrassed, he crawled under a piano."

Rick Is 21, the album that contained "Travelin' Man" and "Hello Mary Lou," spent nearly a year on the LP charts. Supposedly, on his twenty-first birthday Rick had excised the *y* from his name, to indicate that he had "grown up." It was actually a publicity ploy hatched by his press agent. "Let 'em do what they want," Rick said at the time. "Rick, Ricky, it really doesn't matter. My name is Eric."

As he did each year, Eric/Rick/Ricky toured during the summer of 1961. If the self-effacing young star underestimated the extent of his fame, he was reminded of it during an outdoor show for ten thousand at a Wakefield, Massachusetts, amusement park. The band was playing under a canopy, when it suddenly started to pour. Rick's drenched bone white summer suit hung heavy on his shoulders and clung to his legs. He assumed the crowd would scatter, but no one moved.

So the group kept performing, despite the threat of electrocution. Joe Osborn, holding an electric bass guitar connected to an amplifier dripping water, looked up at the angry sky and wondered, *When the hell are we going to get off stage?* Not until the show ended. The fans stayed put, as if oblivious. "It was eerie," Rick mused afterward, "none of those people leaving." The experience heightened Rick's appreciation of his immense power, humbling and unnerving him at the same time.

Eight

"Weren't you jealous?" That is the question David Nelson has been asked throughout his adult life. He denied it then, and he denies it now. "Rick might have been richer, taller, and better looking, but he was never older," he said. "And to a certain point in our lives, that was my saving grace." Friends portray David as tremendously supportive of Rick, but others voice suspicions that he suffered quietly, especially those times when his younger brother's luster seemed more like a blinding glare.

On David's twenty-first birthday, while the family sang "Happy Birthday to You," Lew Chudd barged in to surprise Rick with a gold record for "Be-Bop Baby." "That's been my story," David joked over thirty years later. "At least he could have waited until I blew out the candles." What sibling wouldn't have felt at least a twinge of resentment?

133

The disproportionate amount of attention made Rick uneasy, said Marianne Gaba, his girlfriend at the time. "He was sensitive to the fact that he was getting all the recognition, and I think he felt a little bad for David." In interviews Rick proudly pointed to David's flourishing film-acting career, which his own rock & roll success tended to obscure. David appeared in several pictures and drew encouraging notices for his work in *The Big Show,* with Esther Williams, Cliff Robertson, and Robert Vaughan, and *Peyton Place,* with Lana Turner, Lloyd Nolan, and Hope Lange. The latter role won him *Photoplay* magazine's 1958 award for Outstanding New Film Actor.

But he let his movie career lapse by the early 1960s. "I was being cast in David Nelson–type parts," he said, "and I knew that until the show was over I was never going to graduate to James Dean or Marlon Brando–type roles, I was always going to be David Nelson."

According to David, he and Rick never seriously discussed how either of them felt about their careers. "We joked about it. But Rick and I had a rapport where we could talk without speaking, and that was a tremendous advantage." Their relationship was typical of most brothers, "a little volatile here and there, but overall close," said Skip Young.

He should know, having leased a bachelor pad with them in 1960 and 1961. Erected on stilts, the Hollywood Hills cliffhanger afforded a spectacular, if vertigo-inducing, view from its back porch, which hung precariously over the San Fernando Valley. It amused daredevils Rick and David to execute handstands on the railing.

Rick, then twenty, had never been on his own before and left his imprint all over the comfortably furnished Multiview Drive house. While his roommates were reasonably domesticated (Harriet did their food shopping, and a maid cleaned on Fridays), Rick was the quintessential Helpless Bachelor, dining on Cokes and candy and pounding out Ray Charles songs on the piano until four in the morning.

"He had a habit of stepping out of his clothes and leaving

them on the floor in the same spot," remembered David, whom Rick sarcastically called "Mother." "The house looked like Little Egypt, with this big pyramid of dirty clothes."

Wedding bells broke up the trio on May 20, 1961, when David married June Blair, also twenty-four, at the Forest Lawn Cemetery chapel. A copper-haired actress, June had appeared in two episodes of *The Adventures* the previous fall. Skip Young tied the knot just a few days later, and so the two couples honeymooned together in Anchorage, Alaska. There both bridegrooms appeared in a circus, David as a trapezist, Young as a ringmaster.

Rick's friend Charley Britt, entering his freshman football season with the Los Angeles Rams, took David's room at Multiview Drive. The native Georgian adopted Ozzie and Harriet as his "West Coast mom and dad," he said. "They called David number one, Rick number two, and me number three." Naturally Ozzie was thrilled to make the acquaintance of a professional football player and enticed Britt into joining the cast as one of Rick's fraternity brothers.

That fall Rick and Britt moved into a house Harriet had found for them on winding Zorada Drive, also in the Hollywood Hills, above Nichols Canyon. To ensure Rick's privacy, she purchased the two adjacent lots as well and installed a wrought-iron gate at the foot of the driveway. Both the living room and Rick's bedroom had sliding-glass doors that led to a spacious backyard, with a swimming pool and a panoramic view of Los Angeles. "It was *a trap*," said Britt, "a real good place for a rock & roll star and a football player. We had a lot of 'traffic' "— i.e., endless parties and girls.

Exploiting Rick's Eligible Bachelor status, Ozzie repeatedly cast him on *The Adventures* as a virtuous Don Juan. Rick got to "date" beautiful starlets such as Tuesday Weld, Rhonda Shore, and Linda Evansted, now better known as Linda Evans. In real life Rick was apprehensive about the opposite sex, concerned that women were attracted to him only because he was Rick Nelson. Britt remembered beautiful actress Sherry Jackson (daughter Terry Williams on *Make Room for Daddy*'s first five seasons) "making a huge play for Rick, but he wouldn't pay any attention. He just didn't think she was interested. You got the feeling he was unaware."

In his late teens and early twenties Rick mostly wasted Saturday nights with Hollywood bimbettes and carhops from Tiny Naylor's drive-ins who couldn't speak in complete sentences, he later admitted. Britt assumes credit for breaking that pattern. Over dinner with Rick, Ozzie, and Harriet, he informed his new roommate, "The quality of women around the house had better improve vastly, because *I can't take it.*"

With Ozzie's help, Britt took charge of "quality control." He and Rick used to pick out the prettiest available actresses from the *Players' Guide* casting directory, then Ozzie would call them in for an audition, at which time the two bachelors would just happen to be in Ozzie's office. Sometimes, said Britt, "The girls didn't look like their pictures, so it didn't work out for us. But it usually worked out for them, because Ozzie hired about ninety-five percent." David had used the same technique to meet June Blair, whom he'd seen in a movie called *The Rabbit Trap.*

Surprisingly, Rick carried on few serious affairs. His first love, at seventeen, was Marianne Gaba, a curly-haired blond beauty queen from Chicago. Crowned Miss Illinois 1957, she came out to California for the Miss Universe pageant and landed bit work on *The George Burns and Gracie Allen Show,* also filmed at General Service Studio. One day she auditioned for *The Adventures.*

"It was a small, recurring part as Rick's girlfriend," she said, "and I got it"—both on and off camera. The television role lasted only three episodes; the real-life role, over a year.

Whenever Rick picked up Gaba at her USC dorm for a date, "There were always about twenty girls waiting in the lobby to see him," she remembered. Since venturing out in public presented problems, they spent most of their time at darkened movie drive-ins, after which Rick habitually required a ham-

Rudy Vallee wanna-be Ozzie Nelson circa 1931, the year readers of the New York *Daily Mirror* voted his orchestra the most popular local dance band. First prize: a summer stint at the legendary Glen Island Casino. *Photo by White Studio courtesy of Billy Rose Theatre Collection, New York Public Library, Astor, Lenox and Tilden Foundations*

Hardly resembling the doyenne of motherhood she would later portray on TV, Harriet Hilliard was emceeing a revue at Manhattan's famous Hollywood Restaurant when Ozzie Nelson met her in 1932. *Photo by Murray Korman courtesy of Billy Rose Theatre Collection, New York Public Library, Astor, Lenox and Tilden Foundations*

Repeating a pattern set by both their parents, Ozzie and Harriet's professional relationship turned romantic, and on October 8, 1935, they were married at the New Jersey home of Ozzie's widowed mother. *Photo by Herbert Mitchell courtesy of Special Collections and Archives, Rutgers University Library*

Throughout the late 1930s and early 1940s, Ozzie and Harriet recorded and starred on radio. The same year they wed, their "And Then Some" topped the charts, a feat later duplicated twice by son Rick in 1958 and 1961 and by grandsons Matthew and Gunnar in 1990. *Look Magazine photo courtesy of Special Collections and Archives, Rutgers University Library*

America's soon-to-be Favorite Family in front of what would become the Most Televised Home in America, 1822 Camino Palmero, North Hollywood: (left to right) Rick, Ozzie, Harriet, and David. *Photo by Robert Perkins and Associates courtesy of Special Collections and Archives, Rutgers University Library*

Before transplanting *The Adventures of Ozzie and Harriet* from radio to television, Ozzie test-marketed his family's visual appeal by way of the 1951 film *Here Come the Nelsons*. Rick (second from right) was a natural onscreen, but watching himself traumatized David (far left). *Photo courtesy of Special Collections and Archives, Rutgers University Library*

On Friday, October 3, 1952, the Nelsons moved onto a video block already occupied by the Goldbergs, the Ricardos, the Hansens, and other TV nuclear units. *Photo by John Engstead courtesy of Special Collections and Archives, Rutgers University Library*

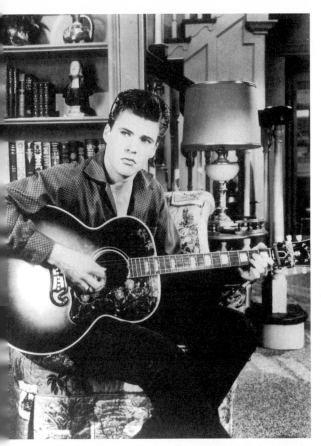

Teenage Rick strumming his guitar in the Nelson living room. Or is that the living room set from the TV show? Hard to say, since both were furnished exactly the same. Inexplicably, though Rick came from an affluent Hollywood family, he felt a kinship with Elvis Presley, Carl Perkins, and other rockabilly singers he heard on the radio. *Photo courtesy of Greg McDonald*

Rick and band-members James Kirkland (left) and James Burton (right) get the kids shakin' at the big dance. An estimated ten million teenagers tuned in *The Adventures* each week to watch Rick lip sync one of his hit records. *Photo courtesy of Greg McDonald*

Rick navigates his way through a predominately female crowd. To protect the teenage idol from paternity suits, handlers set him up with prostitutes on the road. *Photo courtesy of Greg McDonald*

(Above left) With three of the Four Preps (left to right, Marv Ingram, Bruce Belland, and Glen Larson) visible behind him, Rick exhorts the shrieking crowd at Atlantic City's Steel Pier, though it's doubtful anyone heard him. "I used to stand backstage and wonder why he even bothered opening his mouth," recalls cousin George Nelson, a bodyguard on the summer 1950 tour. *Photo courtesy of Greg McDonald*

(Above right) Though at the height of his career, eighteen-year-old Rick knew how fickle the public could be. After the Steel Pier shows, back at his hotel suite, he remarked somberly, "I guess when I'm twenty-one, I'll be a twenty-one-year-old has-been." Hardly. *Photo courtesy of Greg McDonald*

Rick and the Jordanaires (left to right, Gordon Stoker, Neal Matthews, Hoyt Hawkins, and Ray Walker), who added their silvery voices to many of Rick's hits. The quartet had a handshake agreement with long-standing employer Elvis Presley that it wouldn't publicize its association with Presley's foremost competitor. *Photo courtesy of Gordon Stoker*

```
WUX MADISON TENN NL PD JUNE 24 PM 3

HOLD FOR ARIVAL

RICKEY NELSON ROYAL MAWAIIAN HOTEL HONOLULU HAWAII

DEAR RICKEY :BEST WISHES ON YOUR APPEARANCE IN HAWAII BEHALF
ELVIS AND MYSELF WE KNOW YOU WILL RECEIVE THE BIGGEST TURNOUT EVER
WE SINCERELY APPRECIATE YOU TELLING ALL THE FOLKS IN HAWAII HOW
MUCH WE WOULD HAVE LIKED TO BE THERE WITH ALL OF YOU:

    XXX SINCERELY YOUR PALS ELVIS AND THE COLONEL
```

A congratulatory 1959 telegram from friend Elvis Presley, still stationed in Germany, and his manager, "Colonel" Tom Parker. Presley was an ardent fan of *The Adventures* and could recite entire scenes verbatim. *Courtesy of "Colonel" Tom Parker*

By the time of this 1959 photo, Rick was the undisputed star of the Nelson family. When he later contemplated taking a sabbatical from *The Adventures* to appear in the film *Toys in the Attic*, ABC allegedly threatened to cancel the series. Rick subsequently turned down the role. *Photo courtesy of Special Collections and Archives, Rutgers University Library*

(Below) Just as he'd added David's wife, June Blair, to the cast, Ozzie incorporated Kris into *The Adventures*. "It is not only a wholesome show for the whole family," wrote Cleveland Amory in *TV Guide*, "it *is* the whole family." *Photo by P.I.C., Burbank, California*

(Above) On April 20, 1963, Rick married Kristin Harmon, pedigreed daughter of football legend Tom Harmon and actress Elyse Knox. But his heart forever belonged to a teenage prostitute and heroin addict he'd romanced when he was eighteen. She'd left Rick, say friends, because she believed her personal problems would destroy him. *Photo by Hal Mantoen, Glendale, California*

The Adventures followed the Rutgers University motto "Ever changing yet eternally the same," with the Nelsons still convening in their knotty-pine kitchen. Only the fruit in the fruit basket changed. *ABC photos courtesy of Special Collections and Archives, Rutgers University Library*

(Opposite) "Hi, Mom," "Hi, Rick," "Hi Pop," Hi, Dave." *The Adventures of Ozzie and Harriet* lasted fourteen seasons, making it one of the longest-running sitcoms in television history. *ABC photo courtesy of Special Collections and Archives, Rutgers University Library*

Rick, shaggy and resplendent in a rhinestone-embroidered Western shirt, at the October 15, 1971, Madison Square Garden oldies concert he later wrote about in the hit song "Garden Party": "No one heard the music/We didn't look the same." *Photo courtesy of Greg McDonald*

The million-copy success of "Garden Party" in 1972 introduced Rick to a new generation of fans. One concert promoter described his audience as having "the broadest demographic range of any act I've ever booked, from little kids to ladies with blue hair." *Photo courtesy of Greg McDonald*

In the early 1970s Ozzie and Harriet were enjoying their own revived popularity, starring in a new TV series *Ozzie's Girls.* But toward the end of its first season Ozzie began feeling ill. Diagnosed with terminal liver cancer, he died on June 3, 1975, at age 69. *Photo courtesy of Special Collections and Archives, Rutgers University Library*

Not long after Ozzie's death, Rick's life began to unravel. MCA Records bought out his contract, leaving him without a record label, and his marriage was in shambles. *Photo courtesy of Greg McDonald*

Rick, Kris, and close friend Kent McCord, star of the TV police drama *Adam 12* and, years earlier, a fraternity brother on *The Adventures*. *Photo by Frank Edwards/Fotos International*

In a hallowed band tradition, Rick gets pied on his fortieth birthday, May 8, 1980. Kept an eternal adolescent in rock & roll's never-never land, he wistfully asked friends, "Do I have to act like an 'adult' now?" *Photo by Tom McDonald*

Because Rick (shown here with friend Paul Rose and manager Greg McDonald) recorded in an era where singles far outsold albums, several of his LPs didn't turn gold until two decades after their release. *Photo by Michael Zagaris courtesy of Greg McDonald*

By the early 1980s Rick was playing up to 250 dates a year, many of them at small clubs. He had no choice. "The band didn't know that if Rick didn't take the dates," explains his business manager, "he'd have his house repossessed." *Photo by Tom McDonald*

(Above) Rick and Bobby Neal (right) on stage. The talented guitarist became Rick's friend and confidant in much the same way that James Burton had been.
Photo courtesy of Greg McDonald

(Right) Rick in Las Vegas with Greg McDonald (center) and Jerry Lee Lewis (left). The "Killer" once owned the Douglas DC-3 airplane that Rick purchased on May 3, 1985.
Photo by Suzanne McDonald

Rick with "Colonel" Tom Parker (seated), Greg McDonald (far right), and the Jordanaires, whom he hadn't worked with since the mid-1960s. "Most entertainers change tremendously and become completely different people," reflects leader Gordon Stoker, "but Rick was still the same sweet, genuine person he was as a kid." *Photo by Sherry McDonald*

Helen Blair came into Rick's life shortly after Kris filed for divorce in 1980. Some friends say she contributed greatly to Rick's problems with drugs late in life; few, however, deny he cared deeply for her. *Photo courtesy of Marti Blair Ditonto*

Rick and Helen at Christmas 1981. At one point Rick had his manager arrange a wedding in Hawaii, but backed out at the last minute. *Photo courtesy of Marti Blair Ditonto*

In his early forties, still one of the ten sexiest men in America, according to *Playgirl* Magazine. *Photo courtesy of Greg McDonald*

Sons Matthew and Gunnar flank Rick after his August 22, 1985, concert at Los Angeles's Universal Amphitheatre. The twins, then eighteen, moved into their father's house the following month. *Photo courtesy of Greg McDonald*

It took thirty years, but three months before his death Rick finally met his idol Carl Perkins (second from right), shown posing here with Johnny Cash (far left) and Greg McDonald (far right). The occasion: a Memphis recording reunion of Perkins and former Sun Records labelmates Cash, Jerry Lee Lewis, and Roy Orbison. *Photo by Sherry McDonald*

burger and a malt. Then they'd go parking on scenic Mulholland Drive. "He'd play his guitar for me, which of course was heaven."

To commemorate their going steady, Rick gave her his initial ring. As Gaba stood backstage at Rick's 1958 Long Beach Auditorium concert, some girls recognized her from fan-magazine photos. "Oh my God!" one gasped, "is that *his ring?!*" She grabbed for it. "No, no," Gaba quickly replied, "*RN* stands for . . . *registered nurse*. I'm a registered nurse." The bobby-soxers backed off.

Eventually the relationship ran its course. "We were too young to get serious, and he wanted to spread his wings, to experience sex, whatever. People say, 'You dated him and never went to bed with him?' But that was the era and the morals," said Gaba, a 1959 *Playboy* magazine centerfold and now Marianne Starkman, mother of two.

"I was a 'good girl,' and he respected me, although we used to neck *for hours*." When spending the night at 1822 Camino Palmero, Gaba slept in the guest room, "and Rick really did stay in his room upstairs. He'd sneak down and give me a goodnight kiss."

While Rick dated Gaba, his friend Glen Larson introduced him to blue-eyed, pony-tailed Lawrencene (Lorrie) Collins of the Collins Kids. Because both Rick, seventeen, and Lorrie, fifteen, were extremely shy, "We didn't have much to say initially," she remembered. "Thank God there were a lot of people around, including my brother, who was never at a loss for words."

Crewcut guitar prodigy Lawrence, Jr., and Lorrie had learned their first chords from their mother Hazel Collins when they were nine and eleven, respectively, and living on an Oklahoma farm. Two years later the Collins Kids were cutting sassy, ebullient country and rockabilly sides such as "Walking the Floor Over You" and "I'm in My Teens" for Columbia Records. They also appeared on TV with the likes of Gene Autry, Tex Ritter, and Roy Rogers and Dale Evans, and performed at state fairs and rodeos countrywide.

At first music formed the basis of Rick and Lorrie's relationship, but it turned into a serious romance that provoked parental concern on both sides. "We really loved each other and thought it was going to last forever," said Collins. However, the affair ended abruptly when at sixteen she eloped to Las Vegas with her agent, Stu Carnall, a man more than twice her age.

Rick took the breakup hard. "I know it was awful for him. He didn't understand it, and I didn't either," said Collins, attributing her impulsiveness to "being young and foolish." Not long before Rick's death, the two reunited in Lake Tahoe, where she now lives. They made small talk, then Rick finally asked with a smile, "Whatever *happened* to you?"

"We laughed about it," recalled Collins, by then divorced, retired from music, and a successful restaurateur. "There was a nice little spark," she added wistfully, "but when you've been separated for so many years, you can't go back. Still, Rick knew how proud I was of him and his music. I think that meant a lot to him."

Collins, Gaba, and other girlfriends all describe a respectful, romantic young man. Patricia Reed, a former Miss California, compared Rick to "your ideal high-school sweetheart. He brought little gifts like a book, or roses he'd jumped over a fence to steal from next door, which meant even more to me. He knew my mother liked the song 'Stardust,' so for Mother's Day he sang it to her over the phone."

Reed, who dated Elvis Presley, among other celebrities, found Rick "refreshing. He didn't come on real strong and wasn't a big flirt. His shyness was *so cute!*" She recalled hourlong petting sessions on the couch that left hair tonic all over her dress. "Sometimes we'd fall asleep, then he'd get up and take me home.

"Rick was the type you wanted to settle down with," said Reed, and secretly she had hoped to do just that. However, the possibility of a long-term romance faded over the 1961 Christmas holidays, when Kris Harmon came into Rick's life.

Three years earlier, Kris had attended a basketball game

between the Nelsons' Stage Five Productions and USC's Phi Delta fraternity, on whose team her father, former football great Tom Harmon, played as a ringer. In her middie blouse, thirteen-year-old Kris shyly posed for a photograph with Rick, whom she'd dreamed of marrying from the time she was eleven. She hung the picture on her bedroom wall and inscribed it with the prophetic legend "Nothing Is Impossible."

The Nelsons and the Harmons had known one another for many years, and the idea of a match between their children appealed greatly to Ozzie and Harriet and to Tom and Elyse Harmon. Harriet kept prodding Rick, remarking, "You should see Kris now; she's really a lady" and, "I saw Kris tonight at a party, and she's getting prettier." Finally her son took notice.

"You know who's good-looking?" he remarked to Charley Britt. "Kris Harmon." At sixteen she had a dancer's shape, a long Modigliani neck, and luminous hazel eyes. One day Rick wondered aloud who he should bring to a party his parents were giving.

"Why don't you ask Kris Harmon?" his roommate suggested.

"Ask her out? You mean, pick her up, like a real date? I can't do that. She's a friend of the family's."

"Well then, *I'm* going to ask her out." At the time, Britt had befriended Kris's younger sister, Kelly.

"But that's gonna kill Kelly," Rick protested.

"Then ask Kris out."

"All right, I will."

Looking back, Britt said, "I don't think he seriously dated anybody else after that."

The parental campaign to nudge Rick and Kris down the aisle went into high gear. Patricia Reed, "totally crushed" by the budding affair, recalled, "Rick wouldn't go out of his way to date, so his parents found a wife for him. They set up the whole scene. Ozzie and Harriet would lower the lights, have the fireplace going, and Rick and Kris could use the bedroom anytime they wanted. They'd be making out heavily, and the parents would say, 'Good night!' "

There was no question that the young couple was very much in love. "Rick was absolutely smitten," said Bruce Belland. "He talked about Kris in a very different way. She wasn't like the fun-time gals he would take out just for the heck of it." The two could sit for hours communing silently. Reed, who quickly fell into Charley Britt's arms, claimed that on double dates, "Rick and Kris were so into each other, we'd get bored with them and take off." Besides the obvious physical attraction, the two shared much in common: basically quiet dispositions, privileged and public Hollywood upbringings, and domineering, high-achieving fathers.

Thomas Dudley Harmon, son of a Gary, Indiana, steel-mill cop, was an All-America halfback at the University of Michigan and winner of the 1940 Heismann Trophy. A 1941 motion picture, *Harmon of Michigan,* immortalized "Ole 98" 's gridiron career, but his exploits as a World War II U.S. Army Air Corps pilot were equally worthy of cinematic treatment. Within six months Harmon's bomber crashed twice, in the impenetrable jungles of Suriname, South America, and behind enemy lines in China. Both times he was feared dead but miraculously found his way to safety.

After serving four years, Captain Harmon returned to football, playing professionally for the Rams, and to his wife, the former Elsie Kornbrath. As Elyse Knox, the stunning Hartford-born blue-eyed blonde went from John Powers Agency fashion model to B-movie starlet. She appeared in over three-dozen films, mostly lightheaded comedies and musicals with titles such as *Hi' Ya, Sailor!* and *A Wave, a Wac and a Marine.*

During the war she had broken her engagement with Harmon to marry Paul Hesse, an older photographer who'd once pronounced her "the perfect magazine cover girl." But the union ended after just thirteen months, and within weeks of filing for divorce she and the war hero were together again.

For months their lives followed the script of one of her pictures, *Army Wives,* a dreary drama in which military bureaucracy delays a young couple's marriage. On August 26, 1944, they finally wed. In a *Life* magazine piece published that March, Elyse is shown wrapped in a parachute that had saved Tom's life, staring into his eyes. The two claimed she would walk down the aisle wearing a gown made from that parachute.

Ten months later Sharon Kristin Harmon was born, followed over the next six years by another daughter, Kelly, and a son, Mark. At home in North Hollywood, their father often lived up to his college nicknames, "Terrible Tommy" and the "Hoosier Hammer," disciplining harshly and demanding excellence—some would say perfection—from his children. Mark absorbed the brunt of his father's temper.

"That poor kid didn't have a chance," sympathized Charley Britt. "He *had* to perform." During football catches on the front lawn, a single wild toss by Mark would send his father stalking inside, even on the first throw. Dining at the Harmons' one night, Rick's roommate watched in astonishment as a playful punch from the eleven-year-old provoked six-foot-two, 195-pound Tom into a slugging match. "It got to be embarrassing," Britt said.

Kris, by her own admission the family's black sheep, endured her own childhood problems. She had difficulty asserting herself and establishing an identity in a traditional Roman Catholic household where women were expected to be submissive. Kris's outward reticence notwithstanding, she was anything but that.

Friends and detractors alike refer to her as strong-willed, the same adjective often applied to Ozzie Nelson. Rick admired that quality as much in Kris as in his father. And while he'd experienced comparatively few problems growing up the son of celebrities, he was always Kris's empathic ally on that score.

Kris clashed particularly with her mother, for whom appearances and social standing were high priorities. When Kris was little, Elyse ordered her to tweak her nostrils so that they didn't flare. In 1987 Kris told *People* magazine, "I never cared much about being on the covers of magazines. [My mother] did. And cared about her children being there too." At age three adorably cherubic "Sharon" Harmon, wearing a frilly party dress, appeared on the cover of *Life* magazine for a story on Hollywood small fry.

That Kris felt intimidated by her mother later emerged in her painting, for which she gained some recognition. Elyse Harmon had studied design at Manhattan's distinguished Traphagen School of Fashion and was a talented portraitist and realist. Believing she couldn't compete, Kris turned to a freer form, primitivism.

At Bel Air's exclusive all-girls Catholic school, Marymount High, Kris's daydreaming and independence antagonized the nuns. Ann Sothern's daughter, Tisha Sterling, and Mia Farrow were her best friends there. For all intents, she lived a fairy-tale life, and her and Rick's courtship seemed right out of a romance novel. He escorted her to the senior prom, where she was queen, and Troy Donahue, emcee. Sometime around the new year, 1963, the Nelsons' and the Harmons' fondest wishes came true, with the announcement of the couple's impending nuptials.

Although Kris was to become Mrs. Eric Hilliard Nelson, another woman already possessed Rick's heart for eternity. Her name cannot be revealed because evidence suggests that she may still be living but is unwilling to make her life public. Therefore, the pseudonym "Julie" will be used here.

Abandoned in New York City by her mother at an early age, Julie fell in with prostitutes and turned to drugs. Dennis Hopper, then a fledgling movie actor and photographer, befriended her and in the late 1950s took her to Hollywood, where the exotic blond gamine created an instant stir.

"[Julie] was an incredible girl," remembered Mary Jo Sheeley, "one of the original beatniks. And gorgeous. She was delightful, full of energy; one of those people you just loved to be around."

According to Sharon Sheeley, both David and Rick—in that order—fell madly in love with her. As had happened in the past, Rick, then eighteen, stole his brother's girl. "I'm going to stop introducing my dates to Rick; I lose more girls that way," David told a newspaper reporter, who claimed the quote was uttered "more in amusement than chagrin." But when Rick became serious about Julie, David was neither amused nor chagrined, but bitter, and the resulting rift between them lasted months.

Despite a concerted effort by both brothers, Julie could not overcome her heroin addiction. At one point David locked her up in his Pacific View Drive apartment for ten agonizing days of cold turkey, but she went back to the needle. Rick, still living at home then, managed to keep most details of the two-year affair from his parents, though Ozzie gleaned fragments here and there. "He was not real happy," contended one friend, grilled on several occasions by Rick's concerned father. As for Harriet, "I'm not sure she knows too much about [Julie]," Dotty Harmony said.

Rick never knew that he'd made his young lover pregnant or that she'd nearly hemorrhaged to death from an illegal abortion, because he never saw her again. Like Lorrie Collins, she ran off to marry another man: the drug-addicted heir to a family fortune. "It broke Rick's heart," said a friend, "because he didn't know why. [Julie] left only so she wouldn't drag him down. She wanted him to start a life without her. It was a very unselfish act. She told me, 'I love Rick very, very much. And I've never loved anybody in my life. But I'm no good for him; I'll destroy him.'

"Not long after, [Julie] and her husband were busted for heroin," the friend continues. "I bailed her out and brought her home with me. She stayed for three days. Then one morning I woke up and found a note from her saying, 'I've left. I can't involve you with my life. I'll never be well.' And she was never seen by anybody again." Friends speculate that the beautiful waif returned to New York and probably succumbed to street life, though no one knows for sure.

"Nobody who dated that girl ever, ever forgot her," said Sharon Sheeley. Especially Rick, who refused to abandon hope that Julie would reenter his life. Whenever his itinerary took him to Manhattan, he grabbed bookings at intimate clubs like the Bottom Line so that if she attended the show, he could spot her. "But it's been over twenty years," Greg McDonald, his manager from 1976 on, would scoff. "Like you'd recognize her?" Rick insisted he would.

"Rick told me when he was forty-five that [Julie] was the only girl he'd ever really loved," said McDonald. "She was *the one.*"

In the weeks leading up to his wedding day, Rick desperately phoned a mutual friend he thought might have heard from Julie, by then gone over three years. No word, he was told. On April 20, 1963, he and Kris were married in a Catholic ceremony, for which Rick, a nonpracticing Protestant, took religious instruction. Four hundred guests packed the St. Martin of Tours Catholic church in Hollywood.

A daughter, Tracy Kristine, was born on October 25, 1963, making Ozzie and Harriet grandparents for the second time. (A year earlier the David Nelsons had a son, Daniel Blair.) Press releases stated that the four-pound, one-ounce girl had been delivered prematurely but neglected to mention by how long: nine weeks.

Naturally only Kris can substantiate Rick's later claims of a shotgun wedding. "Rick told me that Ozzie basically said, 'You've got to do the right thing, or we're in trouble,'" Rick's friend Paul Rose contended. If true, while Rick was hardly the only twenty-two-year-old in that predicament, he faced unusually severe consequences. Greg McDonald recalled, "Rick told me that in those days, if Rick Nelson got a girl pregnant, Rick Nelson got married."

Would he and Kris have wed otherwise? According to Rick, no. However, he made that claim years later, during and after their messy divorce. Few who knew him and Kris in the spring of their relationship ever doubted their love. Living with little Tracy on Zorada Drive, they appeared a happy, glamourous family.

As he'd always done, Ozzie incorporated his sons' changing lives into the television series. Both wives joined the cast, June in 1961 and Kris two years later. Grandchildren Tracy and Danny appeared on the 1964–65 Christmas episode. "It is not only a wholesome show for the whole family, it *is* the whole family," Cleveland Amory wrote in *TV Guide*.

Ozzie briefly considered a spinoff featuring Skip Young's character, Wally Plumstead, Wally Cox as a college professor, and Rick moonlighting in a straight-man's role while continuing on his parents' program. An *Adventures* installment called "The Fraternity Rents Out a Room" (1961–62) served as the pilot. Although ABC wanted to buy it, Ozzie eventually nixed the idea, because, Young believed, "He would have had to give up control, and he didn't know if he could."

The Adventures already seemed a loosely connected anthology anyway. During its last few seasons story lines alternated among basic character combinations in a wider range of scenes: Rick and Kris; David and June; Rick, David, and myriad college fraternity brothers and sorority sisters; Ozzie and Harriet and neighbors Joe and Clara Randolph; and the extended Nelson family, whose scenes together grew increasingly rare.

Even with its new wrinkles, the show's format essentially followed the Rutgers University motto "Ever changing yet eternally the same," and after eleven, twelve seasons, that created problems. Episodes featuring the "old guard"—the Nelsons and the Randolphs—still elicited laughs. Harriet and ditsy Clara (Mary Jane Croft) conducted their women's club meetings with the secrecy of a witches' coven, while Ozzie and Lyle Talbot almost recaptured Ozzie's and Don Defore's marvelous rapport from the series' early years.

Ironically, though the shows centering on the older characters seemed contemporary enough, Ozzie's portrayal of the college set came across as hopelessly outdated. The sixties generation, raised on rock & roll, was the most politically active since the 1930s, yet on *The Adventures* crewcut fraternity brothers still crooned "Let Me Call You Sweetheart," broke into cheers of

"Hip-Hip-Hooray," and seemed abnormally concerned with pulling pranks.

At ages twenty-five and thirty-five, Rick and Skip Young were still hanging out at the malt shop, and looking mighty self-conscious about it. David admitted, "For the first time, I felt what we were doing on the air as a family really wasn't true." Rick too felt uncomfortable, but out of loyalty to his father perfunctorily recited his lines.

Attempts at capturing something of the real world beyond the tube, such as "Ozzie a Go-Go" (1965–66), in which the Nelsons attend a discotheque, were contrived and as unnatural as Harriet's new pale lipstick and elevated bouffant. That Ozzie, on the cusp of sixty, was falling behind the times was illustrated at one of Rick and Kris's frequent theme parties, for which guests came costumed as their favorite Walt Disney character. Kris dressed up as That Darn Cat, and Rick as Disney himself, in a fake mustache and clutching an Oscar. "Ozzie's idea of a Disney character," recalled actor Sean Morgan, "was a Keystone Cop."

With its 1965–66 season premiere, *The Adventures* now filmed in color, a concession to changing times that Ozzie had resisted for years, but the show seemed an anachronism nonetheless. Another change, moving the entire production to a larger facility, weakened cast morale. Desilu Culver Studios was in Culver City, precluding Ozzie's morning jogs to work; Rick made the hour-plus drive in his Rolls-Royce. "It wasn't home anymore," Connie Nelson said of the new surroundings. "I think that took the starch out of a lot of people."

By December rumors circulated that the show might not be renewed. According to Morgan, some of the cast wanted it to continue, himself included, while "others felt it had run its course. The opinions were about equally divided." When in midseason ABC exiled *The Adventures* to Saturday evenings opposite CBS's top-rated *The Jackie Gleason Show*, "that was the kiss of death," said Skip Young. Its Wednesday-night replacement was truly a mid-1960s timepiece, exploding with gaudy pop-art graphics and high camp. *Batman* finished its abbreviated maiden season as ABC's most-watched show.

On January 1, 1966, "The Game Room"—the Nelsons' 435th and ultimately final adventure—was filmed. Ozzie and Harriet differ over what to do with Rick and David's old room. He wants to install a pool table; she wants to convert it into a guest room. In the end, Harriet, Clara, and their women's bridge club become addicted to the game. "My wife the pool shark," jokes Ozzie, grinning at the camera. Dissolve to credits.

At the wrap party, Ozzie announced somewhat sadly, "This is the first time in fourteen years I haven't been able to say we'll see you next season, because I haven't been told whether or not we're going to be back on the air. I can only say this: It's been the greatest fourteen years of my life. And if I don't see you again as cast and crew, believe me, you have my undying gratitude for having made this show run as long as it has. I love you all."

As for his future, Ozzie said only, "I don't want you to think I'm just going to go to Laguna Beach and sit in the sun, counting seashells."

Sometime after "The Game Room" aired on March 26, 1966, ABC president Tom Moore reluctantly phoned Ozzie with the bad news: The network would no longer carry *The Adventures of Ozzie and Harriet*. This, despite continued steady ratings and plenty of sponsors still clamoring to be part of the program.

With Americans questioning and rejecting many traditional values, the traditional domestic sitcom was doomed. ABC axed two others that spring, *The Donna Reed Show* and *The Patty Duke Show*. Some cast members, however, cite Ozzie's continued 60-percent share of the profits as a contributing factor in the series' demise, for by 1966 most programs were wholly network owned and controlled.

In retrospect, Ozzie admitted, "The show was getting pretty diffuse because of the way the family had grown" and that it

147

had lingered a few seasons too long. But the decision to abandon it "was the toughest of my life," he said, "like killing off a whole set of people loved by millions."

Rick's honest reaction was mainly relief. He'd been working nonstop for eighteen of his twenty-six years, and after having had a camera lens trained on him since age twelve, he looked forward to the relative anonymity. "I didn't have any real interest in a career," he later reflected. "I wasn't in any hurry to return."

Nine

On a transatlantic flight to America, rock & roll idol Carlos O'Connor discusses his flagging fortunes with his manager. O'Connor is hopeful that his longtime record label will renew his contract, but as "Jerome" soberly points out, musical combos, not solo performers, are the current rage. You need a group, he tells his client, then corrects himself. "Carlos, what you need is a miracle."

At a New York City heliport, teenagers in vibrantly colored bell-bottoms and miniskirts await their favorite's arrival, so pumped up with anticipation they literally oscillate in place. "Carlos is getting a little grungy, I guess," one girl concedes aloud, to which a male companion adds knowingly, "after all, he *is* twenty-five." When another excitable fan tells them that the hot new group the Hors d'oeuvres are next door, the "loyal" contingent races off to greet them instead.

Alone in his hotel suite, O'Connor takes an agent's call offering him a demeaning part as a thirsty farmer in an apple-cider commercial. The fading star angrily slams down the phone, then wistfully intones an a capella introduction to a Burt Bacharach–Hal David composition, "They Don't Give Medals (To Yesterday's Heroes)": *They should have been there when I was twenty/ You never heard such applause/But now I'm twenty-five/and hardly anyone knows I'm alive . . .*

Rick returned to television playing Carlos O'Connor in *On the Flip Side*. Though billed as a futuristic fantasy, this ABC musical special contained more truth than creator Robert Emmett realized. When developing the script about an erstwhile teen idol's conflict over pressures to conform to the latest fad, "I wasn't even thinking of Rick Nelson," he claimed. "I had Tony Bennett more in mind." But parallels between Rick and O'Connor are omnipresent.

Emmett, head writer for the trailblazing satirical TV program *That Was the Week That Was,* had created a biting, cynical parody of the music industry. A trio of angels, the Celestials, come to O'Connor's aid, telling him he needs a group—namely them—in order to sound contemporary. "That's what's hangin' you up," says the female of the bunch, Angie (played by singer Joanie Sommers of "Johnny Get Angry" fame), "you're so solitary!"

Together Carlos and the Celestials audition for Vertigo Records, headed by eccentric, narcissistic Donnie Prospect (Anthony Holland), a thinly veiled Phil Spector. (*Prospect* is an anagram of *P Spector*.) When the group plays him "Take a Broken Heart," another Bacharach-David song, Prospect shouts, "I love it!" and orders it be recorded, pressed, and shipped immediately. But the playback reveals only O'Connor's voice and guitar. No angels.

"Just a singer and a song?" the executive sneers. "It's *medieval!*" He calls an influential disc jockey, Hairy Eddie Popkin

150

(Murray Roman) of WEEP, to tell him that the record was sent to his station as a practical joke. Popkin, a composite of Murray the K and other hyperactive announcers, replies that not only has he aired "Take a Broken Heart," he loves it. In the end, the Celestials return to heaven, and O'Connor enjoys success as a solo act.

On the Flip Side aired in December 1966, by which time Rick hadn't placed a record near the top of the charts for almost three years, an eternity in the music business. It is mainly coincidental that his sales diminished once he left Imperial Records at the end of 1962. As Rick's five-year deal with the label drew to a close, others scrambled to lure him away.

"Diskeries Bid Wildly for Ricky," declared a *Billboard* magazine headline. Prospective suitors included independents Dot, Challenge, and Everest, and majors Capitol, Columbia, and RCA Victor. "However, don't be surprised if Ricky decides to remain at Imperial after all," a family spokesman stated. Presumably he was bluffing, for Ozzie loathed Lew Chudd. After the owner had rushed out an unfinished master of one of Rick's first records for Imperial, Ozzie banned him from all future recording sessions.

According to Jimmie Haskell, once Chudd got wind that his top star might not renew, he threatened to release all $750,000 of Rick's excess royalties on one check, most of which would then go directly into Uncle Sam's coffer.

"You wouldn't do that," Ozzie said nervously.

"Try me," retorted Chudd.

On January 3, 1963, Rick signed with Decca Records, a latecomer to the bidding war. Its founder, Jack Kapp, had contracted Ozzie to Brunswick Records back in 1930. The terms from Decca: a guaranteed $1,000 per week against royalties for *twenty* years. Ozzie had sought a long-term deal primarily for tax purposes but also because he doubted rock & roll's longevity and wanted to ensure his son's financial security.

Chudd retaliated by scratching his name on that $750,000 check as promised. "It was the only way he could get back at them," said Haskell. No, not the only way. Imperial inundated the market with seven singles over the next eighteen months, each a retread from an earlier album. "Old Enough to Love," for instance, issued in March 1963, came from 1959's *Ricky Sings Again.*

Imperial was even more shameless with its five post-1962 LPs. Out of all the tracks, only three were previously unreleased. The final indignity: Around the same time that Decca came out with *Rick Nelson Sings "For You"*—on the heels of his hit single "For You"—Imperial advertised an album titled *Rick Nelson Sings for You,* which bought unsuspecting consumers eleven songs probably in their collections already.

In 1963 Rick charted thirteen sides, seven on Imperial, six on Decca. Understandably, the latter company worried it had acquired a depreciating asset when his first two releases, "You Don't Love Me Anymore (And I Can Tell)" and "String Along," fared only modestly. And Decca executives were genuinely annoyed with their expensive new teen idol for relinquishing bachelorhood just four months into the deal. However, Rick's next two singles, "Fools Rush In" and "For You," sold well enough to soothe their ulcers.

Both songs were Ozzie's recommendations, modern treatments of Big Band Era standards. "Fools Rush In" (number twelve, 1963) is driven by a unique double-time drum pattern Rick devised: Richie Frost beats out sixteenth notes on the hi-hat while Rick thwacks offbeats and assorted fills on the snare.

"For You," on the other hand, is one of Rick's dullest 45s, saddled with a boilerplate arrangement and an indifferent vocal. The week it peaked at number six, in February 1964, a quartet from Liverpool, England, was in the midst of a seven-week stay at number one with "I Want to Hold Your Hand." It would be nearly nine years before Rick returned to the Top Ten.

Spearheaded by the Beatles, the 1964 "British Invasion" signaled rock & roll's first period of creative growth since its inception. Though the media fixated on cultural peripherals such as pudding-basin haircuts, Cuban-heeled boots, and collarless jackets, it was a major musical movement that like a great flood displaced all that had come before it. Inasmuch as the preceding years had been pervaded by callow, artless records, few of those performers swept to their commercial demise were missed.

But others were. The irony of the "English Sound," of course, was that it sprang from American rock & roll, country & western, and rhythm & blues. Lamentably, the very artists that had inspired the Beatles, the Rolling Stones, the Animals, the Kinks, and many others were summarily discarded: Chuck Berry, Carl Perkins, Little Richard, Jerry Lee Lewis, Bo Diddley—even Elvis Presley's hits dwindled—and Rick.

The Beatles Phenomenon compelled U.S. record companies to sign every hirsute, accented, guitar-strumming sod they could find, talented or otherwise. In the face of seemingly insurmountable competition, Rick floundered, floating four dispensable albums in 1964 and 1965: *The Very Thought of You, Spotlight on Rick, Best Always,* and *Love and Kisses.* While these hodgepodges had their moments, Rick sounded lost and, worse, bored. Even the singer's cover poses projected indifference, his mouth set in a tight smile as if to say, Let's get this over with.

"I was stale," Rick later admitted. "It was the same old thing over and over again." Not one of the four LPs made the Top 200, the first time that had happened with albums of new material. Decca's Charles "Bud" Dant functioned as recording-session supervisor, though Jimmie Haskell, no longer associated with Imperial either, continued as Rick's independent arranger.

Ozzie, however, was conspicuously absent from these recording dates. Rick had finally summoned up the courage to ask his father to stop controlling his music. This only after years of festering resentment, and Kris's goading him into it. Ozzie, realizing he'd lost his touch, graciously, though somewhat sadly, stepped aside.

Trying to recapture old glories, in April 1966 Rick toured the Far East, where he'd sung to massive throngs six years earlier. Despite his diminishing appeal at home, Beatlemanialike scenes of pandemonium were played out in Japan, Taiwan,

Hong Kong, and the Philippines. The day Rick landed in Tokyo, so many youngsters cut classes and flocked to the airport that authorities granted them an official half-day off. In the Philippine capital a record 72,103 packed three shows at Manila Stadium, with an additional 13,000 turned away. Rick expressed disappointment, though, that he couldn't obtain government clearance for a Vietnam stopover. Opposed to the escalating conflict there, he'd hoped to entertain the troops.

Glen Campbell played bass on the tour because Joe Osborn so feared transoceanic flying, he would break out in hives. His absence was academic, as the group had essentially dissolved. Without hit records to promote, Rick saw no point in touring for the immediate future and no reason to retain a band. Osborn, James Burton, and Richie Frost all quickly became kingpins of the Hollywood studio scene, playing on literally hundreds of pop records.

The luxury of his twenty-year record contract enabled Rick to experiment musically. He made two country & western albums, *Bright Lights and Country Music* and *Country Fever.* Had the country field been the repository for failed pop musicians it is today, his motives might have raised suspicions, but in the first psychedelic summer of 1966, embracing the Nashville Sound hardly assured commercial success.

Recorded in Hollywood, both LPs are as authentic as any cut in the heart of Music City, U.S.A. Supporting musicians included Burton, Frost, Campbell, pianist Glen D. Hardin, the Jordanaires, and guitarist Clarence White, later of the Byrds' final incarnation. Some observers regarded Rick's shift to country as digressional, others as frivolous—that snobbery over his big-city upbringing at work again. But to Rick, then searching for a compatible style, the return to rock's roots felt completely natural.

In contrast to his last few pop LPs, Rick sounds at home essaying Willie Nelson's "Hello Walls," harmonizing exuberantly with Campbell on Doug Kershaw's quaint portrait of bayou life, "Louisiana Man," even affecting a lyrical Cajun accent on his minor 1967 country hit "Take a City Bride." His voice is rich and mellifluous throughout, especially effective on the heartbreaking ballads endemic to country music.

Had Rick persevered, he undoubtedly could have hitched a ride on the profitable country & western wagon train that rumbled across America in 1969, when Johnny Cash's "A Boy Named Sue" restored him to prominence, and TV's top-rated country-music-'n'-corn variety show *Hee Haw* turned Buck Owens and Roy Clark into mainstream stars. But Rick soon abandoned this direction, not the last time he would presage a trend.

A month and a half after *Country Fever*'s release, two explosions violently shook rock & roll's foundations: the Beatles' epochal *Sgt. Pepper's Lonely Hearts Club Band* album, a thematic whole rather than a random collection of tracks, and the Monterey Pop Festival, which unveiled rock's future stars. In an upheaval reminiscent of three years earlier, British Invasion acts were supplanted by talents such as Jimi Hendrix, Janis Joplin, the Grateful Dead, Jefferson Airplane, and Buffalo Springfield.

Their music became a clarion call for the burgeoning youth-culture movement seeking an alternative to what it viewed as the placid, suffocating conventions of American life. In this milieu, Rick's indelible Boy Next Door television image further undermined his credibility with the new rock audience, for whom *The Adventures of Ozzie and Harriet* represented everything the counterculture rejected.

It was a difficult time. Just twenty-six, his artistic prime still ahead, Rick found himself cast out of the musical establishment he'd helped build. He expressed his feelings in the eloquent "You Just Can't Quit" from *Bright Lights and Country Music*. Though the single didn't break the Hot 100, it is as significant as any he ever recorded and was the first in a series of nakedly autobiographical songs. Rick had been writing since he was a teenager, but except for "Don't Leave Me This Way" from

1958's *Ricky Nelson,* he'd felt too insecure to record his own work. Here, in a deceptively subdued delivery, he examines his plight without self-pity or rancor:

> When the whole world puts ya down
> It makes ya feel like a clown,
> That's not it.
> You just can't quit.
>
> Don't feel sorry for things
> 'Cause can't you see,
> I'm still me.
> And I just can't quit.
>
> I can hear the things they're sayin',
> You don't know the price I'm payin' now.
> They all laugh and point at me,
> But I'm gonna laugh the last, you see, somehow.
>
> It's funny how your friends disappear
> Troubles they find,
> But I don't mind.
> I just can't quit.

The song encapsules Rick's attitude during this and subsequent lean times. Even when his records sold poorly, he rarely suffered, or at least suffered to a lesser degree, the anxieties of those who measure their self-worth by public acceptance. Prior to "Garden Party," Rick said, "I don't have to have a hit record to feel good."

However, in the late 1960s Rick no longer seemed to know what was right for his career—only what was wrong, and this he learned from experience. First, Decca Records matched him with a production house, Koppleman-Rubin Associates, which had engineered hits for Gary Lewis and the Playboys, Sopwith Camel, the Critters, and, most notably, the Lovin' Spoonful. Under staff arranger John Boylan, later a respected producer,

Rick recorded two production-heavy albums, *Another Side of Rick* (1967) and *Perspective* (1968). Neither appealed to him nor to record buyers.

Just to be on stage again, Rick made the rounds of nightclubs like Manhattan's Latin Quarter, forcing a smile, finger-popping, and purring "Mame" in a half-hearted lounge-lizard imitation. At the Fairmont Hotel in New Orleans he played to a hardware convention. "Eventually I decided that I'd rather work in a gas station than carry on with that," Rick recalled. "I was very unhappy with myself."

For a few years, he stopped performing altogether while sorting out his plans. All he really knew for sure was that he wanted to remain in music. Rick's waning interest in acting made itself apparent in later *Adventures*, where he went from good to wood. Mary Jane Croft remembered, "It was difficult for him to even get up the volume when we were doing dialogue."

The year before the series ended, Rick starred in his last film, *Love and Kisses*. Kris played his wife; Ozzie produced, directed, and wrote the screenplay; Jimmie Haskell scored; David Nelson, Skip Young, and Jack Ellena put in cameos; and other Stage Five Productions crew members filled various staff positions. Only its length distinguished *Love and Kisses* from *The Adventures*. "Mild entertainment," the *Christian Science Monitor* politely called this frothy comedy, one of the kinder reviews.

Besides *On the Flip Side*, Rick's television appearances through the 1960s were limited to guest spots on series such as the Western *Hondo* and hosting a summer-replacement pop-music program, *Malibu U*, produced by Dick Clark. He also starred in a TV movie with Walter Brennan and Kris (playing the missus again), *The Over-the-Hill-Gang*. Rick appreciated the title's irony.

With few acting commitments and no concerts, he mostly puttered around the Zorada Drive house, collecting a fleet of sports cars, intensifying his karate instruction, lifting weights, and relaxing with his family. On September 20, 1967, it grew from three to five when Kris gave birth to twin boys, Matthew Gray and Gunnar Eric.

Their proud grandparents, Ozzie and Harriet, were only semienjoying semiretirement. Losing the TV series was most painful for Ozzie, about whom Harriet once said, "Work is his hobby, and he's unhappy without it." Having no scripts to write or recording sessions to supervise, he poured his energy into milelong ocean swims, volleyball games with Laguna Beach teenagers, crossword puzzles, and reading, often until sunrise. "I remember Harriet saying he used to run on the beach for hours," said Mary Jane Croft. Harriet adapted more easily, taking up needlepoint, yoga and, after all those years of making believe on television, cooking.

Money was by no means a problem. In 1964 Ozzie had signed a second consecutive five-year guaranteed contract with ABC, and a year after the series ended he sold two hundred installments to Los Angeles TV station KTTV for $500,000. But both grew restless and longed to act again. As Harriet admitted, "Sometimes without working, you find you don't know who you are." They appeared on TV shows such as *Love, American Style,* portraying, of all things, a divorcing couple, and toured the Midwest with two plays, *State Fair* and *The Impossible Years.*

The Nelson to endure the greatest frustration following *The Adventures'* cancellation was David. Finding that his credits directing the family series carried little weight in Hollywood, "He had to go out and re-prove himself," said Connie Nelson, "and it took a lot of time."

Cousin Rich Nelson believes that David may have suffered from whatever enmity Ozzie accrued over the years, turning the Nelson name into more of a detriment than an attribute. When Rich, presently a producer-director at CBS Sports, first auditioned for TV commercial work in the mid-1960s, "I wouldn't say I was related to Ozzie, because I didn't know whose toes he'd stepped on."

In his early thirties David informed his parents that he didn't want to see them as much while struggling to establish himself. It was as though he were going through a delayed adolescence.

"My dad loved us very much and called us all the time," said David. "I had to ask him, 'Can we cool the two-o'clock-in-the-morning phone calls?' I needed to run my own ship, just as my father had run his." The idea, he explained, came from a counselor he and June were seeing. "It was a last-gasp attempt to see if I could save my marriage. I told my mother and father what I was doing and that it had nothing to do with my love for them. It's just that I needed to take over the reins in my house."

"I think David stepped away from the family a little bit harder than he wanted to," contended Connie Nelson, placing the blame largely on June. Her relationship with the family had been strained from the beginning. Ozzie disapproved of June for several reasons, one being her troubled past. She had spent most of her youth in foster homes and orphanages, and the Nelsons' close-knit stability overwhelmed her.

June, classically beautiful, with wide-set eyes, prominent cheekbones, and a stunning figure, was discovered by Warner Bros. and forged a modest career as an actress-model. After she married David, Ozzie offered her a regular part on *The Adventures* as David's TV wife, but she was reluctant to take it, wanting to succeed on her own. June's independent streak bothered the traditionalist, chauvinist Ozzie.

"She was very progressive in her thinking," said Patricia Reed, "and wanted to keep working, which Ozzie didn't like. He felt she should either be at home or in the family show." Not wanting to insult her new in-laws, June gave in and joined the cast. But whereas Kris Nelson was delighted to be billed using her married name, David's wife insisted on the credit "June Blair appeared as June Nelson."

Though it is difficult to gauge June's abilities from the limited, airheaded character she played on *The Adventures*, she projected an appealing vulnerability not unlike that of Marilyn Monroe, speaking in breathy, staccato bursts. "Beautiful girl, wonderful

159

quality," praised Mary Jane Croft. "But she was confined to that one subordinate role, and it made me sorry, because I thought she had great possibilities." June's career never recovered, and after the show left the air she never worked as an actress again, instead staying home with sons Danny and James.

June not only felt personally stifled, she resented Ozzie's domination of her husband, and, like Kris, she expressed her opinion. "June was very good-hearted, but different, not a conservative type like the family," observed Rich Nelson. "She used to tell David, 'Stick up for what you want,' which caused friction." Connie Nelson's blunt assessment: "It was jealously on her part; I don't know why she felt so threatened."

Whether or not June instigated David's estrangement from his parents, Ozzie and Harriet had difficulty accepting that story lines from the TV episodes "The Lonesome Parents" (1961–62) and "Getting Together With the Boys" (1963–64)— in which they feel neglected now that their sons are leading their own lives—had essentially come true.

"I think a part of them understood what was going on," said Connie Nelson, "but a part of them wanted to hold close everything that was dear. If Ozzie had his way, the whole family would have been together twenty-four hours a day. He loved his family. Harriet was fond of the family," she added with a laugh, "but I don't think she needed *that* much togetherness."

The sad irony is that once their television image faded to black, the Nelsons finally became the "average" family they never were. And like many American families in those years, they felt the buffeting effects of the generation gap. *Esquire* magazine documented their conflicts in a lengthy 1971 article that once again held up "The Happy, Happy, Happy Nelsons" as a societal barometer, only this time to exemplify the breakdown of The Family.

Among the story's more fascinating revelations was the brothers' apparent role reversals. After years of buoying the Nelson image, perhaps at his professional expense, David now exposed the family as myth, telling writer Sara Davidson, "The Nelson family as the great American pastime is sinking. Ricky is likely to dive in and try, until his last breath, to prop the whole thing up. I'm likely to stand on the rocks watching, with my arms folded, and say, 'I told you so.' "

Indeed, Rick minimized David's comments in a subsequent *New York Times* interview, saying, "I don't believe Dave said anything about our family not being real off stage and that we were now falling apart. He certainly doesn't believe that." David, used to dealing with a less critical media, today calls the *Esquire* article "a complete double-cross" and claims his comments were strictly off-the-record. But he does not deny making them.

The piece's "on-record" quotes were just as revealing. Sounding defeated, the doyenne of motherhood, Harriet Nelson, remarked: "The whole institution [of family] seems to be in trouble. We're just as confused as everybody else. And we all used to be so sure about what we wanted, what was good.

"We're three separate families now. It's kind of sad."

Ten

In early 1969, five years after his last big hit, Rick finally recommitted himself to making music. More observer than participant during that time, he'd been listening to rock & roll with fresh ears again, and at twenty-eight felt the same enthusiasm and sense of discovery he'd experienced at fifteen. The music industry barely resembled what Rick remembered from when he began, but most of the changes encouraged him.

On the whole, musicians had wrested artistic control away from hit factories and producers that for years imposed their songs and sounds on stables of acts. Rick especially inclined toward literary singer-songwriters in the folk-music tradition such as Bob Dylan, Tim Hardin, Randy Newman, and Eric Andersen, who chronicled a-changin' times and crystallized emotions with journalists' eyes and poets' souls. On his 1969 *Perspective* album Rick had interpreted Newman's "I Think It's

162

Gonna Rain Today," Paul Simon's "For Emily, Wherever I May Find Her," and Harry Nilsson's "Without Her."

"Rick had a real reverence for that kind of writing, the ability to express yourself," said Eric Andersen, Rick's close friend and mentor during this period. Like the other Eric, Andersen was of Scandinavian ancestry and occasionally hindered by his handsomeness. Warner Bros. Records once embarrassed him with an ad that read, "Anybody Who Looks This Good Shouldn't Sound This Good," a neat summation of a common critical bias.

Andersen remembered Rick as "very shy, but the most hilarious person I've ever met. He was very curious about the possibilities of songwriting and had an urge to write himself, so we talked a lot and listened to a lot of writers. I played him people like David Blue and Fred Neil, and he played me his new songs all the time. He wrote some beautiful songs."

Bob Dylan's just-released *Nashville Skyline* struck Rick with the same force as Carl Perkins's "Blue Suede Shoes" years before. Its songs ("Lay Lady Lay," "Girl From the North Country") were country-flavored, melodically simple, and lyrically romantic and direct. "I listened to that album for days," Rick recalled. "Suddenly I knew where I wanted to go."

He also realized that he missed the camaraderie of a band. If he could have afforded him, Rick would have tried coaxing James Burton back. As it was, later that year Burton accepted the lead-guitar spot in the group Elvis Presley was assembling for *his* return to the concert trail. He stayed with Presley until the legend's death in 1977.

Rick spent nights at the Troubadour in West Hollywood, seeking musicians. The 350-capacity "Troub," opened as a folk club in 1961, became the mecca of Los Angeles's country-rock movement and the workshop for Jackson Browne, Linda Ronstadt, J. D. Souther, Don Henley, and Glenn Frey.

Country rock crossbred country's melodicism and rock's aggression, minus the former's flag-waving conservatism and the latter's instrumental excess. The Byrds, the Dillard-Clark Expedition, Poco, the Flying Burrito Brothers, and particularly Buffalo Springfield (the first group to desecrate the Troubadour's folkie ambiance by playing electric guitars) are generally credited as the genre's founders. Rick, however, had been making country rock, or its direct antecedent, rockabilly, most of his career, and in 1969 the "new" style came as second nature to him.

At the Troubadour Rick had seen Poco, a group founded by ex-Springfield members Richie Furay and Jim Messina, and coveted bassist Randy Meisner for his remarkable vocal range and distinctive keening tone. Not long after Rick watched the transplanted Nebraskan from the darkly lit Troubadour bar, Meisner became a free agent, quitting Poco while recording their debut album.

One night at the club a friend of Meisner's recognized Rick, hidden inside a fur parka and chain-smoking menthol cigarettes. "I was really crocked," Miles Thomas, a former Springfield roadie, recalled. "I sat down next to him and said, 'What's it like being Ricky Nelson?' a great opening line that got me a very strange look." When Meisner's name came up, Rick said, "Boy, I'd like to have a guy like that in my band."

"I can do that for you," Thomas replied, and did.

Meisner rounded up two other players, Allen Kemp and Pat Shanahan, whom he'd worked with in a pre-Poco outfit called the Poor. Kemp, a slender, sharp-featured guitarist, had idolized Rick while growing up in Denver. "I used to comb my hair back into a ducktail, leave it long on the sides, roll up my sleeves, and try to emulate him," he said. "I'd put a bunch of Rick's forty-fives on the stereo and stand in front of the mirror." Jazz-based drummer Shanahan also hailed from Denver, where the Poor began under the name Soul Survivors (*not* the New York group of "Expressway to Your Heart" fame).

Aiming for the big time, the Soul Survivors relocated to Los Angeles and were taken under the wing of Buffalo Springfield's management, which rechristened them the Poor "and proceeded to make us poor," Kemp said dryly. He and Shanahan shared a house on Stone Canyon Drive, in Sherman Oaks. One spring afternoon in 1969, their roommate Richard Schnyder came home to find "a real neat Mercedes convertible outside. I walked into my room, saw guitars all over the place, and there was Rick Nelson in the next room, jamming."

Rick named the new group the Stone Canyon Band. Initially they rehearsed at the Sherman Oaks house in conditions more fitting an amateur garage band. "It was an eight-by-ten room," Shanahan recalled, "completely insulated with blankets and rugs so that we didn't disturb the neighbors. In the summer it got so stiflingly hot, we had to go outside after playing just one or two tunes." They soon moved to a more comfortable Burbank office Ozzie owned.

The group played together four, five days a week, working on Rick's original songs and jamming on selected oldies—but only after Kemp, Shanahan, and Meisner convinced him that if they were going to tour, the public would demand at least some of his hits. Understandably, Rick was wary of reliving a past he'd been unfairly made to feel he had to live down. He worried about audience reaction to his most famous work and considered revising lyrics, such as the reference to going steady in "Believe What You Say."

The Stone Canyon Band's musical signature would be its prominent use of pedal-steel guitar, an instrument still relatively exotic to rock & roll. Rick hired "Sneaky" Pete Kleinow, an older, respected player from Indiana, and also a licensed pilot. The day of the Stone Canyon Band's concert debut at the Troubadour, Kleinow phoned from Las Vegas during equipment soundcheck to say he was grounded there by fog and wouldn't be able to make the date. "We had a hard time believing there was fog in Las Vegas," said Kemp, thrust into service as main soloist for the evening.

Despite having to go on as a foursome and improvise arrangements, the group thoroughly won over its opening-night audience, many of whom, *Rolling Stone* magazine reported, "had come as much to scoff as out of curiosity." The more sophisticated fans of the late 1960s listened attentively, and it was a wonderfully strange experience for Rick to not have adolescent screams drown out his voice.

Shortly thereafter Kleinow hooked up with former Byrds Gram Parsons and Chris Hillman in the Flying Burrito Brothers, and was replaced in the interim by Buddy Emmons. In December, just days before recording his first live album, Rick recruited Tom Brumley, who for the next nine years would fill a role similar to James Burton's, both professionally and personally.

Thin and boyish, Brumley came from a musical Missouri family; his father composed the gospel favorite "I'll Fly Away" and some six hundred other songs. The steel guitarist joined Buck Owens's Buckaroos in 1963, just as Owens began his remarkable streak of twenty-five Top Ten country hits. Weary of touring after six years, Brumley had quit to manufacture pedal-steel guitars, but quickly came out of retirement to play with Rick.

Twenty-four hours after his first rehearsal, Brumley sat next to Rick on the Troubadour's cozy stage, playing for posterity. Cables snaked across the club's floor and into a decrepit mixing board wired to a remote recording unit. The idea to tape four nights of shows for an LP had come from Rick's new manager, Joe Sutton, the same Joe Sutton who'd grown up around the corner from the Nelsons. He now also guided Neil Diamond's and Lou Rawls's careers.

It was a commercially risky concept: a live album of mostly unfamiliar songs. But *Rick Nelson in Concert*'s main purpose was to prove that Rick had grown up. He was less interested in selling records than in being judged by the new rock standards, high on the list of which was musical virtuosity. So for those cynics to whom he remained the trifling teenage idol, Rick and his splendid quartet presented their music pure, free of studio trickery.

Rick Nelson in Concert stands as the singer's benchmark, crackling with confidence—and a measure of defiance, as Rick and the band sense they are gaining converts with each song. The rollicking opener, "Come On In," one of four Nelson originals, is both a warm welcome and a peace offering to the audience. Leading into the chorus, Rick sings, *We'd like to try to make you happy/You can be just what you want to be/So let's be friends no matter what you see,* referring to the changed, mature Rick Nelson standing before them in bell-bottoms and a blue pullover, with longish hair and thick sideburns.

From there the band drops easily into "Hello Mary Lou," performed true to the original, save for Brumley's embroidering throughout. "Believe What You Say" also receives a conservative reading. But the third oldie, "I'm Walkin'," is infused with a country-swing rhythm and joyful three-part harmonies. Curiously, Rick sounds self-assured premiering his new songs, yet self-conscious rendering the hits.

He introduces "Believe What You Say" with a cautious "Here's an old rock & roll song that I recorded about eight or nine years ago." (Actually, almost twelve.) Then he pauses, holding his breath for any heckling, before proceeding. Rick's lack of showmanship did not escape Ozzie, who attended nearly every show with Harriet. One imagines the elder Nelson gesturing from his seat for Rick to smile.

Between sets Ozzie made his way into the Troubadour's cramped dressing room and offered some stale jokes Rick might use to enliven his stage patter. But his twenty-nine-year-old son wasn't listening anymore. "Rick never answered him," said Tom Brumley, "he just kept combing his hair," staring into a mirror. "So Ozzie said, 'Don't *you* think so, Tom?' and wound up talking to me!"

Eric Andersen, who authored the liner notes for the resulting live LP, was also present. "I got a little bit pissed off," he said. "It was as if Ozzie still viewed Rick as a kid. You could see Rick's jaw clench, but he listened politely, because he had almost a southern sensibility, always the perfect gentleman to his father."

Rick also breathes fresh life into Andersen's fragile "Violets of Dawn," Tim Hardin's "Red Balloon," and three Bob Dylan

167

songs. A studio version of "She Belongs to Me" was just then peaking at number thirty-three, Rick's highest-ranking single in over five years and his first entry onto the Hot 100 since 1965. With this album and 1971's *Rudy the Fifth*, Rick covered five Dylan numbers and established himself as one of Robert Zimmerman's most sensitive interpreters. The summer following Rick's death, Dylan returned the compliment, covering "Lonesome Town" on his 1986 world tour.

Explaining his approach to Dylan's songs, Rick said, "They're not difficult to sing. People get so hung up on trying to do them differently. . . . It's all there. You don't have to embellish the songs at all." He did, however, to great effect, on "She Belongs to Me," fashioning an airy three-part-harmony chorus, *ba-dada-da-da*, from the basic progression. Dylan's spartan original had consisted only of multiple verses interrupted by one of his trademark asthmatic harmonica solos.

Rick reveled in Kemp's and Meisner's vocal abilities, and blended himself in ringing harmonies at every opportunity. Meisner's voice was so high that several record reviewers assumed they were hearing a female backup singer. On "Believe What You Say," the choruses' fiery responding "I believe"s lend the song an almost gospel feel.

The album closes dramatically with Rick's own "Easy to Be Free" and Dylan's "I Shall Be Released," their meanings amplified by the circumstances. On the latter, one wonders if Rick wasn't singing about himself while shouting out the chorus, as if at last emancipated from his past.

Issued in early 1970, *Rick Nelson in Concert* met with ecstatic reviews. *Rolling Stone*'s Lester Bangs praised, "A brilliant collection of gutsy originals and exquisitely rendered favorites. Listening to this album and recalling Nelson's early work, the extent of his influence on styles of composition and delivery of [Bob Dylan, Buffalo Springfield, and the Byrds] becomes obvious." The LP sold respectably, climbing to number fifty-four and remaining on the charts through early summer.

Rick had to re-establish himself as a concert draw, his bookings restricted mainly to sweaty clubs such as the Cellar Door in

Washington, DC, Mr. Kelly's in Chicago, Boston's Unicorn, and Greenwich Village's famed Bitter End. Summer state-fair dates were also scheduled, reminders of a time when Rick routinely played to tens of thousands rather than to hundreds.

He was starting over again, yet even when confronting conditions that rock & roll neophytes would have deemed intolerable, the onetime idol gamely carried on. Miles Thomas, hired as road manager, recalled one particularly dreadful concert at a Fairbanks college, "arranged" through a shifty promoter:

"No one even knew we were coming. There was no stage, no lights, no nothing. So we got them to build us a small low-rise stage, went to a music store and bought some el-cheapo microphones, plugged them into the guitar amplifiers, and Rick did a show in a college cafeteria for about thirty people.

"Looking back," said Thomas, "it gives me a warm feeling, because I worked for so many egomaniac performers that would have walked out of much better situations. I know it really pissed Rick off, but he didn't let it show. He was the total trouper."

Rick's dedication inspired the Stone Canyon Band, which Allen Kemp called "the kind of group I missed so much afterward. We had an all-for-one togetherness, and Rick let everyone be a part of the whole thing." Following the example set by Ozzie, of whom trumpeter Holly Humphreys said, "No bandleader treated his musicians better," Rick truly respected his sidemen. Were it not for Joe Sutton's and Decca Records' vociferous objections, he would have omitted *Rick Nelson and* from the Stone Canyon Band name.

Rick always flew the same class as the band and hauled his own baggage, a private hotel room his one allotted privilege. "He was no aristocrat," said Richard Schnyder, Miles Thomas's successor as road manager, "and he worked as hard as everyone else." Rick's deep-rooted family values influenced his affinity for intragroup equality. But his lifelong desire to fit in, to be *one of the guys*, also played a part, as did sporadic bouts of artistic insecurity.

At one point the entire band except Tom Brumley moved

to Laguna Beach, renting houses on two acres of beachfront property once owned by actress Bette Davis and rehearsing in a garage. Rick's family stayed in a charming red cottage atop an eighty-foot cliff, where motion-picture stars Howard Duff and Ida Lupino had honeymooned.

Camaraderie, however, couldn't always compensate for moderate wages and a punishing schedule. Randy Meisner and Miles Thomas quit after a grueling monthlong winter-1970 tour of U.S. Army bases in Europe that Thomas called "a nightmare from the book of bad road dreams." With dates scattered throughout Germany, Rick and the band were confined to a hotel in centrally located Frankfurt. During the day they languished in their rooms, then at night were driven to officers' and enlisted-mens' clubs as far as one hundred miles away.

Their long hair did not sit well with the GIs, who heckled, "Where's your miniskirt?" and blew kisses. Afterward the group was deposited back at its hotel. Depressed roommates Meisner and Thomas gave notice on the flight home. Tim Cetera, brother of the jazz-rock septet Chicago's Peter Cetera, replaced the bassist for one record before Meisner rejoined a year later.

In another change, Rick acquired a new manager, and as per Nelson custom he was family. Cousin Willy Nelson, the second youngest of Al and Kay Nelson's five boys, had been involved in music since recording for Liberty Records in 1958 at age fourteen. A sandy-haired, rugged version of Rick, he moved west in 1964 to sing on the rock TV show *Shindig*. But all along, Willy said, "I was more interested in the business end," and he left performing for artist management in his early twenties.

Rick released his eighteenth studio album of new material, *Rick Sings Nelson*, in September 1970. For the first time he composed every track, publishing each under Matragun Music, an acronym of children *Mat*thew, *Tra*cy, and *Gun*nar. His burst of creativity continued with 1971's *Rudy the Fifth*. Though neither LP sold well, their songs, evoking James Taylor's plain-spoken style, are windows into Rick's soul. More than most songwriters,

170

Rick's lyrics merit examination because they reveal so much about him.

Due to his inability to express himself clearly in interviews, his stoicism in *The Adventures'* later years, and his most personal music going largely unnoticed, Rick was often presumed superficial. The self-produced *Rick Sings Nelson* and *Rudy the Fifth,* both the works of a surprisingly existential man, invalidate that perception.

Jack Ellena, Rick's bodyguard in the 1950s and 1960s, remembered the teenage star studying the Bible, "learning and reaching out, trying to find out more about life." Kahlil Gibran's *The Prophet,* which Rick gave to girlfriends as gifts, affected him strongly. Years later, so did Hermann Hesse's allegorical *Siddhartha,* the inspiration behind Rick's delicate "Easy to Be Free," a Top Fifty single in 1970. Like all of the German writer's major works, this one concerned the search for self and knowledge. Rick saw himself in the story's protagonist, a privileged yet dissatisfied young member of Hindu society's highest class, the Brahmins.

> Love stirred in the hearts of the young Brahmins' daughters when Siddhartha walked through the streets of town . . . But Siddhartha himself was not happy . . . Dreams and a restlessness of the soul came to him . . . He lived a good life . . . but even he who knew so much, did he live in bliss, was he at peace? Was he not also a seeker, insatiable?

While "Easy to Be Free" offered the answer to life's riddles (*I'll take you there with me/And maybe then you'll see/It's easy to be free*), the diarylike songs "How Long" and "Life" make no such claims. They hint darkly at some underlying discontentment: about the state of Rick's career? his marriage? "How Long," from *Rick Sings Nelson,* is a somber acoustic meditation with imagery similar to Eric Andersen's "Time Run Like a Freight Train." Rick asks, *How long before the train goes by?/It never seems to get here/How long before the train goes by?/Will I just sit here forever?/How long?*

171

And in "Life," from *Rudy the Fifth*, Rick demands, *Life, before you're over/I'd like something to show for/all my trouble,* then concludes by imploring, *Tell me, life, what are we here for?* As a teenager he often wondered why everything came so easily to him; now Rick questioned why things seemed so much harder.

Despite favorable reviews, *Rick Sings Nelson* withered on the bottom of the album chart. So to promote *Rudy the Fifth* Rick agreed to take part in a Madison Square Garden Rock & Roll Revival concert on October 15, 1971. Promoter Richard Nader had contacted him several times before about appearing on one of his bills but was always rebuffed. "Rick had never done a packaged rock & roll show before and was skeptical," said Nader, originator of the live-oldies format. "And he didn't want to be labeled an oldie."

Rick relented, but on the condition that Nader, one of the rare people Rick openly detested, rebill the show from "Rock & Roll Revival" to "Rock & Roll Spectacular." While he'd never disowned his past, Rick wanted no part of trading in nostalgia. Each of the other acts—Bobby Rydell, Bo Diddley, the Shirelles, the Coasters, Gary U.S. Bonds, and headliner Chuck Berry—was at least seven years removed from its last hit record. But the lure of playing to an audience of twenty thousand at the Garden swayed Rick.

As soon as he walked into the dressing room, the evening's "Special Added Attraction" realized his mistake. The capacity crowd came garbed in Eisenhower-era memorabilia probably not worn since high-school proms, as if their collective yearning for the supposed good-old days might whisk them all back in time. "True fifties people," Rick called them, "who wear their saddle shoes and sweaters and really *believe.*" By contrast, Rick and his group, in their bell-bottom jeans, denim shirts, vests, and cowboy boots, resembled a band of desperadoes.

The set's first half, featuring old hits, elicited delighted screams of recognition. But with "She Belongs to Me," the audience's enthusiasm dampened, turning to outright hostility when Rick finished pumping out "Honky Tonk Women."

Richard Nader recalled, "They started booing—that's a New York crowd—to tell Rick they were displeased he'd interrupted the ambience of the evening. For two hours up to that point they'd been able to escape the seventies. But 'Honky Tonk Women' jarred them back to reality, that it was nineteen seventy-one."

At the sound of the boos, Rick's face turned ashen. Twenty thousand howling faces seemed to whir above him and the band, their jeers swelling. "We were all terrified," said Kemp. Despite the predictable cheers for the planned encore, "Travelin' Man," Rick, who rarely swore, trudged off stage and asked his manager, "What the fuck's going on?"

"I don't know," Willy Nelson replied grimly, "let's just keep walking." They filed up an aisle, past the fans in the seven-dollar orchestra seats and on to the dressing room, where Rick sat in stunned silence.

Tom Brumley, trying to console him, said, "I didn't think it was that bad, Rick. I saw the people, and they enjoyed what you were doing."

Brumley may have been right. Though there were unmistakable catcalls, whether or not they were directed at Rick remains the subject of controversy. Nader subsequently learned from a Madison Square Garden official that as Rick was finishing "Honky Tonk Women," security guards were forcibly evicting a section of rowdy patrons. Neighboring fans booed in protest, then others in the crowd followed.

What really occurred that night? There seem to be as many opinions as eyewitnesses. Over the summer Randy Meisner had left the band again, to back Linda Ronstadt and within months to cofound the Eagles. His replacement, Stephen Love, stood to Rick's right. "We weren't getting the audience off," he said firmly, a belief supported by Kemp, who was on Rick's left. Tom Brumley, however, accepted the security-guard scenario. And Pat Shanahan, fortressed behind drums and cymbals, said with a laugh, "To this day, I still can't tell you what happened."

Pete Fornatale can. A popular New York FM-radio disc jockey, he was in the audience. "I've heard all the stories," he said, "and it was booing. There is no doubt in my mind that the crowd was intolerant of what Rick was doing. It was a typical Richard Nader show, where part of the game is, You step out exactly as you were. Dare to change a phrase in your song or a lock of your hair, and we'll get you for it. 'Honky Tonk Women' just made the place go berserk."

Rick never would accept that the audience booed the guards and not him. He'd seen the incredulous expressions on the faces in the front rows. As he recounted to *Rolling Stone* in 1972, "They kept looking at me and my long hair as if they couldn't believe I was the same person. But I couldn't have done it any differently, except by getting my hair cut and putting braces on my teeth."

> When I got to the Garden Party
> They all knew my name.
> But no one recognized me,
> I didn't look the same.

Rick's bitter Madison Square Garden experience typifies the complicated ties between stars and their fans. Dr. Raymond A. Moody, Jr., best known for his landmark studies on near- and post-death experiences, explored these ties in his provocative book *Elvis After Life*. Moody believes that we create celebrities "to impose some sort of order" on increasingly chaotic lives and then relate to them in oversimplified, idealized and unrealistic ways.

Fans presume to know their idol, when in fact all they have knowledge of is that portion of his character displayed to the media. While fame affords our cultural heroes wealth and power, they do not control this relationship. Fans often view an artist's success as a blessing they bestowed upon him or her by purchasing a record or a concert ticket. *Just as we made you,* goes the rationale, *we can break you.* And in the commercial arts, especially in America, all too often they can.

If Moody is correct, it follows that the public expects from celebrities a consistency. Let them stray too far afield creatively, and, depending on the prevalent cultural climate—progressive (the late 1960s) or regressive (the late 1980s)—fans may snap the leash and bring the artist to heel for more of the same. We seem to forgive our icons almost anything except growing up, growing old, or growing at all.

> I played them all the old songs.
> I thought that's why they came.
> No one heard the music,
> We didn't look the same.

Naturally the crowd's antagonism hurt Rick, but he also understood it. Deeply aware of how an entire generation associated him with its youth, he frequently joked about being an "age gauge" for his peers. In public fans scrutinized Rick's face, wincing at the tiniest wrinkle.

"Rick was extremely conscious about his image and what he looked like when he went out," said a friend, Alan Bush. "I don't think he ever left the house without shaving two or three times [Rick had an extremely heavy beard] and wearing brown pancake makeup for some facial color. He always prided himself on looking picture-perfect."

However, Rick, who possessed an absurdist sense of humor, couldn't resist debunking that image. He'd put people on, cornering strangers and deadpanning, "Let's get naked and dance to Hitler speeches," knowing it would be doubly shocking because it came from him. Drummer Ty Grimes, a later Stone Canyon Band member, remembered Rick one day telling the group about his and David's old trapeze act.

"Rick," Tom Brumley asked, "is there anything you *haven't* done?"

Placing a hand over his mouth, Rick affected a pensive expres-

175

sion, then cartoonishly jabbed a finger in the air. "I've never fucked a chicken," he answered brightly, a picture of mock innocence.

"Can you imagine *Rick Nelson* saying that?" Grimes asked. "When he was around the band, he was a riot; my face used to hurt from laughing. But the minute a fan came up, he was Mr. Prim and Proper."

Rick also took perverse pleasure in portraying sinister television characters during the 1970s: a murderous pimp on *The Streets of San Francisco;* a singer accused of murder on *Petrocelli;* a serial killer on *McCloud;* and a pornographer and rapist on *Owen Marshall: Counselor at Law.* But "a *nice* rapist," he clarified to a magazine reporter, smiling at the incongruity.

For some time, friends George Harrison and Elton John had been urging Rick to tour England, which he'd never played despite having sailed nineteen singles into the British Top Forty. Still despondent over the Madison Square Garden nightmare and *Rudy the Fifth*'s failure to nick the charts, Rick looked forward to performing for fans who knew him only as a musician.

When the group landed at Heathrow Airport in February 1972, a fervent reception warmed their spirits. "Nelson At Last!" trumpeted the front-page headline on a London daily. "They treated us like royalty there," recalled Allen Kemp. The eight-person entourage traveled the countryside in two rented Daimlers, the Royal Family's official limousines.

England was then mired in a crippling seven-week coal-miners strike, leaving most of the country without electricity or heat. By the time Rick and the band pulled into Liverpool, the strike had been settled, but power was still sporadic: four hours on, four hours off. Rather than cancel, as they'd had to do in Manchester, Willy Nelson rented generator trucks and parked them outside the venue, an old dance hall the Beatles used to play.

"We knew the lights were going to go off at a certain time," he explained. When the theater went black and the amplified sound ebbed midway through "My Babe," ten hired hands started rotating the generator drums. *Thwap! Thwap! Thwap! Thwap!* The portable arc lights flashed on, the electric guitars fired up again, and the band played on almost as if nothing had happened, although, Stephen Love recalled, "our amps' tones went up and down every time the generator turned."

The two-week tour ended in triumph on February 28, at London's famed Royal Albert Hall. "That crazy round building," Rick called it. The packed house, which included Elton John, Olivia Newton-John, and Cliff Richard, went wild over essentially the same set Rick had presented at the Garden, only stocked with more new songs. Fans loudly demanded four encores, and the mob scene outside the stage door afterward was reminiscent of a bygone era. "The crowd picked all five of us up in the air," Love remembered, "and carried us about thirty, forty feet. And some girls ripped Rick's shirt off. Kris was pissed."

If Rick's commitment to forging ahead had ever wavered, it was renewed that night. After Albert Hall he came to terms with what had happened at Madison Square Garden. "Considering where I was musically," he reflected later, "I had no business doing a nostalgia concert." He realized that "when I have a hunch deep down that something is wrong for me, and I go against that judgment, I always end up regretting the experience."

> But it's all right now.
> I learned my lesson well.
> You see, you can't please everyone
> So you got to please yourself.

Rick walked away from the Garden show with not only a valuable lesson but grist for a new song. Though it came to him in one sitting, "Garden Party" had been stirring in his subconscious for months. One spring night in 1972 Rick slipped off to the game room of his Zorada Drive home to play guitar. He often did this, finding music therapeutic.

177

As if he were channeling from an outside source, lyrics materialized before him on a single sheet of paper. "I didn't want to *move*," he recalled. The result was an incisive, detailed account of that fateful evening:

> I went to a Garden Party
> To reminisce with my old friends.
> A chance to share old memories
> And play our songs again.
>
> I said hello to "Mary Lou."
> She belongs to me.
> When I sang a song about a honky tonk;
> It was time to leave.
>
> Someone opened up a closet door
> And out stepped Johnny B. Goode.
> Playing guitar like a ring an' a bell
> And lookin' like he should.

Only a line from the second verse strays from the factual narrative:

> People came for miles around.
> Everyone was there.
> Yoko brought her walrus.
> There was magic in the air.

The "walrus," as anyone even vaguely familiar with Beatles trivia knows, is John Lennon. But no one recalls seeing either him or Yoko Ono at the show that night. Why Rick added the famous couple to the song remains a mystery. In a less decipherable clue, the same verse mentions another Beatle:

> And over in the corner,
> Much to my surprise,
> Mr. Hughes hid in Dylan's shoes,
> Wearing his disguise.

178

"Mr. Hughes" was Rick's Hollywood Canyon neighbor George Harrison, who attended the show with Bob Dylan. At the time, Rick was upset that the former Beatle didn't come backstage to say hello. But, said Willy Nelson, in retrospect Rick understood Harrison's reticence. "He said, 'I went through my own Howard Hughes period, trying to hide from the public.'"

The morning after "Garden Party" came to him, Rick called his cousin-manager and announced excitedly, "Willy, I wrote one! I think I just wrote a hit."

Eleven

If Rick was convinced he'd penned a smash single, he was about the only one.

"I don't think anybody expected it to be a hit," admitted Stephen Love. When Rick played "Garden Party" for Tom Brumley at a rehearsal, the steel guitarist wondered aloud if the sentiment might not be too strong. Rick's back stiffened. "He looked at me, his eyes beaded, and he said, *'No, it's not too strong,'*" Brumley recalled with a laugh. "Rick was gonna do it, and that was the way he was gonna say it."

Like the lyrics, the music took shape in one session, Rick producing "Garden Party" exactly as he'd heard it in his head. The simple backdrop suggested Johnny Cash and the Tennessee Two, a creeping guitar run and a *boom-chick-a-boom* rhythm, topped by Rick's intimate vocal and tagged with a guitar coda he called his "Carl Perkins ending."

After a sluggish start, the June-released single caught fire over the summer and peaked in October at number six. Ironically, Chuck Berry, chided in "Garden Party" for his complacency (*Someone opened up a closet door/And out stepped Johnny B. Goode*), had his first and only number one that month with a juvenile novelty, "My Ding-A-Ling," the artistic nadir of a once brilliant career.

"Garden Party"'s appeal was twofold. As with an earlier 1972 hit, Don McLean's "American Pie," identifying its rock & roll allusions turned into a parlor game. But most of all listeners were struck by Rick's honest conviction, expressed in the chorus and the memorable final half-verse:

> If you gotta play at Garden Parties,
> I wish you a lot of luck.
> But if memories were all I sang,
> I'd rather drive a truck.

"That was one of the greatest instances of snatching victory from the jaws of defeat," said Pete Fornatale, the first American disc jockey to air "Garden Party," on WNEW-FM in New York. Rick metaphorically transformed a mere oldies concert into a battlefield on which to take a moral stand. Understandably, the song held special meaning for other artists.

"I think it spoke for most of us of that era," said Del Shannon, whose debut, "Runaway," had preceded Rick's "Travelin' Man" at number one in May 1961. Shannon, a suicide in 1990, had also been steamrollered by the British Invasion and at the time of "Garden Party" was trapped in the crosscurrents of his past and the present. John Fogerty called it "the all-time anthem for wanting to go on and be creative." Carl Perkins, Rick's first idol and inspiration, also asserted, "That song said a lot to me." But most fulfilling for Rick was the secretary who accosted him in an airport, recited the chorus, and declared, " 'Garden Party' changed my life."

And Rick's too, for a while. His *Garden Party* LP charged to

181

number thirty-two, its stunning cover photo visually comple-
menting the title song's sentiment. Trim in a velvet jacket and
a white open-collar shirt, his hair glistening, Rick locks eyes
with the camera and grips his black Gibson Les Paul electric
guitar defiantly, as if to say, *Just you* try *taking this away from
me.* On the back of the album, designed by Kris, is a picture
of the original sheet on which he'd scribbled "Garden Party" 's
lyrics.

Concert ticket sales rose in proportion to record sales. Bill
Hollingshead, then entertainment director for Knott's Berry
Farm, presented Rick more than any other promoter. "The
John Wayne Theater there sat twenty-two hundred people,"
he said. "When we first booked Rick, in 1971, he filled it three
times in one evening. But after 'Garden Party' he was able to
do as many as seventeen shows a week, including four shows
on Friday, Saturday, and Sunday. And it was the broadest demographic range of any act I've ever booked, from little kids to
ladies with blue hair."

Toward year's end Willy Nelson asked his cousin, "Feels great
to have a hit again, doesn't it?"

"Yeah," Rick replied, "but I can't go Christmas shopping
anymore!" People constantly stopped him on the street to offer
congratulations, seeming to share in his victory. It was like
the old days.

The press too rallied around Rick, including those counterculture journalists who'd previously seemed indifferent to his comeback. Rick accepted their support as evenly as he had the lack
of it. Going over interview commitments with publicist Sandy
Friedman one afternoon, Rick started laughing.

"I can't believe it," he said. "The same people who didn't
want to talk to me before want to talk to me now. But I'm the
same guy."

Friedman observed, "He knew that when 'Garden Party' went
down the charts, the phones would stop ringing."

While cooperative, Rick was by no means forthcoming, fending off personal questions. "It was always like pulling teeth,"

recalled Pete Fornatale, who interviewed him several times over the years. According to Rick's friend Paul Rose, "He would give short replies or stammer through an answer, trying to think out precisely what he wanted to say." Consequently, "Some people misunderstood and thought Rick was either dumb or 'out there.'" His dry humor only furthered that impression. An interviewer would ask, "Did you and David have any problems growing up on television?" and Rick would crack straight-faced, "No, although I only wear *one* pump," an inside reference to a 1950s pulp magazine's lurid claim that teenage Ricky had once been arrested in Griffith Park wearing women's hi-heels. The reporter would write it down.

In Rick's mind vindication would not be complete until his scheduled return to New York City for a Carnegie Hall show. Just two weeks before the March 30, 1973, date, however, band members Kemp, Love, and Shanahan quit over a salary dispute, boycotting the gold-record presentation for "Garden Party."

"Childish," Love admitted in retrospect, Shanahan adding, "We were young. If I had to do it all over again, I'd have stayed with Rick." Believing they could procure their own record deal like Neil Young's much-heralded backing group Crazy Horse, they carried on with a fourth member and Richard Schnyder as manager, but were never signed and soon disbanded.

In the late 1970s and early 1980s, all three went on to play with the New Riders of the Purple Sage, founded as a country-rock side group by several of the Grateful Dead. One of the New Riders' best-known songs, coincidentally, was an update of "Hello Mary Lou."

Through a single phone call, Willy Nelson found Rick three new musicians. The publicity director at MCA Records, newly formed out of the Decca, Kapp, and Uni labels, recommended guitarist Dennis Larden, who in turn suggested bassist Jay White and drummer Ty Grimes. Larden, a singer-songwriter from Brooklyn, had briefly enjoyed pop success in 1967 with a group called Every Mother's Son ("Come On Down to My Boat").

One night in early 1973 he caught Rick singing on the *Tonight* show.

"I nodded at my old lady," he remembered, "and said, 'You know, that wouldn't be a bad gig for me, playing acoustic guitar and singing harmony.' She said, 'Yeah, yeah, sure, sure.' " Two weeks later Larden was at an elegant Manhattan hotel suite, preparing to play Carnegie Hall.

The night of the show, nerves bristled backstage. "Rick definitely had that General MacArthur 'I shall return!' syndrome going," said Larden. His white satin suit had ripped in back, and Kris, having flown in for the show, safety-pinned it together while Rick chain-smoked cigarettes. "He was terrified," remembered Ty Grimes. "He said, 'Man, if I get booed off the stage again . . .' "

There was no need to worry. The reverent audience sprang to its feet at the introductory chords of *Rudy the Fifth*'s "Gypsy Pilot." At Madison Square Garden Rick had cut the song from the set for fear of further antagonizing the crowd. Clearly he wanted to jolt Carnegie Hall with his most uncharacteristic selection, on which guitars are pushed to distortion level, pulsating bass resonates chest cavities, and Rick sings in a searing voice about the music that shaped his life. The Garden audience would have plugged their fingers into their ears, but here "Gypsy Pilot" set the appropriately radical tone.

One of Rick's quietest compositions, however, "The Last Time Around," provided the show's highlight. Open to other interpretations, its lyrics touch upon reincarnation, which Rick believed in. Two years earlier, while in New York to promote the "Life" single, he and Willy Nelson had stopped at an East Side bar. There an old black man, not knowing who Rick was, engaged him in besotted conversation about the afterlife.

"You've been here before, and this is your last life," he told Rick, who back at the Warwick Hotel wrote: *This is my last time around/And I don't know where I'm bound/But I'm leavin' now, so don't look back at me. . . . Don't ask me how I know/But I've been here before/And the things that seem important aren't, you see.*

At Carnegie Hall the new Stone Canyon Band ended it with a tricky fade-out. "The house lights came down with us," Larden remembered, "and it was like staring into the face of a cobra; hypnotic. Then the music disappeared, and everything went black. And in that moment before people started clapping, there was just this peace, this nothing. You could *feel* the air. It was amazing."

"From that point on, we were home free," said Grimes, "and we knew it." The audience, now crowded around the stage, called the band back for three encores until it had exhausted its repertoire. Striding back to the dressing room, Tom Brumley paused to smack an open hand against a wall. "Damn!" he exulted. "That was only the fourth time we played together!"

Afterward the band took limos to a private party at a club called Hippopotamus. Andy Warhol, one of many celebrities in attendance, made little effort to conceal his amorous interest in the guest of honor. But Rick barely noticed. Buoyed by a feeling of redemption that erased the painful memory of his last New York appearance, "Rick was ecstatic," said Larden. "We were all so happy for him."

Rick wasn't the only Nelson making a comeback. The night he headlined Carnegie Hall, his parents were treading the boards in *The Marriage-Go-Round* at a New Jersey theater. Later that year Ozzie published his autobiography, which coincided with his and Harriet's return to weekly television.

Ozzie's Girls starred the Nelsons as themselves, of course, still living in the same replica of 1822 Camino Palmero. The knotty-pine kitchen and other old sets were taken out of storage and reassembled on General Service Studio's stage five, though Harriet insisted on some redecorating. Her top priority: doing away with the American eagle that had hung conspicuously over the Nelson fireplace. "If there's one thing I got sick of looking at after fourteen years," she said, "it's that goddamn eagle."

Numerous alumni made up the cast and crew: Connie Nelson,

Parley Baer, Sally Hughes, Sean Morgan, Jack Iannarelli, Jack Wagner, Frank McKelvey, and David, as associate producer and part-time director. Apart from Rick and David's onscreen absence, the half-hour syndicated series could have been a continuation of *The Adventures*. Ozzie wrote and directed. Even the basic premise—two college coeds rent the boys' old room—was loosely based on a vintage episode, "Ozzie's Daughters" (1958–59), only here one girl was white and the other black.

"When I walked back on the set," said Morgan, "I thought, *God bless Ozzie, this is wonderful*. It was a real déjà vu. Everything was the same, including my cardigan sweaters and pullovers, except that I walked past the mirror, and I'd gotten seven years older."

But Ozzie could not generate that old spirit among the cast, especially with his two young costars, Susan Sennett and Brenda Sykes. "We had a lot of fun," said Iannarelli, "but there wasn't that family feeling."

The original program's easygoing charm was also missing. Taking his cue from such topical sitcoms as the top-rated *All in the Family* and its spinoff *Maude*, Ozzie awkwardly ventured into racial humor. In one episode he prepares to meet Sykes's black boyfriend by reading up on his native Chad. Only it turns out the boyfriend hails from Chad, Indiana, not Chad, Africa. Ahem.

Harriet drifts through scenes even less frequently than before. She was not keen on returning to the daily grind and did so only for Ozzie's sake. One columnist critiqued the show with: "What it seems to prove is, You can't stay home again." Another called it "a ludicrous program" but marveled at Ozzie's vigor, writing, "The guy looks better than most people in their forties."

Those on the set knew otherwise. "Ozzie wasn't feeling too well," remembered Iannarelli. "He seemed pale and grayish." Sitting next to the prop man one day, Ozzie suddenly clutched at his right side.

"Jesus Christ, Jack, I've got this pain that's killing me!" An ambulance rushed him to a Burbank hospital for tests. Doctors found nothing wrong, telling Ozzie that physiologically he was a decade younger than his sixty-seven years.

Yet Ozzie kept complaining of fatigue so severe that he discontinued the television series. Two months after Kris gave birth to his sixth grandchild, Sam Hilliard Nelson, on August 29, 1974, Ozzie again entered the hospital. This time the surgeon detected terminal liver cancer. (No one outside the family knew that Ozzie had a malignant colon tumor removed in 1967.)

"How long do I have?" Ozzie asked his doctors. Six months to two years, he was told. "Two years?" he replied. "Gee, if I have two years, I can walk outside and get hit by a truck. I thought you meant next week."

Ozzie handled his illness in characteristic fashion. He plunged into writing a second autobiography, which was never published, and putting his financial affairs in order. "My father never gave up thinking he could beat the disease," said David. "His only fear was that there would be some cowardice toward the end. There never was."

Like most people afflicted with a terminal illness, Ozzie reacted bitterly at first. How could a man who neither smoked nor drank develop cancer? "If I wasn't in such good shape, it wouldn't be so hard to die," he said to Harriet.

But he came to accept death philosophically. And, as his own father had done when in terrible pain from bone cancer, Ozzie tried to spare family and friends. At the Nelsons' annual Christmas celebration that year, "Dad didn't want the grandkids to see him in his condition," said David. "It was a struggle for him to come downstairs. But he did it."

Once the ravaging disease had extracted seventy pounds, leaving him gaunt and listless, Ozzie refused all visitors except for the immediate family. "I'd call him at least once a week and ask if I could come see him," said Jack Iannarelli. "Ozzie would say, 'Jack, do you remember what I looked like? Just remember me that way.'"

As the end drew near, Rick curtailed concert dates to be with his father, and David, in the process of divorcing June,

187

visited the house daily. Ozzie now occupied his oldest son's former bedroom, which Harriet had wallpapered with a flowered pattern he liked. The early morning of June 3, 1975, David stood vigil at his father's bedside. Tubes extended from Ozzie's nose and throat. Except for the sound of his labored breathing, it was quiet, and dark outside.

David gazed out the window at the backyard swimming pool, reflecting on a childhood memory of the family looking at the expanse of grass below and saying, "Someday we're going to build a pool here." Suddenly he felt a rush of energy leave the room. When he turned around, Ozzie was still.

"There was such a sense that my father was gone," David said, noting the parallels between Ozzie's and George Nelson's passings. Ozzie too had been staring out a window, then turned around to find his father dead.

Ozzie's death affected Rick and David in ways as different as the brothers themselves. As much as David missed his father, he was finally free to be his own man. Rick, on the other hand, felt lost. "It took a lot of the fire out of him," Tom Brumley observed. In his cluttered guitar case Rick saved a yellowed newspaper clipping about his father the Rutgers University football player. Months before his own death Rick reflected, "Dad did everything for us. He was always there when you needed him. Things really changed after he died."

Rick's life indeed began unraveling within just months. By 1975 the flame of renewed popularity "Garden Party" ignited had flickered, then died. Rick's ethereal, hypnotic "Palace Guard" reached number sixty-five in early 1973, his last appearance in the Hot 100. Instead of capitalizing on "Garden Party"'s momentum, Rick coasted, composing only two songs for 1974's lackluster *Windfall*.

In the long run, "Garden Party" turned out to be both a curse and a blessing. With that million-selling record Rick proved his artistic legitimacy. Few comebacks have been as poetically just. How do you top a thrill like that? Judging from his musical output in the mid-to-late 1970s, Rick seemed to feel he couldn't. He considered "Garden Party" his ultimate statement. Rather than pleasing himself, as the chorus goes, he became a bit too pleased with himself.

Windfall's recording sessions were maddeningly full of distractions. To ensure that work got done, Dennis Larden was in charge of delivering Rick to the studio. "Kind of like the guy that puts the robe around James Brown," he said jokingly.

"I'd get to Rick's house around eleven, and it was always, 'Oh, oh, I just, uh, want to get a pack of cigarettes,' or, 'Why don't I meet you there? Tracy's got this thing at school . . .' Hours and hours would go by, with the band sitting around the studio waiting, burned out." Then Rick would buzz merrily into the room: "Hi, guys! How's it goin'!" Said Larden, "It ate up a lot of time, energy, and money."

MCA Records was deeply concerned about the latter, having sunk $60,000 into *Windfall* and seeing little return. Company president Mike Maitland told Rick bluntly, "You spent too much; you need a producer." Rick did not cotton to this, and wouldn't for a long time. Like Ozzie, he craved control, enjoyed the security of a small, closely knit group, and regarded outsiders warily.

Which was unfortunate, for Rick would have benefited greatly from an objective ear, especially when recording his own material. Too often he undermined potential hits with Byzantine arrangements or by switching tempos in midsong. His version of Chuck Berry's "I'm Talking About You" from *Garden Party* barrels ahead in 4/4 time on the verse and chorus, then detours abruptly into a tangential jazz guitar solo that disrupts the groove and practically gives the listener whiplash.

Though MCA was right to insist Rick accept a producer's guidance, it had badly mishandled him since he formed the Stone Canyon Band. Beginning with the late-1960s emergence of album-oriented FM-rock radio formats, the music business had shifted its focus to LPs. Inexplicably the company continued marketing Rick as the singles artist Decca had signed in 1963. As "Garden Party" moved up the Hot 100, Willy Nelson was embroiled in a heated battle to get an album bankrolled. The label's go-ahead came too late; by the time *Garden Party* was finally set loose in late November 1972, the smash single was dropping off the charts after five months.

"MCA didn't understand or care about the record business," claimed A&R man Charles "Bud" Dant, who quit in disgust after fourteen years. "They acquired Decca only because they wanted Universal Pictures, which Decca owned." The new hierarchy, Allen Kemp said, "considered Rick a novelty act and made it real hard for him to come back. We hardly received any promotion until 'Garden Party' hit, and that did it on its own."

In December 1975 Rick accepted MCA's offer to buy out the remainder of his $1-million twenty-year contract, as glad to flee the label as it was to unburden itself of him. Just three years after his biggest-selling record since "Travelin' Man," Rick found his career at a standstill.

But another serious matter monopolized his attention: At the same time Rick and his record company were divorcing, he and Kris were on the verge of breaking up. The couple had contemplated separation much earlier. Charley Britt remembered Rick sounding him out about their becoming roommates again in 1967.

"We were riding down Sunset Boulevard, and he said to me, 'After Kris and I split up, maybe you and I can get a house together again. Imagine all the chicks we'll have!'

"I said, 'Now, hold on. Man, you've got the prettiest little daughter in the world. Do you want to share a house with me, or do you want your marriage to work?' He thought about it for all of ten seconds and said, 'I want my marriage to work.' "

Britt drove Rick back to the Zorada Drive house, then took Kris out for a drink, to hear her side. "At the end of this whole conversation about her and Rick, she said, 'By the way, Charley, if you want to hear the crusher, I just found out today that I'm pregnant.' " With the twins.

" 'Well, doesn't that solve everything?' I said. All of a sudden they were back together, and everything was fine, or so I thought."

As can be surmised from a number of Rick's personal songs, everything was not fine. The achingly sad "The Reason Why," an emotional plea to Kris written in 1970, laments two lovers grown irrevocably apart:

> Can't you see the reason why
> I walked in, I sat right down and cried.
> Can't you see the reason why
> I looked at you and knew it meant good-bye.
>
> You said that you loved me once before
> And now you don't want me anymore.
> Well, I tried, baby, I tried . . .
>
> Can't you see the reason why
> I try so hard to stop the tears I cry.
> Can't you see the reason why
> There's nothing here without you,
> You're my life.

"Rick knew there was trouble," said Connie Nelson, "and he was devastated at the thought he might be losing Kris. He once said to me that if anything ever happened to their marriage, he'd never marry again; that whatever their problems were, nobody could come close to what Kris was." What she was, in essence, was the opposite of Rick: as unpredictable as he was constant; as temperamental as he was easygoing; as easily dissatisfied as he was easily contented.

Theirs was a compensatory relationship in which each admired the other's contrary, and ultimately incompatible, nature. Why did they remain together for so long, so unhappily? Like many couples, for the children's sake. But too, Kris knew that if she bailed out of the marriage, she'd find no parental parachute to float her to safety, for both Tom and Elyse Harmon disapproved strongly of divorce. And as we've seen, Rick dodged

191

confrontations. So they remained husband and wife, leading mostly separate lives.

Miles Thomas observed them during their seventh year as marrieds. "On a real personal level, Rick and Kris never should have happened," he said. "I don't know how much love there was in the relationship; it was hard to judge. They both fooled around a lot and were all over town. It was a real Hollywood thing. Kris ran around with her friends, and Rick ran around with his."

The conflict's roots go back to the cancellation of *The Adventures of Ozzie and Harriet*, which is when Kris's disillusion with her storybook marriage set in. Her first three years as Mrs. Rick Nelson had been everything she'd dreamed, transforming her into the much-envied young bride of an international star and a budding celebrity herself. Then, like Cinderella at the stroke of midnight, everything vanished—the family show, Rick's musical popularity, and her path to Hollywood stardom. She wasn't yet twenty-one.

At first Kris seemed satisfied to funnel her considerable creativity into home life, imaginatively decorating their house, entertaining guests, and raising the children. This she did largely on her own. Rick, something of a big kid himself, freely admitted he'd never win any awards for fatherhood. He acted more like a big brother to Tracy, Matthew, Gunnar, and Sam than a disciplinarian or adviser, responsibilities Kris had to assume.

How puzzling that Rick should wind up the antithesis of his own father. Was he wary of overprotecting his kids as Ozzie had him? Though well intentioned, Ozzie's compulsion to control his son's life left Rick overly dependent on others, handicapping him when it came to functioning in the real world. Or, as some friends suggest, was Rick simply unprepared to be a father? No one truly knows, for it wasn't a subject Rick liked to discuss.

This is not to say that Rick wasn't loving. "When he was home, he was a good daddy," said Connie Nelson, "and the kids just adored him. He played music to them, he was patient with them, he had a sense of humor with them, and he went to their activities. Of course," she added, "his wife had to drag him."

As Kris's younger siblings surpassed her in public accomplishments, she grew resentful and restless. Kelly, a tawny five-foot-eight beauty once married to General Motors executive John DeLorean, modeled and pitched products in television commercials. And Mark, an actor, was on his way to becoming a national sex symbol. "Meanwhile," said David Nelson, "Kris was kind of left at home holding the frying pan."

The Mrs. Rick Nelson she played on TV was intensely jealous, another of Ozzie's true-life characterizations. As the years passed, Rick himself became the object of her envy. Coming from such a competitive family, Kris began vying with him for the limelight.

She did gain a measure of acclaim through her painting, which Rick had encouraged her to take up. Some of Kris's primitive canvasses fetched as much as $10,000 from such prestigious clients as Robert Kennedy, President Lyndon Johnson, and George Harrison. Yet Kris's obsession with acting did not fade. She continued to study drama and dance, and pressured her husband into abandoning music for movies.

Kris understood that Rick's resuming acting would give her greater entrée and that so long as he remained a singer, she would always be excluded from his work. Her motives weren't wholly selfish; indeed, Kris's ambitions for Rick probably exceeded his.

"Rick could never do enough about his career to suit Kris," said Charley Britt. "Once they got married, she became really critical of the way he handled things. He wasn't enough of a go-getter." Kris apparently believed Rick would find greater success as an actor, although infrequent casting calls did not support such optimism.

Rick, coming into his own musically, wouldn't go along with his wife's program. Didn't she understand? He hadn't merely portrayed a musician on television all those years, he *was* a musician. His failure to cooperate set off Kris's fuse. Allen Kemp recalled:

"Every time we'd get ready to go on the road, she'd cause problems to make Rick feel like he shouldn't be going." Kemp, who quit the New Riders of the Purple Sage after nine years to be with his family, added, "It's always stressful to tour when you've got kids, but Kris made it doubly hard for him."

According to Rick, his marriage unofficially ended the week "Garden Party" went Top Ten, ensuring him at least a while longer in the music business. For years Kris forbade him to bring his guitar into the house; to her it symbolized everything wrong with their life. One night she flew into an incendiary rage after discovering Rick's mistress lying on their bed. It wasn't another woman but his six-string acoustic, the one with *Rick Nelson* emblazoned across its white leather face.

Kris's incessant meddling drove Willy Nelson to step down as his cousin's manager in 1976. "It became a strain," he explained. "What Rick and I discussed was between us, and Kris would get upset when I didn't tell her things about the business. "I'd say, 'Your husband has to tell you.' It came down to a choice between career and family, and family was too important to me and to Rick. I honestly think Kris felt she should be managing Rick, controlling him, which was never going to happen."

Jack Brumley, Tom's younger brother and Rick's booking agent of four years, took over as manager. The band always welcomed concert dates close to home, so when a Palm Springs, California, promoter named Greg McDonald wanted to present Rick there, Brumley drove down to meet him. The stocky twenty-seven-year-old self-made millionaire had been peripherally involved in the music industry since he was a teenager, assisting Elvis Presley's manager, "Colonel" Tom Parker, to whom he was something of an adopted son.

Though the proposed show never came off, Brumley recruited McDonald as comanager, figuring that any connection to the Presley organization certainly couldn't hurt. In October 1976 McDonald, by then the sole manager, landed Rick a new recording contract with Epic Records.

Because of McDonald's close relationship with Tom Parker, shortly after Elvis Presley's death on August 16, 1977, reports circulated that the sixty-eight-year-old Dutchman would now mastermind Rick's career. Although the two never formally discussed working together, "The Colonel," deeply fond of Rick, came to function as a casual adviser, as he had for Ozzie years earlier. When in Palm Springs Rick frequently dropped in at the Parker home, even if it meant having to sample his host's godawful fishhead stew at backyard cookouts.

Afterward, as Rick desperately sought shade, Parker lounged in the baking sun and pontificated show-business theory. "There weren't too many people in the music industry whose opinions Rick respected," said McDonald, "but he went to 'The Colonel' about all sorts of things, even personal matters, and could really talk openly with him."

McDonald's first day on the job, he met with Rick's business manager from the trusted firm Jess S. Morgan and Co., the Nelson family's longtime representatives. After offering his congratulations, Wally Franson announced, "Now for the bad news: Your client is practically broke."

McDonald couldn't believe his ears, naturally assuming Rick never had to work another day in his life. For the next five hours Franson outlined how years of overspending had eroded Rick's wealth.

At twenty-three Rick had an estimated $1 million in the bank after taxes, seemingly enough to ensure permanent financial security. However, over the next decade, Rick saw his major sources of income evaporate: He made no movies after 1965, the family's ABC contract expired in 1969, and, unbelievably, his music career consistently lost money.

From 1969 to 1976 Rick toured only intermittently. As a result, his annual gross of approximately $175,000 put him $50,000 to $75,000 in the red after he paid the Stone Canyon

Band's salaries, management and booking-agency commissions, travel expenses, and so on. And although Rick pocketed an average of $50,000 a year[1] from Decca (later MCA) he saw no record royalties—not even from "Garden Party"—because he hadn't generated enough total sales for the label to recoup its $1 million advance. In fact, when Rick and MCA split in 1975, the company had earned back only about half that.

McDonald shook his head as Franson went on. As Rick's net worth plunged, the family made no adjustments in its extravagant life-style: ski weekends in Aspen and Sun Valley, lavish parties, private schools and horses for the kids, maids, nannies, and birthday presents of Mercedes-Benzes and Porsches.

In 1973 they'd moved from Zorada Drive to "The Farm," a barnlike, yellow-and-white three-story house Kris discovered on a hilly, densely wooded acre in Studio City. As always, she decorated its fourteen rooms exquisitely, and expensively, in an Early American motif. The kitchen, featuring a reconditioned 1920s stove and oven and a parquet dining table custom made from an old London ballroom dance floor, cost over $70,000 in renovations alone.

"Kris had no concept of two and two equaling four," said Bill Hoyt, a successor to Wally Franson. "If she wanted something that cost a thousand dollars, she'd buy it, even if she had only ten. One time I sent Kris out to get her car fixed. I wrote on the check, 'Not to exceed twenty-five dollars,' and signed it. She came home with *a new car.*"

It's unfair to blame Kris alone. Why didn't Rick put a stop to his wife's spendthrift ways? And why didn't he grasp the gravity of his economic situation in the first place? Here again we see how Ozzie's shielding young Rick from everyday responsibilities later boomeranged.

Because Rick depended on Kris to run the household and in general to help him "keep everything together," as he used to say, in his eyes she became an authority figure like Ozzie. And Rick responded passively to most authority figures. He

[1] With his customary prudence, Ozzie anticipated falling record sales and had wisely structured the 1963 deal so that Rick's yearly advances increased.

could confront Kris about her chronic acquisitiveness only through music. "Something You Can't Buy," a song on his 1977 album *Intakes*, contains the scathing lines *You get everything you see, then you wonder why/What you got you don't need, and you can't be satisfied.*

"Boy, this is really gonna piss Kris off," he cracked while recording it.

As for why he didn't realize his cash flow had slowed to a trickle, Rick's grasp of finances was on par with the average banker's knowledge of chord progressions.

Psychologically Rick was a perpetual adolescent on a weekly allowance, doled out either by his parents or by accountants. If he wanted a new car, for example, he simply contacted his business manager, who arranged payment with the dealership. He didn't write a check until he was in his early forties, and did so with such infrequency that he had to go over each one painstakingly to make sure he'd filled it out correctly. Another foreign concept, credit cards, also gave Rick fits.

One time while out on tour, Greg McDonald handed him the night's receipts, several thousand dollars. Rick flipped through the wad of bills in astonishment.

"You know something?" he said. "I've made millions of dollars, but I've never actually *seen* more than two or three hundred at a time."

The sky was darkening outside Wally Franson's Wilshire Boulevard office when he finally finished painting Rick's bleak financial picture for McDonald, who kept running a hand through his hair. "You've got to find dates within two weeks and create income for Rick," the business manager said firmly. "We're running out of money."

The starting pistol had been fired, and the endless, nerve-racking race to keep Rick ahead of mounting bills and fast-gaining creditors was on. Ironically, money—which he'd gladly never concerned himself with before—would now become a constant worry.

197

Twelve

To make money and to escape friction at home, Rick took to the road. That is where he mainly spent the rest of his life. He was in Monroe, Louisiana, in October 1977 when Kris notified him she'd filed for divorce. Having spoken to her husband the night before, she knew precisely what time he'd be leaving for the local fairgrounds, where a young director named Taylor Hackford was filming a TV documentary about Rick. Kris deliberately picked that moment to call his hotel room.

"I was already in the limousine waiting for him," recalled Greg McDonald. "Rick got in, completely devastated, of course, really upset and hurt. And then he had to go do a television special." Minutes after learning his marriage of fourteen years had apparently crumbled, Rick sat in his dressing room, calmly answering interview questions and preparing to perform before thousands of fans. Unaware of what had transpired, the Stone Canyon Band wondered why he'd suddenly added "Something You Can't Buy" to the set and why he sang it with uncharacteristic venom.

Marital and financial problems notwithstanding, Rick toured simply because it fulfilled him like nothing else. "He loved it," said former band member Stephen Love. "I remember Rick telling me, 'That's what I know how to do best.' Entertaining was his life's calling, he felt, and a good one."

It wasn't just the hour on stage. With the exception of early wake-up calls, Rick relished all aspects of road life. The traveling. The companionship. The *room service.* Some might consider it a sad commentary on his values, but the truth is that Rick felt most at home on tour and more comfortable fulfilling obligations to nameless fans than to his own family. Two weeks of off-time back in Los Angeles, and he was antsy to start singing again.

"Rick would call and ask, 'What've we got booked? I'm tired of sitting around in my robe,'" said Greg McDonald. Rick rarely got dressed the entire time he was home. "Once we hit the airport, though, you could see the new Rick. He picked up his step and didn't slow down until he got back. He was happy, up, and laughing."

Embarking on a tour is like entering a bizarre dimension where the rules governing civilized society are suspended. Days blur into one another. Everything, in fact, seems the same, from hotel restaurants' ersatz nautical decor, to framed frozen New England landscapes adorning sterile hotel-room walls. After a while the veteran campaigner awakens remembering neither the town he's in nor the name of his bed partner, and what's more, doesn't care. For a man-child like Rick, continually rebelling against the constraints of adulthood, it was the ideal environment.

The day began with trying to rouse Rick, a formidable challenge for road managers because, like Ozzie, he rarely went to sleep before dawn. Richard Schnyder, during his three years with the band, occasionally resorted to ice-water "alarm clocks"; Greg McDonald literally dragged Rick out of bed by his ankles. Then the grumpy entourage checked out of their hotel after breakfast and hurried to the airport.

Rick remained one of the country's most recognizable celebrities. While he waited for his flight, fans casually approached him. Not as a star but an honorary family member. A waitress pouring his morning coffee would nonchalantly inquire, "Hi, Rick, how're you doing?"

"Fine."

"How's your Mom?"

"Fine."

"And brother Dave; is Dave all right?

"Oh yeah, he's fine too."

Rick treated all fans courteously and graciously, Ozzie having impressed upon him at a young age that signing autographs, posing for pictures, and such were an entertainer's duty. People walked away from Rick satisfied they'd met the person they presumed to know from television.

Dave Morgan, band pianist in the early 1980s, recalled, "Rick often had to be rescued from autograph seekers because he couldn't sign for one person and then tell the next person in line, 'I'm sorry.' He didn't know how to be rude. Sometimes it was somebody's job to say, 'Rick, we've got to catch the plane. Sorry, folks, see you later.'" Even thirty thousand feet in the air, the parade of autograph seekers continued. "He'd never get to touch his food," said Dennis Larden. "The guy would shine on without something warm in his belly, just to talk to a couple of giggly girls."

As surely as Rick could be counted on to sing "Hello Mary Lou" in his show, whenever a group of admirers surrounded him, there was always one who'd say, "Rick, I'm going to ask you a question I'll bet you've never heard before—"

"Let me guess," he'd interrupt. "What did my father do for a living on the show?" It was about the only thing that could set Rick's eyes rolling.

Upon landing in the Next Town, Rick and the musicians

were whisked to the hotel, while the stage manager headed to the concert site to check out the sound and lighting systems. As Rick's schedule expanded to over one hundred shows in 1977, the size and quality of venues fluctuated. He still had enough of a following to get weekend bookings at state fairs, colleges, and theaters, some of them grand old halls that his parents had worked in the 1930s and 1940s. At Milwaukee's Riverside Theater, an elderly stage manager showed Rick a cracked and faded datebook recording the bills presented over the years. Rick carefully opened it to his birthday, and there, inked in next to May 8, 1940, was the name Ozzie Nelson.

With country rock dying and "Garden Party" nearly qualifying as a golden oldie, Rick was what the music industry calls a soft draw. So he had little choice but to take weeknight dates at stale bars and suburban supper clubs accustomed to smarmy polyester-jacketed lounge singers.

The first lesson itinerant musicians learn is to demand compensation up front and in cash. As Ozzie advises Rick in an old *The Adventures* episode: "When we had our band in college we always used to insist on getting paid before the dance started." ("Your band was pretty bad, huh?" the sixteen-year-old replies.) At some of the disreputable joints Rick played, he was lucky to see his money at all.

One Florida club owner declared flat out between sets, "I ain't paying ya," so Greg McDonald vaulted the bar and went from cash register to cash register, emptying the tills, as a pack of burly bouncers hustled toward him. Just as they were about to pounce, a band member came to his aid with an upraised bar stool and fended them off long enough for McDonald to race into the dressing room with the money.

Another time, in Joliet, Illinois, Rick's manager refused to let him go on until they had been paid in full, as contractually agreed. With a house of over two thousand simmering, the small-time hood in charge finally handed over the cash, growling at Rick, "You're never going to sing again. We're gonna *kill* you."

He wasn't bluffing. In a replay of the scene in which Ozzie

201

and Harriet are pursued along a dark country road, a couple of thugs tailed Rick and McDonald back to their hotel suite after the show.

"Where's McDonald!" Rick and his manager nervously peeked through a window at the two men pounding on the door, revolvers conspicuous in their waistbands. *"Open the door!"*

"We thought it was all over," McDonald remembered, "that these guys were going to kick down the door and shoot us both. Rick and I actually hid in the shower, shaking hands good-bye, saying, 'Well, this is it.' " As it turned out, the menacing pair did not draw their weapons. But come morning they were still lurking outside, dispersing only after police arrived to escort Rick's group to Chicago's Midway Airport and onto their plane.

These less-than-prestigious bookings provided writers ample opportunity to portray Rick as a despondent down-on-his-luck has-been. Down on his luck? True. A has-been? Perhaps, although as Rick often pointed out, "A career is a series of comebacks." But despondent? Never.

Naturally Rick preferred big fairs and quality showcase clubs to converted steakhouses and shabby bars. He especially enjoyed college dates, where he could reach young people unfamiliar with his past. But in every setting he was just happy to be making music, always radiating genuine pleasure on stage. Pat Upton, a member of the band from 1979 to 1982, said, "Rick played as hard for sixty people as he did for twelve thousand."

In cities across the country Rick still commanded loyal contingents of fans. "No matter where we went," recalled Dave Morgan, "we always recognized some of the people in the front row." Francine "Frenchy" Falik, last met here as a starstruck eleven-year-old in 1960, attended his Houston concerts year after year "for the memories." Others came to hear the current songs that constituted the bulk of the show as well as the oldies.

As in the old days, many of the women in the audience bought tickets as much to watch Rick as to hear him, something he considered when structuring the set. "We can't do anything 'serious' until the third song," he'd explain to the band, "because for the first two all they want to do is see what I look like." Judging from lusty female shouts of "Take your clothes off!" and the numbers of women congregated at the foot of the stage, hoping for a kiss, they found him as appealing as ever at age thirty-seven: outfitted in snug silver-belted black pants, a flowing black satin shirt, and snakeskin boots, his immaculate hair shorter than in the early 1970s, blown dry and combed back.

After the final encore Rick, soaked with perspiration, strode directly into a waiting limousine that whisked him back to the hotel. For many performers, the postshow period is the most difficult part of the day. Adrenaline still surges through their veins, making sleep several X-rated videos away, but what's there to do in Grant's Pass, Oregon, or Potsdam, New York, at 1:00 A.M.?

Reconciling the imbalance between pent-up energy and limited outlets requires a juvenile resourcefulness and mischievousness, traits few rock & rollers seem to lack. In pitch blackness Rick and the group might race rental cars through bumpy, weedy fields behind the hotel, trying to get them airborne.

"Everybody would be screaming at the top of his lungs, just going crazy," remembered Steve Duncan, Stone Canyon Band drummer in 1976 and 1977. "One time in Cicero, Illinois, the car went so high in the air that when it hit the ground, all the fan belts popped off and it died in the parking lot. We called the rental company. 'Something happened to the car . . . No, I don't know what.'

"A tow truck took that sucker away and brought us another."

Most nights, Rick retired to his hotel suite, savoring the lazy early-morning hours like a child permitted to stay up past his bedtime. "I'm a master of doing nothing," he liked to say, perfectly content just to joke and watch television with the band.

Occasionally they caught a rerun of *The Adventures of Ozzie and Harriet.* Everyone would crowd around the set but Rick, who'd sit back and observe his buzz-cut younger self onscreen with amused detachment. All the while he'd supply a running commentary that kept the group in stitches.

Rick regarded his entourage almost as a surrogate family, perhaps to compensate for the one slipping away from him at home. "He never acted like the superstar he was," said Eddie Tuduri, Steve Duncan's predecessor on drums. "He was one of the guys. I've toured with a lot of different bands, and usually you're treated like a sideman. But I always felt I was working *with* Rick, not for him. It was the most pleasurable time I've ever had anywhere."

Certainly membership in the Stone Canyon Band had its privileges, not the least of which was the persistent groupies who roved hotel lobbies and dressing rooms. "There were always lots of elegant, fine-looking women around," recalled Ty Grimes. "At one show in Atlanta I looked out the backstage door and said to Rick, 'We're going to have to get more guys in the band to handle all these girls; there's not enough of us to go around!'"

Recreational sex is as much a part of touring as boredom and lost luggage, considered by many musicians rightful recompense for the life's many drawbacks. It is a male adolescent's ultimate fantasy fulfilled, where women become the predators and men the prey. Brazen female fans repeatedly snuck naked into Rick's hotel room, disrobed in elevators, slipped keys under his door, or simply led him off by the hand.

A stewardess once escorted him downstairs to the cramped galley of a Boeing 747. While engaged in the act, Rick suddenly felt the heat of passion quite painfully when he accidentally backed into a hot oven, searing a bright red stripe across his bare buttocks. "My racing stripe," he kiddingly called it.

As tour's end approached and the scorch mark hadn't faded, though, Rick began to worry. His marriage had been sexless for some time, but how would he explain the mark to Kris? Rick's predicament became a topic of discussion among the band for days. "Maybe you can paint it," one musician suggested. "How good are you with makeup?" another asked.

204

"Boy," Rick concluded wryly, "this is really *my ass.*"

Rick had a voracious carnal appetite and a casual attitude toward sex. "Getting laid is like a good sneeze," he often said. Like music, it freed him of inhibitions. An entourage member recalls lying in bed one night at Chicago's Hyatt Regency Hotel and hearing a commotion from the adjacent balcony.

Peeking outside, he saw Rick, stark naked, with a stunning nude woman on his shoulders. Despite subfreezing temperatures, both were laughing hysterically as Rick enacted the part of Luke Skywalker from the recent movie *Star Wars,* vanquishing imaginary aliens with a makeshift light saber—actually a futuristic fluorescent lighting fixture from his room.

Rick, not prone to exaggeration, once estimated he'd bedded literally thousands of women. Yet he frowned on the macho, misogynistic behavior typically exhibited backstage. "Rick used to call it the 'big-man routine,'" said a friend. "If anybody ever got too self-important or into that rock-star syndrome of '*Hey, baby,*' he had a way of putting them in their place.

"Rick was nice to people, groupies included. He'd pass on absolute beauty queens who seemed to know it and go out with their so-so-looking girlfriends instead. This sounds terrible, but he'd say, 'You know, some of those girls that aren't real pretty are so . . . appreciative.' He was almost looking for acceptance, not just to bang 'em and leave."

As for the common postshow ritual in which roadies gather a selection of willing women that the star then reviews, "Rick thought that was embarrassing and pretentious. If anything, he did his best to get the bachelors in the band laid.

"Although," the friend hastened to add, "Rick wasn't a total philanthropist."

Up to a dozen women would pour into Rick's suite for a promised "party" that differed little from the usual late-night routine of smalltalk, TV, and guitar picking. Gradually couples paired up and drifted out, leaving Rick with his evening's companion or alone, eagerly awaiting sunrise before finally retiring.

Then: *Ring!* Kris, well aware of her estranged husband's

habits, called virtually every night, hoping to forestall Rick's affairs by keeping him on the line—sometimes for as long as three hours. But her efforts were to no avail. "The girls would wait," said Greg McDonald, "and Rick knew it. He was undaunted by this stuff. If they left, that was okay, and if they didn't, that was okay too. He'd just play along.

"Kris couldn't beat him. She couldn't out-wait him, because Rick had *patience*. She never won that game. She probably thinks she did over the years, but she never, ever won that game."

Band members and friends contend that Kris was no model of fidelity herself. Her liaisons are alleged to have included Rick's arranger and producer John Boylan, a Los Angeles Lakers basketball star, a Hall of Fame NFL quarterback, a popular crooner, an ex-Beatle, and a seventeen-year-old Ron Reagan, Jr.

The future First Son met the thirty-year-old mother of four on the ski slopes. With his parents away for the weekend, Ron invited her to the Reagan home for an intimate candlelit dinner. The two wound up in Ronald and Nancy Reagan's bed, where a team of secret-service agents discovered them after Kris accidentally pressed an alarm button.

Ronald Reagan, about to declare his candidacy for the 1976 Republican presidential nomination, was secretly relieved to learn of his son's first sexual affair, having suspected him of being gay. Wife Nancy, however, exploded and is said to have warned Harriet Nelson to keep her lecherous daughter-in-law away from young Ronnie.

Only a few hours after Rick's head hit the pillow, the cycle began all over again: check-out, airport, travel, check-in, gig, back to the hotel, with unforeseen catastrophes inserted wherever least convenient. Each day of a tour seems more arduous than the last, culminating in a general physical and mental collapse. Musicians casually refer to this condition as road burnout, the symptoms of which would constitute grounds for institutionalization in other walks of life.

Rick, who slept less than anyone, believed he could hypnotize himself back to full vitality. "He was a master at it," said Dennis Larden. "He'd duck into the bathroom on a plane, touch up his mind, and come out and be that nice guy, shaking hands and smiling even though he was so tired that his face was cracking and his teeth were throbbing like the rest of us." Rick called this technique his "Eleanor Roosevelt," based on a childhood image of the First Lady riding in a tickertape parade, mechanically waving and smiling, smiling and waving . . .

Rick returned from a weeklong tour promoting his new *Intakes* album to find he no longer lived at The Farm. Kris picked him up at the airport and silently drove him to an unfamiliar address off Mulholland Drive. "What's this?" asked Rick. "You live here now," she informed him, having taken the liberty of renting a house and moving his belongings there in his absence.

If Kris's motive was to punish Rick, she'd picked the wrong house, a sunny bungalow overlooking the San Fernando Valley, with windows on all sides and a glass-enclosed Jacuzzi in the middle. Rick hadn't been there a month when his estranged wife caught him frolicking in the foaming water with two Los Angeles Rams cheerleaders he'd met on a TV-movie set. After observing the *ménage à trois* through a window, Kris stormed inside, smacking the naked women and screaming for them to get out, while Rick hid in a closet. He always believed she'd set him up, hoping to catch him in an incriminating act that could then be used against him in court.

Not only was Rick's private life in disarray, but the Stone Canyon Band as well. Still a solid unit on stage, it had become a liability in the studio. While recording *Intakes*, original producer Keith Olsen pulled Rick out into a hallway and told him bluntly, "Your lead guitarist can't play." Olsen, who'd recently produced the four-million-seller *Fleetwood Mac*, insisted a studio pro be brought in to overdub solos, a standard practice. But Rick, blindly loyal to his musicians, wouldn't hear of it and finished the album himself.

Two years earlier producer Jerry Fuller had the same complaint during Rick's final recordings for MCA. "It was more like the *Stoned* Canyon Band," he said. "I couldn't stand them, except for Tom Brumley, who of course is an excellent steel-guitar player. He'd come over to me and ask, 'You're not going to use that take, are you?' How could I? The guitar playing wasn't making it; the guy couldn't keep in tune. Tom would cringe like me, but everyone else was oblivious."

By late 1977 intraband dissension was brewing over several issues: the quantity and quality of dates, but mainly the addition of oldies to the live show. Greg McDonald had made this suggestion after a somnolent performance at an Illinois supper club. While Rick and Dennis Larden perched on stools, strumming acoustic guitars and singing Bob Dylan songs, he refunded disappointed customers their money.

Back at the hotel, McDonald facetiously called his client a crook.

"What do you mean, a crook?" Rick asked, folding his arms and clenching his jaw, the posture he adopted at his height of anger.

"People are coming to see Rick Nelson, and they're getting Bob Dylan," McDonald said. A "Hello Mary Lou"/"Lonesome Town" medley and a finale of "Believe What You Say" were the set's meagre concessions to Rick's past. Dennis Larden, who today writes music and screenplays under his legal surname Sarokin, overheard the conversation. He piped up, "If you think I'm going to sing *'I was a fool, oh yeah'* "—mimicking the famous Jordanaires backing vocals—"you're crazy."

John Beland, Larden's eventual replacement on lead guitar, observed, "For years Rick was surrounded by musicians and producers who downplayed his role in rock & roll, whereas I was a big fan of his. At one of my first rehearsals, I said, 'Hey, Rick, let's play "It's Up to You," ' and he rolled his eyes, like he was embarrassed." Kris too used to tell her husband, "Don't play those old songs, they date you," until Rick, plagued by self-doubt, came to believe it.

To prove McDonald wrong, the next day Rick hastily taught

the group "Poor Little Fool" and three other old songs for its evening show at the same supper club. "Naturally they brought down the house," said his manager. "You didn't have to be a rocket scientist to know that if Rick Nelson played his hits, audiences would go nuts. But it really surprised the hell out of him. As soon as we got back to Los Angeles, Rick modified the act and immediately started getting more dates."

The band was unhappy, seeing the change as a raised white flag, an admission that the Stone Canyon Band had lost its commercial viability.

Which, in fact, was the grim reality, made painfully evident by *Intakes*' abysmal reception and failure to kindle rock radio's interest. Compared to the harder-edged pop acts glutting station playlists in 1977—Boston, Heart, Fleetwood Mac, Foreigner— Rick sounded tepid. Even Randy Meisner's group, the Eagles, country rock's most successful proponents, had played down the country and amplified the rock on that year's multiplatinum *Hotel California*. And Rick's laid-back country rhythms paled alongside disco music's tyrannical urban *thump-thump-thump-thump*, then vibrating dance floors nationwide. Ironically, after eight years the Stone Canyon Band had become as archaic as the 1950s songs they objected to playing.

Things came to a head during a showcase performance of *Intakes* for Epic Records' West Coast staff at the Roxy Theater in Los Angeles. As a treat, Rick digressed into a block of old favorites, which of course were ecstatically received. Larden, however, rolled his eyes and mugged comically throughout. When Rick found out afterward, he angrily dismissed Larden and White, bandmates of nearly five years. In the heat of the moment he also let go Steve Duncan, one of country music's finest time-keepers. It was a move Rick quickly regretted.

Only Tom Brumley, promised a job for life, remained. But a year later he too was gone, worn out by the road. "When I joined the band, we agreed never to be away more than ninety days a year," he explained. "My last year with Rick, we worked twice that, and I just got ulcers over it. Plus, I wanted to get my kids out of L.A. and raise them in Texas." Indicative of Rick's desire to move away from country rock, pianist Bobby Craig replaced the steel guitarist, who had been with Rick for more than nine years. After a decade of relative stability, the Stone Canyon Band was to become a revolving door for musicians.

The Roxy engagement turned out to be the highpoint of Rick's relationship with Epic Records. The label shelved his next two LPs; odd when you consider that its executives had dictated the musical direction of each. The first, recorded in spring 1978, was helmed by Al Kooper, a solo artist as well as a producer, and ex-leader of the influential 1960s groups the Blues Project and Blood, Sweat and Tears.

Kooper, deciding this album should depart from Rick's country-rock sound, assembled an unlikely group of musicians: New Orleans pianist Dr. John, the Doobie Brothers' Jeff "Skunk" Baxter and Michael McDonald, and members of Rod Stewart's backing band. Rick had little input and found himself a virtual spectator on his own record. John Beland, one of the few band members to participate, called it "a three-ring circus, with Al Kooper as ringmaster." Epic rejected the LP, titled *Back to Vienna*, for bearing too much of its producer's imprint.

The company then suggested Rick return to his rockabilly roots and, furthermore, that he go directly to its source, Memphis, to record. Rick had long been disenchanted with modern studio techniques, which for him stole the excitement and rendered record making clinical. He also missed the immediacy of recording two decades earlier, when he could cut a side in a few hours and see it in the stores just days later.

Rick never had more fun than recording in winter 1978–79 at Memphis's Lyn-Lou Studio, a converted grocery store that reminded him of the old Master Recorders. This was the first time Rick recorded outside Los Angeles. Free of personal distractions, he fell back into the schedule he'd kept as a teenager: working from night to morning, fueling himself with cheeseburgers and handfuls of M&Ms.

210

After sessions, before sunrise, he, Greg McDonald, and John Beland drove around Memphis. Naturally Rick had to stop and pay his respects at 706 Union Street, where the Sun Studio stood empty. (It reopened in 1987.) "I remember hanging out front in the middle of a snowstorm at three A.M.," said Beland, a former sideman to Linda Ronstadt and Dolly Parton. "We sat talking about what it must have been like in the old days and how many hits came out of that little building.

"Then we drove over to Graceland and hung out in front of that for a little while." Only Elvis Presley's still-grieving father Vernon and paternal grandmother Minnie Mae now lived in the two-story house at 3764 Elvis Presley Boulevard. Rick had last seen his friend two years before at the Las Vegas Hilton.

The sight of a bloated Elvis slurring his words and lumbering about the stage in a spangled, studded jumpsuit had been too painful to watch. "He doesn't like this," Rick observed over the music. "He's not having fun up there. He's doing a parody of himself, and it's really scary." Normally Rick would have visited backstage, but he felt too embarrassed for Presley and wasn't sure he could keep a straight face looking at the gaudy costume.

Like many people, Rick preferred remembering Elvis in his prime: sleek as a panther, eyes burning, sex personified. *That* Elvis pervaded the studio while Rick recorded at Lyn-Lou. One late night he started picking "That's Alright Mama," just fooling around. Guitarist Beland and the other players, handpicked by producer Larry Rogers, joined in.

The track wound up opening the LP, *Memphis Sessions*. One of Rick's best, it includes crisp, lean rock & roll (Buddy Holly's "Rave On," John Fogerty's "Almost Saturday Night") and intimate pop balladry ("Send Me Somebody to Love," "Sleep Tight, Good Night Man"). Rick, more satisfied with this record than any he'd made in years, felt as if he'd rediscovered himself musically. "It was a very intimate album," said Beland. "Rick really had an artistic high doing it."

As soon as the sessions ended in February 1979, Rick flew to New York to host *Saturday Night Live,* then at its peak of popularity. Appropriately, instead of the customary opening monologue, Rick let his music speak for him, though his few introductory lines brimmed with humorous irony:

"This is probably the first time most of you have ever seen me in color, I guess, huh?" he deadpanned. "But if you feel it's not the same as it was, and you'd rather have the old black-and-white Ricky, then turn the color control down on your TV a little bit, and maybe it'll be just like the old times."

With that, drummer Billy Thomas rapped out the clip-clopping intro to "Hello Mary Lou," followed by "Travelin' Man" and "Fools Rush In." Of the sketches Rick appeared in, the highlight was a *Twilight Zone* parody. The cast and writers wanted to satirize *The Adventures of Ozzie and Harriet,* but out of respect for his mother and late father, Rick wouldn't allow them to be spoofed. He was adamant about it to the point of threatening to walk off the show.

Dan Aykroyd then brainstormed the idea of stranding Rick in a black-and-white domestic-sitcom purgatory, unable to find his way home. He mistakenly enters the kitchen of one famous 1950s TV family after another: the Cleavers of *Leave It to Beaver,* the Andersons of *Father Knows Best,* the Williamses of *Make Room for Daddy,* and the Ricardos of *I Love Lucy,* each time calling out the familiar "Hi, Mom, I'm home!"

Aykroyd and John Belushi, the manic, creative heart of the original Not Ready for Prime Time Players, were thrilled to have Rick on the show. Over a late-night Japanese dinner, following an exhausting weekday rehearsal, Belushi lobbied Rick to let him produce his next album. "We'll sing together, man," the comic enthused, waving his chopsticks in the air.

"We'll get Duck Dunn, Steve Cropper, Steve Jordan, to play on it . . ." He gobbled a bite. ". . . be fuckin' incredible." As their alter egos the Blues Brothers, Jake and Elwood, Belushi and Aykroyd currently claimed the country's number-one album, *Briefcase Full of Blues.* Depending on your perspective, it was either an affectionate tribute to or a grotesque travesty of blues and soul-music standards.

212

Rick, while appreciating Belushi's good intentions, was not about to entrust himself to a novice of dubious musical talent. Typical of his penchant for putting people on, however, he replied sincerely, "Well, why don't you fly back to California and stay with Greg here"—he pointed to his manager, who practically gagged on his sushi—"and I'll meet you there to discuss it."

A harried McDonald spent the next week rescuing Belushi from fistfights with Palm Springs maître d's and carrying him half comatose out of local clubs. "Every day," he remembered, "I'd be on the phone to Rick, pleading, 'When are you coming down here for that meeting?' and he'd just laugh." Following a night during which Belushi raced around his house acting out scenes from the movie he was writing, *The Blues Brothers*, McDonald tactfully suggested the comedian might be more comfortable in a nearby hotel. The creative pow-wow between Belushi and Rick, of course, never took place.

Doubling as musical guest on *Saturday Night Live*, Rick performed a fourth song, his sensuous treatment of the late Bobby Darin's "Dream Lover," arranged in the same understated style as James Taylor's and Art Garfunkel's recent soft-rock covers "Handy Man" and "(What a) Wonderful World." It was to be his new single, and Rick and the band felt confident they had a smash on their hands.

"The two weeks after playing *Saturday Night Live* were like Ricky Nelson back in the fifties," remembered John Beland, "with kids screaming for him and ripping his clothes. It seemed like we were right on the comeback."

But Epic held up "Dream Lover"'s release for several weeks to overdub a *conga drum*, thus failing to capitalize on Rick's *SNL* appearance, one of the most popular in the show's history. The 45 made only *Billboard*'s Hot Country Singles chart, in April. Then the label—which had recommended Rick go back to basics in the first place—junked the Memphis album, pronouncing it unsuitable for a pop marketplace then dominated by new-wave acts.

In 1986, after Rick's death, Epic finally issued the LP as *Memphis Sessions*. Original instrumentation was wiped out, and with it, John Beland and Larry Rogers feel, the gritty rockabilly sound Rick had intended. "They totally bastardized it," said the guitarist. "I thought it was a real slap in the face to Rick's memory." Rogers, replaced by Nashville producer Steve Buckingham, added, "Rick would have had a fit. He didn't like anybody messing with what he was doing."

Epic had previously tampered with the same tracks. In 1981, two years after Rick left the company for Capitol Records, it put out four of the songs as an EP titled *Four You,* overdubbing applause onto "Rave On" so that it sounded like it had been taped live. "They even added on the liner notes that it was recorded during a hot, sultry Memphis night," Beland said with disgust. "We recorded it in January during a *blizzard.*"

According to Greg McDonald, Rick bristled with anger when he heard *Four You* and learned that Buckingham had been given production credit over Rogers, one of the few producers he'd enjoyed working with. "That was the maddest I'd ever seen him, over the fact that someone had the balls to ruin what he thought was a good record."

"When I was with Epic Records," Rick later reflected, "everybody there had different ideas what I should be doing. I was trying to listen to them all, and it wasn't a workable situation." The chorus to "Call It What You Want," a song from his 1981 Capitol album *Playing to Win,* was obviously directed at the label. *Call it what you want, it's all right,* Rick sings bitterly, *it's rock & roll to me.*

While still under contract to Epic, in 1978, Rick had reconciled with Kris and moved back to The Farm. Not for long. The next year they sold the Studio City home and purchased a sprawling Connecticut-style farmhouse at 3100 Torreyson Place. Decades before it had been more infamously known as Mulholland House, the pleasure palace of original occupant Errol Flynn.

The Tasmanian-born movie actor designed and built the two-story estate for $125,000 in 1938, the year he starred in *The Adventures of Robin Hood*. Nestled on three forested acres above Mulholland Drive, it was graced by a stone-edged black-bottom swimming pool, a tennis court, four fireplaces, and five bedrooms, as well as several unusual features for facilitating Flynn's sexual fetishes.

An enthusiastic voyeur, he bugged the women's powder room so that he and his male cronies could eavesdrop on female conversations. Flynn also installed a one-way mirror in the spacious first-floor master bedroom. During parties, he, David Niven, John Barrymore, and other Hollywood pals snuck upstairs for poker, pausing between hands to peek through the mirror, located under the table, and observe the activities below. For the same purpose, Flynn drilled a peephole into the ceiling of the pine-paneled den.

Rick secretly fancied himself a dashing swashbuckler like Flynn and loved 3100 Torreyson, saying it gave him a special feeling. Harriet later told him that Ozzie used to play tennis there and had also dreamed of owning it someday. Against the advice of business manager Bill Hoyt, Rick paid $750,000 for the house.

He and Kris resumed their reckless spending. During 1978, 1979, and 1980, the couple's living expenses averaged approximately $300,000 annually, including such sums as $4,080 for flowers, $12,000 for psychiatrists, $30,000 for a maid (in 1980 alone they hired seventeen housekeeping employees), and $24,000 in miscellaneous cash payments to Kris.

When she and Rick bought the Flynn house, Hoyt allocated Kris $10,000, not a penny more, for refurbishing. But she spent nearly ten times that amount, filling the home with Victorian furniture, antiques, and contemporary artwork. "Everything had to be the best," said Hoyt, offering an example: "You know how you go to a paint store, pick a color, and buy the paint? Kris had to hire a guy for thirty dollars an hour just to *mix* the paint. Nothing could be standard."

Interestingly, Kris had hired Hoyt to investigate and indict

Greg McDonald, whom she accused of cheating Rick and causing their dire financial straits. "She considered Greg McDonald the thing that came between her and her husband, and wanted him out of the way," said the CPA. "Kris was trying to gather data to give over to the district attorney."

Hoyt reviewed Rick's business records and found no improprieties. McDonald's commission, 15 percent of the gross, was standard for the industry. "Greg wasn't cheating," said Hoyt, "he was very honest. He wasn't the greatest record-keeper, perhaps, but when you're on the road all the time, you don't run around with file cabinets. You're in hotels with a guy [Rick] who doesn't care about money. Greg did the best he could under the circumstances."

Hoyt's cordial relationship with Kris quickly cooled "once she saw I was one of 'them,' one of the boys; when I didn't turn out to be an ally. Instead I turned out to be another guy telling her to stop using her credit cards. I put Kris on a two-hundred-dollar-a-week budget for food." Did she abide by it? "No," said Hoyt. "It was cash, so she started overdrawing the account." The couple dug themselves deeper into debt, eventually overdrawing their personal bank account by $30,000.

Just as Rick's and Kris's monetary problems persisted, so did their irreconcilable differences over his career. If anything, they worsened, due to Rick's heavy workload. Until the mid-1970s he'd never played more than three dozen days a year, his musicians dubbing themselves "the Weekend Warriors." Now Rick traveled eight months out of twelve. Kris certainly wasn't being unreasonable in wanting him home more. But, in a textbook catch-22, her spending, coupled with Rick's indifference, forced him into playing 250 dates annually just to stay solvent.

Maintaining their extravagant life-style was desperately important to Kris, who turned thirty-five in 1980. In addition to her successful siblings, friends such as Mia Farrow and Tisha Sterling were well into glamourous careers. Because Hollywood rarely recognizes motherhood as an achievement in itself, one level on which she could compete was by owning the fabulous house, throwing the fabulous party, living the fabulous life. Rick understood her needs, confiding to friends, "In my heart of hearts, I know that if I don't keep it up at home," meaning supporting his family in the manner to which it was accustomed, "I'll probably lose my wife and kids."

The reunited couple quarreled more than ever. "It was pretty crazy," said John Beland. "Rick would call me up at one o'clock in the morning. 'Uh, hey, John?' I could tell from his voice that something was wrong. He'd start humming the theme from *Jaws*—*dum-dum, dum-dum, dum-dum, dum-dum*—and I'd say, 'I'll be right over.' We'd spend all night together in the music room, because Kris would have the door to the bedroom closed."

Kris occasionally accompanied Rick on the road, but no matter how much a wife ingratiates herself with the band and joins in on hotel horseplay, amid the male fraternity of rock & roll she's bound to feel like excess baggage. Kris would then create embarrassing scenes to get Rick's attention.

"Rick was playing a huge Wang Computers convention at the Princess Hotel in Acapulco, Mexico," recalled Greg Mc-Donald, "a black-tie affair. Kris walked into the ballroom wearing nothing but a slip and a Wang Computers banner that she'd ripped down and wrapped around her. Rick, who was very conservative and careful in public, turned white as a sheet; he didn't know what to do.

"Kris knew that these crazy public displays would drive him nuts."

McDonald is no admirer of Kris's, a feeling that is undoubtedly mutual. "Rick dreaded Kris coming to shows," he continued, "like local dates at Knott's Berry Farm. She wouldn't tell us if she was coming or not, so that if she did show up and we didn't have the best seat in the house reserved for her, she could complain to Rick, 'They don't want me here, and if I'm not welcome, I'm leaving.' And she would leave just before the show.

"Rick knew her like a book and had already predicted this

scenario, which Kris would play out. It became an us-against-her thing, which was real divisive. Musicians—the whole music industry—were a waste of time for Kris. If it wasn't film, it was trash."

Under pressure from his wife, Rick played the part of a grandfather in a charming children's short for *The CBS Library* called "A Tale of Four Wishes." Road manager Alan Bush drove him to location in Ventura, California, each morning at four and helped Rick study his lines. "I probably knew them better than he did," Bush said with a laugh. "I could see that he didn't like acting."

On one of their predawn trips, Rick confided, "I can't believe Kris. She wants me to give up singing and get back into acting, or else she said she's going to leave me. But I can't give up my music," he said emphatically. "It's what I *do*. Acting is what I *did*. Music is *me*."

This time the impasse over his career permanently doomed Rick and Kris's marriage and made life at home wretched for both. Rick sought refuge on the road, which only exacerbated Kris's unhappiness. She started drinking, "quite heavily," she later admitted.

Things deteriorated to a point where Kris holed up at her Hollywood art studio for days at a time, leaving the children in the care of household help. And when Rick left for tours, she hurled his bags out the door, screaming, "Get the fuck out of here!"

Thirteen

n October 1980, three years after their first separation, Kris left Rick, this time for good. For a woman who'd never been independent before, it was a brave decision, and ultimately the right one for both of them. As miserable as they were together, Rick never would have taken that step himself, partly because drastic actions weren't his way, and partly because, having observed his parents' model forty-year marriage, he equated divorce with personal failure.

"I was with Rick in Cincinnati when he got the call," said his friend Paul Rose. "For twenty-four hours he wouldn't talk, he wouldn't move, he wouldn't shave. He was totally depressed." Typically, Rick expressed himself through song, composing the dirgelike "The Loser Babe Is You" for the album he was completing, *Playing to Win:*

I know you think I'm crazy,
Burned out and lazy,
Winning days are through.
Am I mistaken? Have you been takin' more than you can use?
By the way, the loser, babe, is you.

I hear you think I'm used,
Overworked and abused.
If what you say is true,
Why'd you do me? I thought you knew me,
I've never been your fool.
By the way, the loser, babe, is you.

The ensuing divorce ultimately made losers of the entire family. Kris's long-smoldering frustration burst into an inferno that raged out of control for more than two years, eventually consuming all of Rick's money. "If Kris couldn't have him," said Alan Bush, "she was going to take everything she could and make sure Rick spent everything he had on defense until he had nothing left."

David Nelson commented, "It was a long divorce that never should have happened. Kris somehow felt there was a pot of gold, which just wasn't there. The money had been spent long ago. Though not by Rick," he added, "because my brother lived on cheeseburgers and Cokes."

In January 1981 Kris's own attorney noted in a concise memorandum that Rick's assets were insufficient to warrant drawn-out proceedings, concluding, "The $1 million that Rick had tax-free in the bank approximately fifteen to eighteen years ago has been used up over the years to finance the negative touring expense and the negative living expense."

Furthermore, he found that Rick, sleeping in $50-a-night hotels, was hardly squandering money on the road. "There is not a judge in the world," Kris's counsel wrote, "who would order a performer of Nelson's stature to stay in a thirty-dollar room to save money." His memo essentially advised, *Settle now, while there's still something to be had.* That lawyer was soon replaced by "a bomber from New York," in David's words, who allegedly boasted he would leave Rick Nelson in the gutter. From a financial standpoint, he succeeded.

The sad case of *Nelson* v. *Nelson* can be neatly summed up like this. What Kris didn't get, attorneys and accountants did, siphoning over $1 million. Not only did Rick have to pay his own legal expenses but his ex-wife's as well, eliminating any incentive on her part to settle equitably. The costs were astronomical, one independent accounting firm alone charging $240,000 to assess Rick's rapidly plummeting net worth.

"These lawyers and accountants are getting money I earned when I was ten years old," complained Rick, though he still managed to maintain his sense of humor. Hit with yet another enormous bill, he'd comment dryly, "Well, there goes 'Travelin' Man' "; "Whoops, so much for 'Lonesome Town.' "

By June 1982 he was overdrawn at all his banks. Juggling creditors, Rick fell behind on some, including tuition for the boys' private schools. Had his manager not bailed him out on several occasions, both his sons would have been expelled. Fourteen-year-old Matthew did, however, once suffer the humiliation of being barred from a final exam at the exclusive Crespi School due to an outstanding bill.

"Those things ultimately got paid," said Gary Olsen, Rick's accountant, "but it wasn't real comfortable. That hurt Rick a great deal, to think people could think of him as not being a good father."

Rick's manager and business manager, meanwhile, hustled and scrounged for money, trying unsuccessfully to borrow against Rick's Screen Actors Guild retirement funds. Rick had already borrowed $50,000 from a bank and $50,000 from Harriet. Asking his mother for money was "the single toughest thing he ever had to do," said Greg McDonald.

McDonald continually approached affluent businessmen, often longtime fans of Rick, about investing in his client.

"Greg managed to come up with people all the time," said Bill Hoyt. "I'd just shake my head and ask, 'Where do you find them?' But they always came through and paid. There was always somebody that wanted a ride into show business, and Greg was willing to sell it to them."

One such benefactor, Dick Heckmann, had served as associate administrator of the Small Business Administration under President Jimmy Carter before moving to the securities firm Prudential-Bache as senior vice-president.

"I grew up listening to Rick Nelson songs," he said. "I remember singing 'Travelin' Man' when I was in the Air Force." Rick performed at an Idaho ski resort Heckmann owned, and the two subsequently became good friends. "I never expected such a big star to be such a nice, humble guy," he recalled.

Heckmann, admittedly stunned to learn of Rick's financial bind, offered assistance. "I financed a couple of concerts," he explained. "When Rick had bills that had to be paid immediately, I'd front the money and then get reimbursed from whatever the receipts were. I also helped him to refinance his house.

"Rick never came to me personally," he emphasized. "There were never any embarrassing or demeaning scenes: 'Hey, Dick, can you help me?' It was never like that. Greg did it all, which is the way I preferred it. And clearly it was the way Rick wanted it. Rick could not have survived without Greg," Heckmann added. "He saved Rick's bacon time after time after time."

Even these loans and favors couldn't offset Rick's mounting debt. Both McDonald and Hoyt eventually advised him to declare bankruptcy. Rick mulled it over back at the Torreyson house, where thirty years earlier Errol Flynn, $2 million in debt, had been forced to consider a similar plea from his attorney.

"Somehow," the actor wrote in his autobiography *My Wicked, Wicked Ways*, "the thought of what my father would think entered my mind. I said no." Out of pride and the belief that a bankruptcy proceeding would ruin his reputation and career, Rick too refused.

Through it all, Kris never truly left Rick's life; she had him served with papers right before going on stage or called his hotel room just before showtime to detain him. "It was like telepathy," said Alan Bush, responsible for escorting Rick to the venue. "I'd open the door to leave, and the phone would ring. 'Should we answer it?' 'No, we can't.' Sometimes we didn't. Once Kris got Rick on the phone, laying into him for something or other, she wouldn't let him get off."

Paul Rose added, "She would try to get Rick into court when he was on the road and interfere with the tours; do anything she could to cause him grief." Ironically, having to return to Los Angeles for court appearances or depositions only further prevented Rick from meeting his obligations. His attorney complained in a letter to Kris's counsel, "Mr. Nelson turned down a number of tour dates to be available for two aborted trial dates, causing him a substantial reduction in cash flow."

Depositions were "sheer torture, an affront to Rick," said Greg McDonald. "Rick was a very private guy, and Kris's lawyers would ask him highly personal questions and financial questions he didn't know the answers to, making him seem like a fool."

Why was Kris so seemingly bent on revenge? Alan Bush cites a perceptive observation of Harriet's. "She pointed out to me that deep down inside, Kris was really in love with Rick. Having attorneys fight him over one thing and another was a way of keeping in communication with him, even though it was such a bitter way of doing it."

Rick's outward response to Kris's actions was surprisingly mild. "Usually it was a resigned, 'Kris did this' or, 'Kris did that,'" said Bush. "The one time I heard him get really angry was when one of the lawsuits came in: 'Aw, shit, I don't believe that bitch.' For Rick to throw out a couple of cuss words was pretty amazing." Occasionally he'd deliver his ultimate insult, calling Kris "a waste of skin," then quietly correct himself. "Nah, I shouldn't say that."

Connie Nelson, who believes Kris has been unjustly vilified, said, "Though Rick and Kris could never like each other, they still had a great mutual admiration." Greg McDonald concurs. "Rick used to say about Kris, 'Boy, she sure has balls, doesn't she?' almost enamored of her. His favorite expression was, 'The girl's a criminal genius.' He had tremendous respect for her intelligence."

As happens in many divorces, the Nelsons' four children were trapped in the middle, used by one parent against the other. "Kris placed a lot of restrictions on the kids," said Bush. "If Rick got home from a tour one day after visiting day, too bad, he didn't get to see them. That definitely hurt him."

Risking groundings from their mother, the twins snuck up to the Torreyson house. And Tracy, by then living on her own, brought Sam there too whenever possible. Rick worried that Kris would accuse him of encouraging these unscheduled visits, thus jeopardizing his already limited visitation rights. "It was a crazy no-win situation for him," said Bush.

Rick regretted being away so much but felt no more guilt than his own parents had for leaving him in his grandmother's care when he was a baby. He justified his career by saying, "Some guys are electricians and work nine to five. This is what I do. I really wouldn't be happy being at home and not doing what I do, and I couldn't make them happy because I'd be unhappy." He knew it was an imperfect arrangement, "but this is the best it's going to be," he said.

Though Rick rarely shared family matters with the musicians, John Beland recalled, "He always talked about Sam a lot. He really loved his other kids, but he had a special fondness for Sam." Rick barely got to know the boy, placed in Tom and Elyse Harmon's custody when he was six because of Kris's alcohol abuse and unpredictable behavior; one of her psychiatrists warned the court she'd been suicidal at times. Upon turning seventeen, Tracy moved in with her father, as for a while did the thirteen-year-old twins, despite the original agreement that they live with their mother while Rick toured.

In a declaration to the court, Rick claimed that when the boys stayed with Kris in her rented Valley home, his housekeeper had to awaken at 5:00 A.M., drive over there, fix Gunnar and Matthew breakfast, and take them to and from school, "as Pe-

224

titioner [Kris] would not tend to these chores." Moreover, the children alleged that their mother pocketed money intended for their use only.

Tracy, who'd inherited Rick's blue eyes and Kris's blond hair, understood and suffered the most. She told *People* magazine in 1982 that her mother and father "were too young when they decided to have a family." Tracy also recounted a sad childhood memory of once dressing up as a mermaid every day for a week just to attract their attention.

Early in 1982 Kris appeared ready to settle, requesting a meeting with Rick, sans lawyers, at her place. Greg McDonald and Tom Harmon joined them. The divorce had been distressing for Kris's parents, who liked Rick a great deal and still maintained their close friendship with Harriet.

"Kris and her father decided they should get it over with once and for all," said McDonald. "It was actually a nice evening. The four of us sat around a table, and everyone was agreeable. We even determined how much Kris would get a month, which was pretty simple—they didn't have that much to divide anymore. At the end of it, Rick and Kris were hugging and saying, 'All right, this is finally over. We're going to tell the lawyers in the morning.'

"Tom left, and Kris wanted me to leave Rick alone with her; she was going to try to get him back. But Rick didn't want to hear about it. That was the first time I'd ever seen him stand up to her and say no. Kris promised blood to her father that she was going to stop, but the next day both Rick and I received telegrams from her attorney: 'Cease and desist talking to my client.'" The case, originally scheduled for court in February 1981, dragged on practically into 1983.

Rick's mother and brother remained surprisingly distant from the turmoil overtaking his life. Kris felt closer to her mother-in-law than to her own mother, and Harriet refused to take sides. Perhaps as a woman continually outshone by the men in her life, she empathized with Kris's feelings of neglect and frustration. During the marriage Harriet encouraged Kris to pursue painting and dancing and to find her own happiness.

More pragmatic than passionate about her work, Harriet had opted for a stable family life rather than a film career. Did she fault Rick for not settling down and for being away from his children so much?

"No, Harriet never made a judgment call on that and never even thought it inside," Connie Nelson asserted. "I think she wished his business didn't make it necessary for that, but she realized Rick was doing exactly what he wanted to do, and you don't stop someone from what they want to do."

David was less impartial, furious with Kris for her shabby treatment of his second wife, Yvonne, whom he married shortly after divorcing June in 1975. Alan Bush recalled, "Kris would say to Yvonne and David how Rick hated coming over to their house and how he thought Yvonne was the worst thing that ever happened to David," when in fact he thought the world of her. "She was saying things that weren't Rick's words, and it created a lot of tension."

But David's involvement too was minimal. "Rick called me up one time and asked, 'Would you mind driving me down to the courthouse? I don't want to burden you with any of this stuff, but . . . I don't know how to get there.'" David laughed. "So, the first couple of times, I drove him down." He and Yvonne once testified on Rick's behalf as to the kind of father he was, angering Kris.

Greg McDonald remembered, "One time during the divorce when Kris was being just awful, Rick said to me, like a little kid, 'If my dad were here, boy, he could handle her.' It was funny, because he was forty years old at the time." Since Ozzie's passing, the Nelsons had drifted apart like planets whose sun has gone cold. "Nobody cared if they were all together at Christmas anymore," Connie Nelson reflected sadly. "Everybody just went in the direction of their own immediate family."

By 1982 Connie and Don Nelson were divorced. June Nelson,

the perennial outsider, was essentially excommunicated from the clan. Ozzie's mother, Ethel Orr Nelson, had died in 1966. Ozzie's brother Alfred passed away in January 1982, only months after his wife, Kay. Harriet's parents were also deceased, Roy Hilliard having died in 1953, and Hazel Hilliard, in 1971.

Six years after her husband's death, Harriet was still deep in grief. "She'd been a rock all the way through Ozzie's illness," said Connie Nelson. But afterward, "It was devastating for her, and she handled it not well at all." Though not a churchgoer, "Harriet has a very strong religious belief that really helps her. Outside of that, I'm sure she just wanted to climb in a hole and pull the dirt over her."

In an unusually candid 1981 interview with the *Los Angeles Times*, Harriet said of her and Ozzie's relationship, "We were almost like one person, and I don't know that it should be that way." Feeling alone in the big house on Camino Palmero, she sold it in 1979 after thirty-eight years. Its new owners are said to believe that Ozzie's ghost haunts the Colonial Cape Cod, opening and closing doors, and turning lights and faucets on and off.

Aside from occasionally acting in TV movies and guest-starring on series such as *The Love Boat* and *Fantasy Island,* Harriet sequestered herself in Laguna Beach. Her six grandchildren and three step-grandchildren (from Yvonne Nelson's first marriage) were her happiness, as was her closeness with David. After Ozzie died, "She relied very heavily on David," said Connie Nelson. "Still does and always will."

Rick, however, saw his mother and his brother only on Thanksgiving and Christmas. Between songs at his concerts audience members frequently hollered, "Where's David?" Rick, honest to a fault, replied from the stage, "I don't know, he never writes." Months often passed without the two brothers speaking.

One time, though, in Detroit, when the predictable yell came, before Rick could answer, a voice in back spoke up, "Here I am!" It was David. The audience went wild. Rick, scanning the house for his brother, said into the microphone, "David? I never hear from you; you never write." Later the two of them spent the night catching up at Rick's hotel.

For the Nelsons to get together only twice a year would have been inconceivable when Ozzie was alive. But since his death, strain had crept into Rick's relationships with both Harriet and David, and he increasingly kept them at arm's length. Harriet would attend a show and ask Greg McDonald for a tour itinerary. Then, after she'd left the dressing room, Rick would say to his manager, "You don't have to send it; I'll call and tell her." He never did.

Rick even refused to participate in a television special that aired on Los Angeles's KTLA, *An Ozzie and Harriet Christmas*, for which the Nelsons' living room was re-created and old friends from *The Adventures* dropped by. "It was very well produced and very well received," said McDonald, who tried in vain to convince Rick to appear. "He never really gave me a reason why he didn't want to do it, except to say, 'I don't want to go back to *that time*.' Rick got a lot of nasty letters from fans for not doing it."

Just why Rick grew estranged from his family is unclear. Having been its most independent star for years, perhaps he didn't want to divulge his financial and personal problems. Or maybe the personality differences that had always existed were simply magnified now that Ozzie was gone. Some suspect that disagreements over money matters, a subject the Nelsons rarely discussed, were partly to blame. Kris had long been of the opinion that David, in charge of selling *The Adventures* to local television markets, wasn't negotiating the best deals possible. And David objected vehemently to Harriet's lending Rick more money to pay off the Internal Revenue Service, which was then threatening to attach his receipts from the road.

"For the last years of Rick's life, he and David wouldn't stand in the same room," said a friend of both. "They'd always get into fights, and not the type of banter you saw on the TV show. It was, 'You're an idiot!' I never could figure out what the exact problem was. They were just drastically different people, and they argued about everything."

Adding to Rick's woes, in 1981 a New Jersey woman filed a paternity suit against him. Greg McDonald maintains that as far as Rick was concerned, Georgeann Crewe was simply "just another girl on the road," but to hear her tell it, their one-night stand ignited an everlasting love affair.

Crewe, then thirty-five and married, met Rick at the Playboy Resort in Great Gorge, New Jersey. She remembers the date: May 16, 1980. No groupie lying in wait, Crewe insists, she and her sister just happened to be vacationing there in a room opposite Rick's suite. Alan Bush recalled that both girls were invited to a party.

"Actually," he said, "I think Rick was more involved with the sister. He went into the bedroom with Georgeann, then came out and spent the night with her sister." According to Crewe, who claims that Rick instantly recognized her from a chance encounter nearly twenty-five years before, "This was a very deep thing Rick and I experienced. I deeply loved him, and I'm sure he felt the same way at that time." Crewe says that the next morning, "Rick wanted me to go to Kentucky with him, but I couldn't just drop everything and take off."

She became pregnant and on Valentine's Day 1981 gave birth to a son, Eric Jude. A 1985 blood test substantiated that Rick was indeed the father. Although he agreed to pay $400 a month support, he wanted nothing to do with the boy. Crewe insists this was only because "Rick wasn't fully aware of the circumstances; he was put in a situation where he had to do what his business people told him. He was a very sensitive person. I can guarantee you that he loved Eric and wanted to do right by him."

Whenever Rick was in the vicinity, Crewe says that his road manager called and invited her to his hotel suite. Out of fear, she didn't go. "It was very hard for me to refuse to see Rick, but I had a son to raise. I couldn't put myself in a position where someone might drug me—and I never take drugs, ever—

and say, 'Well, she was a druggie and died of an overdose.'

"I was never afraid of Rick," she emphasized. "I was afraid of Greg McDonald." Rick's manager had threatened Crewe with a restraining order and dismisses her claims of a profound requited romance as pathetic self-delusion.

In desperation, she and her parish priest confronted Rick as he exited a small Jersey Shore club a few months before his death. "Father Joe approached him first," said Crewe. "Then I walked over, and of course Rick knew who I was. We stood there holding hands for about ten minutes. Father Joe said to him, 'Rick, Georgeann needs your help with your son. She can't do it alone.' Rick said, 'I understand.'"

Crewe alleges that Rick agreed to meet and discuss the matter sometime soon. Then he climbed into his limousine. "As Father Joe and I started to walk away, the limousine stopped, and out came Rick again. He said, 'I *will* make the time. When do you want to do it?' Rick gave me a hug, smiled, and said, 'We will talk. I want this whole thing straightened out. I care about you, and I care about Eric.'

"But then," Crewe said mournfully, "the plane crash happened . . ."

Greg McDonald's version of these events differs drastically. "Rick called me the minute he got back to the hotel, and he was in a fit. He said he got to his limousine and found this preacher blocking his path, so he politely waved to Georgeann, dashed around to the other side of the car, ducked inside, and ordered the driver to tear the hell out of there. The two of them did not have any discussion.

"He told me over the phone, 'Don't *ever* book me in New Jersey again! This girl's a nutcase, and she's chasing me!' We turned down a number of lucrative dates in Atlantic City for fear she'd show up."

Eric, now a stocky eleven-year-old, has been blessed with Rick's stunning blue eyes and pouty mouth. "He knows quite a lot about his dad and the Nelson family," said his mother. "I play *Ozzie and Harriet* videos for him, and he enjoys that. But on the other hand, he feels kind of left out. He wonders

230

why Rick's family won't accept him. I can't tell him it's because people aren't happy with what his father and I did. So I tell him that some people just don't understand, but maybe one day they will. I say, 'I'm sure that if they did meet you, they'd love you just as much as Mommy does.'"

Even after a decade of battling Rick and later his estate for money, Crewe said, "I've never held anything against Rick, because I know what his true feelings were. There were moments we shared that no one else in the world could ever know. We were really happy."

The ongoing divorce took an enormous toll on all that Rick had left: his music. He'd already been treading rough financial waters for some time. Now he had to swim furiously upstream. This meant accelerating his already punishing pace on the road just to survive. As a rule, tours lose money, but with luck that is offset by increased record sales. Rick, however, had to profit on the road, and managed to do so, netting around $500,000 in 1981.

"Everything was for today, to get money," said Bill Hoyt. "Rick never could do any long-range career planning." The ongoing financial crisis made even planning just a week in advance difficult. Although Rick grossed between $7,500 and $10,000 a show, the net varied due to the unpredictability of expenses. If management had sufficient time to reserve economical flight and hotel rates, Rick might come away with $5,000. For a last-minute booking, he might only break even. Regardless of how he fared, employees had to be paid. Given the choice between a day off in a strange town and performing, Rick preferred to play. Anywhere.

"The Friday- and Saturday-night gigs and the fairs were big," said Hoyt, "but what do you do on Tuesday in the winter? How do you pay your thirty-thousand-dollar overhead in December, when nobody works then except for New Year's Eve?" By playing what Rick half-jokingly called "skull orchards."

Because few of the musicians understood the magnitude of

their leader's monetary woes, they grumbled and wondered how he could lower himself to appear at the sleazier venues. "The band didn't know that if Rick didn't take the dates, he'd have his house repossessed," said Hoyt, adding, "That came close to happening four times."

There was no mistaking the emotional hardship from the divorce. "It had a tremendous effect on him," Tom Brumley said sadly, "his personality, his work, not getting new albums out. Rick was so undone by the personal situation that he didn't have the energy to keep that going. He didn't have time to write."

Rick composed only two songs for *Playing to Win,* his disappointing Capitol Records debut. The label signed Rick on the basis of the rockabilly he'd cut in Memphis when still with Epic. Earlier in 1980, the operatic glam-rock British group Queen reigned at number one with a rockabilly-style record, "Crazy Little Thing Called Love." But producer Jack Nitzsche, once an architect of Phil Spector's famous Wall of Sound, compiled faceless midtempo rock and sleepy ballads for Rick to sing.

"He wasn't the right guy," said John Davis, Rick's bassist from 1978 to 1983. "If he was, he would have brought in the right material and stood up for what he believed in." Standing up, period, was a problem for Nitzsche, charged the year before with attempting to murder actress Carrie Snodgress.

Greg McDonald recalled the opening session: "Jack's trying to put down the first track," John Hiatt's caustic "It Hasn't Happened Yet," "and he's smashed, telling Rick over the talkback mike, 'This should sound like "Happy Trails." You remember "Happy Trails"? *Da-da, da-da . . .*' Not real coherent, slurring his words. His manager, this nice young guy, is assuring Rick, 'Don't worry about Jack, he had some dental work done today, and he's not feeling well.' Just then Jack falls face first into the mixing board and passes out. We hadn't been in the studio more than a minute.

"Rick picks him up, like it was his kid. He thinks this is just

232

great. He's walking out the door carrying Jack Nitzsche and says, 'Y'know, I think this is going to work out.' We all knew he meant, *This guy's never gonna get through the record, and we get to do it ourselves,* whether that was good or bad."

Rick would have much preferred working with Paul McCartney, who'd offered to oversee an album of rockabilly at the deserted Sun Studios, using a mobile recording unit. This was before stars' rescue missions of their idols' careers (Bruce Springsteen's 1981 salvaging of Gary U.S. Bonds; John Cougar Mellencamp's less successful 1983 attempt with Mitch Ryder) were commonplace.

The two had met in 1976 when McCartney was playing the States for the first time since the Beatles' 1966 retirement from the stage. Bob Dylan, Cher, Elton John, and Natalie Cole mingled among the four hundred guests at the tour-ending bash held at the Harold Lloyd estate. McCartney spotted Rick and loped toward him, singing, "Stood up, broken-hearted, a-gain." During soundchecks on their spring tour, McCartney and Wings had played both "Stood Up," one of the first songs he learned on guitar, and its flip side, "Waitin' in School."

"Ricky Nelson!" he shouted. The ex-Beatle took him upstairs and spent the rest of the evening asking questions about his favorite Rick Nelson records. Three years later, McCartney contacted Rick about producing a rockabilly album for him. "Listen, man," he said, "I'll design the album cover with Linda, write some songs, play bass, and sing harmonies."

Greg McDonald immediately phoned Capitol Records. "Guess who wants to produce Rick?" he practically shouted. "Paul McCartney!" Amazingly, A&R executive Rupert Perry nixed the idea, claiming, "Paul's never been successful at producing other people." McCartney's only outside productions up to that point included a movie soundtrack and albums for brother Mike McGear and singer Mary Hopkin, whose "Those Were the Days" hit number two in 1968. The real reason for Capitol's lack of interest: McCartney had recently jilted the label for Columbia Records.

Aided by a media blitz, *Playing to Win* went to number 153, distinguishing Rick as the only artist in rock & roll history to chart LPs of new material in the 1950s, 1960s, 1970s, and 1980s. It was Rick's last album to be released during his lifetime. The label scuttled the follow-up midway through, and once again Rick found himself without a record company when Capitol dropped him in October 1981.

What could Rick have done to reverse his sliding career? Realistically, very little. Rock & roll music, at its best, defines a moment in time, and we associate performers with their particular moment. Few artists escape this link, which for many turns into a ball and chain. Rick's peers from the 1950s, Carl Perkins, Jerry Lee Lewis, Fats Domino, Chuck Berry, may still perform and in some instances record, but they are not contemporary. They are, and will forever be, of their time: the past.

Arguably, Rick was the only singer of his era to transcend his past, even if just briefly. That a new generation of listeners considered him current in the 1970s must be recognized as a doubly remarkable achievement because of his musical and television fame. And that he had a record contract for as long and as consistently as he did placed him ahead of virtually every musician his age. But to compete against younger acts for the attention of 1980s rock fans required an extraordinary—and most likely futile—effort that Rick was no longer willing or able to give.

"I was always on him to do things to help his career," said Paul Rose, then a Capitol Records marketing executive, "and Rick's comeback was always the same: 'Look, I've had lots of hit records, and I'm real happy with that. I love to record. But I don't have the energy to go out and do all *that stuff* to have another hit record. If it happens, it happens.' "

After *Playing to Win* sank, "I tried talking him into making a record with either Linda Ronstadt or Pat Benatar," said Rose, "because Rick had a lot of fans in the music industry who'd grown up with him and would show up at his concerts. But he wasn't interested. We'd argue about it. Rick felt that if getting a hit record was dependent on singing a duet with someone else, he didn't want to do it."

For the same reason, Rick declined offers of payola. "We were paying off radio stations all the time," claimed Rose. "Rick said, 'Don't spend three hundred thousand dollars and buy me a fake hit. If the record isn't good enough to be played, then it shouldn't be played.' "

The severest test of Rick's inflexible idealism had come in 1977. "Colonel" Tom Parker arranged for him to work in Las Vegas, which was finally recognizing rock & roll's power to draw aging Baby Boomers. The Las Vegas Hilton offered Rick a long-term contract for $400,000 to share equal billing with comedian Bill Cosby. Four option periods raised its potential worth to $1.4 million. Naturally Rick would be expected to conform to Vegas's production values: orchestra, choreography, costume changes. Or, as Rick referred to it, "a balloons and feathers show."

"Rick could have become an instant millionaire doing one of those big productions," said Greg McDonald. "With his looks and all those hits, all he had to do was walk out on stage and smile." Only weeks before, business manager Wally Franson had transmitted his SOS concerning Rick's desperate financial position. "Rick didn't even blink," said his manager. "He just couldn't do it, and he passed. Wally almost had a stroke."

Rick understood what he was turning down. "This is the big one, isn't it?" he said. "But I can either do what I do, or roll over." Rick laughed. "I know: Maybe I'll get a nice *jumpsuit*, some studs . . ." When he made his Las Vegas debut in 1978 at the Aladdin Hotel, he performed his usual rock & roll show.

"One night," McDonald recalled, "we were sitting in a penthouse suite at the Sahara Hotel, eating cheeseburgers and talking. As we looked down the Strip, we could see from all the marquees who was appearing there: Roy Clark. Wayne Newton. Mel Tillis. Rick had more Top Forty hits than everyone else on the Strip combined, yet he wasn't making near the money they were, because he was playing showrooms with a five-piece band in jeans."

Although Rick never abandoned his principles, by late 1982 he'd lost his hunger, exhausted from the road and preoccupied by ongoing divorce proceedings. And at age forty-two, the stress was beginning to show, just a year after *Playgirl* magazine had selected Rick as one of the country's ten sexiest men.

"I think Rick was feeling the strain," promoter Bill Hollingshead observed. "He almost had a little paunch on him, which was very sad, because he'd always been so athletic-looking. His complexion was very sallow. Rick just did not look like he was in good health."

He turned into a recluse at home, padding about in his towel, playing piano to Carl Perkins records, watching sports on TV, and going grocery-shopping at 2:00 A.M. to avoid autograph-seekers. "I tried to get him out more," said David. "Like when he was in Las Vegas, I'd say, 'Let's play tennis or something.' He wasn't quite up to doing that, which was very unlike Rick."

Most of the time in L.A., Rick longed to hit the road again. "To escape the process-servers," David explained dryly. But even on tour, things had changed. Jay White rejoined the group briefly in early 1983 and was disheartened by what he saw. "In the old days Rick used to hang out with the band," the bassist said. "But now he was very much apart and spent a lot of time in his hotel room. The band wasn't like a family anymore."

Throughout his life, things had always come easy to Rick. "Maybe too easy," David suggested. "He was a natural at everything he did." In that respect he was the direct opposite of Ozzie, who overcame his moderate talents with sheer ambition. Until his later years, Rick had never felt compelled to overcome anything. He never had what he desperately needed now: drive. Disappointment, fatigue, and personal unhappiness had ground him down, and for the first time, Rick—the escape artist—found himself cornered.

Fourteen

ric . . . Hilliard . . . Nelson.
Rick set down his pen,
looked up, and grinned. "There, it's over," he said. "Finally."
He'd just autographed a thirty-page Marital Settlement Agreement, officially ending an extraordinarily acrimonious divorce.
The couple's signatures told the story of the past two-plus years:
Kris's, bold and angry; Rick's, feeble and ragged.

Though he didn't realize it at the time, in December 1982,
Rick's problems were by no means over. The earthquake may
have subsided, but years of aftershocks would follow in the
form of continued legal warfare. Rick strolled out of the notary
public's office feeling as if a tremendous burden had been lifted,
and he gradually regained something of his old enthusiasm
and easygoing manner.

Soon after, Rick harked back to rockabilly, rebaptizing himself
in its rushing rhythms. He drastically revamped his live set to

include the classics "Stood Up," "Waitin' in School," "My Bucket's Got a Hole in It," and "Milk Cow Blues."

One of 1983's biggest acts happened to be the Stray Cats, a young American trio that wrote its own neorockabilly songs, introducing the MTV generation to this genre. Some of Rick's former musicians insist that had he recorded in that vein right then, he would have been assured another comeback. It's unlikely, for the Stray Cats' fleeting popularity hinged mainly on the novelty of their 1950s-burlesque look and stylish videos, and in no way signified mass acceptance of rockabilly.

Nonetheless, performing his old songs upped Rick's value on the concert circuit. Promoter Bill Hollingshead said, "As a buyer, it was something I'd commented on, that Rick wasn't doing enough of his hits. I think his attitude was, That was then and this is now." Through the early 1980s, the first rider in Rick's contract clearly stipulated, "Artist to be called Rick Nelson, not billed as Ricky!!"

By 1983 Rick's resistance had melted. He even allowed the *y* to be reappended to his name. A sign of resignation? "No," said Hollingshead, "I think it was a sign of maturity, of facing reality. There was the realization that he was who he was. He had all those hits"—twenty-seven Top Twenty smashes, more than any touring artist from the early rock & roll era—"and he should sing all those hits."

Had Rick not previously declared, *If memories were all I sang, I'd rather drive a truck,* he probably would have felt less skittish about performing his best-loved songs. That line came to haunt him the same way that the Who's Pete Townshend has had to live down his smug "Hope I die before I get old" from "My Generation." Memories weren't all Rick sang, though. At the time of his death he was at work on an album, and in concert he made it a point to follow "Garden Party" with a new song.

In his forties, Rick came to accept his place in rock & roll. Increasingly, accolades like *patriarch* and *legend* popped up alongside his name in newspaper articles. Friends nicknamed him *Ledge,* short for *Legend.* "You know," Rick used to joke, "through attrition, one day I'm going to become the king of rock & roll."

He could now enjoy the irony of headlining a Madison Square Garden oldies concert called "Garden Party Reunion," which brought together the original lineup from 1971, minus Gary U.S. Bonds. "Boy, this is really asking for it," Rick worried beforehand.

When he came out on stage, the audience—acutely aware of what had transpired twelve years before—responded with a standing ovation that froze Rick in his tracks before he reached the microphone. As he stood there, astonished, flashbulbs exploded and fans raced down the aisles to get a closer look. Rick's four-piece group had to vamp the musical introduction for several minutes until the crowd finally quieted down enough for him to sing.

"The outpouring of affection really got to him," said Ray Walker of the Jordanaires, supporting Rick on stage for only the second time. Poetically, he closed with "Garden Party," which received the loudest roar of the night.

The Jordanaires (in 1982 Duane West replaced the late Hoyt Hawkins) expressed surprise at how little Rick had changed in the nearly twenty years since they'd last worked together. "Most entertainers change tremendously and become completely different people," said Gordon Stoker, offering Elvis Presley in his later years as a grim example. "But Rick was still the same sweet, genuine person he was as a kid." Comparing Rick the adult to the teenager of a quarter-century ago, Jordanaire Neal Matthews observed, "He was more open than he was before, speaking up, joking, and laughing."

It is not unusual for performers traveling the oldies circuit to play with house bands or hastily assembled pickup groups. Chuck Berry is notorious for arriving minutes before showtime, collecting his nightly fee, then alternately sleepwalking and duckwalking through his set backed by a crew of unrehearsed local amateurs, with frequently embarrassing results. But throughout his career, including when he could least afford it, Rick surrounded himself only with top musicians.

What would be the final configuration of Rick's group was among his best, put together shortly before the Garden Party Reunion show. Rick wanted to recapture an authentic rockabilly sound, so he hired Pat Woodward, an acoustic slap bassist as well as an electric player. Bearded, balding, he looked menacing on stage, arms bulging from a leather vest, but in private the towering bassist was warm and soft-spoken.

Woodward brought along twenty-one-year-old drummer Ricky Intveld, who must have reminded Rick of his younger self. Instead of the modern hard rock and new wave the other kids at Garden Grove High School championed, Intveld listened to the same records that had seduced Rick. He was a passionate fan of Elvis Presley, Gene Vincent—and Rick Nelson. The tall, slim youth from a close-knit Dutch family even resembled Rick in his early twenties, with a moderate pompadour and clear, piercing eyes. Pianist Andy Chapin, the last member to join, had played keyboards with Steppenwolf and the Association.

The previous band's lone holdover, lead guitarist Bobby Neal, had been with Rick since 1979. Raised on an Arkansas farm, Neal met Rick during the recording of *Memphis Sessions* at Lyn-Lou Studio, where he served as staff guitarist.

"Bobby was a rock & roll historian," said producer Larry Rogers. "He loved Rick and the idea of playing with him." A storehouse of rockabilly riffs, the huskily built guitarist could duplicate James Burton's licks note for note as well as improvise his own crackling solos. Aside from the illustrious Burton, Rick considered Neal the best picker he'd ever played with.

Neal, perennially smiling and full of southern charm, also provided the sort of friendship Rick had missed since Tom Brumley's departure. Alan Bush recalled one time during the divorce when Rick, feeling tired and distracted, wanted Neal to take over the song-ending guitar lick to "Garden Party."

"Bobby kept flubbing it, like, twenty times in a row, saying,

'Gee, Rick, that's a weird fingering; I can't get it. That's your line.' " Bush added skeptically, "Now, there wasn't *anything* that Bobby couldn't play on guitar." Out of love, concern, and respect, he subtly pushed Rick and bolstered his spirits.

Rick's friend Paul Rose commented, "Rick really enjoyed working on the road with Bobby and the band. He liked doing rock & roll again, and loved the response he was getting; the girls were still screaming, and stars were coming out to see him. Even though he wasn't able to come up with hits, he was having a lot of fun." In Hermann Hesse's book, an aging Siddhartha tells an old friend, "I am not going anywhere. I am only on the way." At this stage of life, simply being "on the way" brought Rick satisfaction enough.

His happiness was evident in a more energetic performance, never one of Rick's strong suits before. During a mid-1970s concert at Knott's Berry Farm, a subdued Rick kept tuning up between songs, taxing the audience's patience. Finally, late in the show, past eleven o'clock, an agitated voice from the last row broke the silence: "For God's sake, sing 'Garden Party' already, so we can go home!" Bill Hollingshead remembered, "There was virtually a five-minute roar of laughter, and it embarrassed Rick."

But now Rick was animated, pumping his fist in the air to accent final notes, exhorting Bobby Neal and Andy Chapin during solos, and shaking hands with the front row. Rick developed into more of a showman, playfully exploiting his abundant sex appeal with a wiggle that sent young girls screaming and older women fanning themselves.

Rick had another cause for contentment: Helen Blair, a girlishly pretty blonde sixteen years his junior who played a major yet puzzling part in his life. Those who observed the pair during their five years together held sharply divided opinions about Helen, her effect on Rick, and the nature of their relationship. However, there are three points on which most everyone agreed:

that she was sweet, madly in love with Rick, and had endured a dismal childhood.

According to older sister Marti Ditonto, their mechanic father and secretary mother "were very strict and had strange ideas. Helen had a hard time growing up with them." As soon as she escaped high school, Helen fled South Orange, New Jersey, for Florida and then moved to California, working as a part-time model and as a trainer of exotic animals.

Rick and Helen met in 1980, only weeks after Kris walked out on him for the last time. "Helen was at the Riviera Hotel in Las Vegas to sleep with [a band member], whom she'd slept with before," Paul Rose explained. This musician had committed the tactical error of inviting two other out-of-town girlfriends to his hotel room. "I've got to move some of these women around," he said to Rick, panic-stricken. "Will you take one?" Helen was the one.

"When she came into the room," recalled Rose, "Rick's eyes lit right up." With his wife and kids gone, "He'd been very lonely. He used to drive me and Greg McDonald nuts calling us at two o'clock in the morning, wanting to talk. Rick needed somebody to stay up with him at night." Helen, smitten with Rick since girlhood, happily obliged. She was the only woman he dated seriously following the breakup of his marriage, and it wasn't long before Helen confided to her sister, "Someday I'm going to marry Rick Nelson."

Within weeks, Helen became Rick's constant road companion. This did not endear her to his manager and business manager, who viewed her, at the very least, as an economic liability. Aware of their feelings, Helen tried to prove herself an asset, organizing Rick's day and acting as fan-club liaison at the shows.

"Helen was a real support mechanism for Rick, helping him to be at his best," said the band's copilot, Ken Ferguson, "yet she was very careful about not drawing attention to herself and always remained in the background whenever Rick was in public." Ferguson kept a watchful eye on Helen at shows, especially at some of the seedier clubs. "The last thing Rick

242

would say to me before going on stage was, 'Stay with her, please,' because she was an attractive young woman and very much a target."

In 1982 Helen moved in with Rick. Between her two longhair cats and Afghan hound, and his four dogs, most of the Torreyson house's furniture was covered with fur. Two years later, for Christmas 1984, Rick gave his live-in lover a diamond engagement ring. The fact that they hadn't set a wedding date didn't seem to bother Helen. Her sister Marti recalled, "She said that if they stayed engaged for the rest of her life, she wouldn't care."

Some friends credit Helen with making Rick less reclusive. "She got him out of the house more," said Alan Bush. "Rick would go shopping downtown during the day, which was something I'd never seen him do before, and he became freer with his emotions." Bobby Neal's wife, Phyllis, observed, "Helen just did something different to Rick. I think that he wanted a family life again, and he loved this woman to death."

At the same time, many of Rick's friends who knew her as a drug abuser wondered what he was doing with Helen and sometimes got up the nerve to ask him. "You couldn't do it too often," said Rose. "You had to catch him just right." One night when they were alone together in a hotel room, Rose asked point blank, "Rick . . . Why Helen?" Rick's answer revealed a great deal, not so much about his fiancée, but about his self-perception.

"Let me tell you something," he said quietly. "Look at my life-style: I sleep during the day, I'm up at night. In general, I don't go to restaurants, I don't go to movies, I don't socialize. Most girls would never put up with that. I need somebody like Helen who's willing to just throw away all that stuff to adapt to my life-style."

But instead, the reverse appeared to be happening—Rick adapting more to hers—at a time of so many positive changes in his life. Reexamining Rick's romantic history points up that his dating Helen, a woman bedeviled by personal problems, was totally in character. The parallels between her and "Julie," the heroin-addicted waif, the love of Rick's life, are striking.

No one seems to know what drew Rick to troubled women from dysfunctional families. As a friend observed, "The guy had the possibility of dating anyone, but he loved those street girls." Realizing that, a worried Ozzie and Harriet had steered their twenty-year-old son toward a girl of some pedigree: Kris Harmon.

Rick's mother and brother both disapproved strongly of Helen, and those feelings undoubtedly contributed to the coolness between them and Rick. When Harriet learned that Rick and Helen were engaged, she threatened to write him out of her will. Magazine articles from after the plane crash claiming that Harriet, David, and Rick's children were fond of Helen seem to have been promoted by her family, who wanted their estranged daughter buried beside Rick at Forest Lawn. Harriet wouldn't hear of it.

Behind the scenes, Rick's manager and business manager also lobbied for Helen's ouster. Not only was she addicted to cocaine, she was a chronic shoplifter. One afternoon Greg McDonald received a phone call from the manager of a Minnesota hotel gift shop. "Are you Rick Nelson's manager?" she asked.

"Well, Rick Nelson is in here with a young blonde. She's on the other side of the store, and as we're speaking, she's filling her pockets. Now, I'd rather not embarrass Mister Nelson, so if I keep account of what she's taking, will you pay for it?" McDonald had to call the road manager and have him cover the amount, $50. This happened on other occasions as well.

Another time, in Miami, Rick and Helen accompanied Paul Rose to the house of a wealthy record-business friend. The man was such a fan of Rick's that he secretly set up a video camera on the second floor balcony and aimed it down at the living room to record the visit for posterity.

"At one point during the evening," Rose remembered, "we were all in the kitchen. Helen snuck into the living room alone and emptied my buddy's girlfriend's purse of five hundred dollars." The theft was captured, of course, on videotape. This time McDonald made Rick hand over the money himself.

Rick's defense of his fiancée was always the same: "You have to be patient with Helen; she had a terrible childhood." Some friends say that Rick had finally run out of patience and wanted to terminate the relationship but that Helen threatened him with a palimony suit. She'd apparently done this before.

"Her ex-boyfriend called my office to warn Rick about her," said McDonald. "He said they'd lived together in Florida and that as soon as Helen moved out, she sued for palimony but later dropped the suit."

Others insist Rick had no intentions of ending the romance. "He loved Helen," asserted Alan Bush. "I don't care what anybody says. Greg and Bill Hoyt would have done anything at all to get her out of the picture, but there was no way to do it, because Rick found a lot of support in Helen." Even Mc-Donald conceded, "Rick genuinely cared about her. I think he thought he needed her." Sharon Sheeley, providing an insight based on knowing Rick almost thirty years, felt that he probably stayed in the relationship "because it was comfortable."

But would Rick have married her? Soon after their engagement, he impulsively announced that he and Helen planned to wed in Hawaii. "I want you to be my best man," he told McDonald, "and your wife to stand up for Helen."

From Florida, McDonald reluctantly made the arrangements.

"Everything was all set: They were going to get married at the Hilton Hawaiian Village. We had the preacher, the reservations, and the planes booked. The guys in the band couldn't believe it. I remember all of them, to a man, sitting downstairs in the coffee shop, shaking their heads. 'Why would he want to marry *her?*' 'I'll believe it when I see it.'

"The last thing before we left was for Rick to call my wife back in Palm Springs and ask her to be a part of the ceremony."

But Sherry McDonald, who'd joined Rick on countless road trips, cutting his hair and sewing many of his stage outfits, stunned him by refusing.

"As your friend," she said, "I can't do it."

"Usually when Rick made up his mind about something," McDonald went on, "you couldn't sway him. But after speaking to Sherry for about an hour, he came out of the bedroom and told Helen and me, 'I've changed my mind; I just can't do it right now.'

"Helen didn't say anything; she just spun around on one heel, locked herself in the bathroom, and promptly got blasted. Later Rick told me, 'I respect Sherry for what she said. Helen's obviously wrong for me.' He never mentioned marriage again."

For Rick's forty-fifth birthday, in May 1985, Helen threw a surprise party at the house. About thirty people, including Harriet, David and Yvonne, Don Nelson, band members and their wives waited for Rick to return from a business meeting in Palm Springs.

When Rick walked in the door, he took a whipped-cream pie square in the face, courtesy of sons Matthew and Gunnar. "Happy birthday, Pop!" they choroused. Harriet appeared shocked, but pieing the birthday boy was a hallowed band tradition, one that had cost Rick quite a few dollars in hotel-room damages over the years. Toward the end of the otherwise quiet celebration, Helen brought out a huge cake decorated with an icing silhouette of Ricky the Rocker in his youthful prime.

Rick had no intention of aging gracefully. "I don't really see myself growing old," he told an interviewer. "It doesn't happen with what I'm doing." Kept an eternal adolescent in rock & roll's never-never land, Rick was neither emotionally nor spiritually ready for senior citizenhood. The thought of what he'd have been like at fifty-plus is inconceivable to friends, as it was to Rick.

His forty-fifth birthday was easier on Rick's psyche than turning forty had been. Then he'd wistfully mused aloud, "God, I'm forty. Do I have to act like an 'adult' now? Act differently? Do I have to quit wearing jeans? I guess I'm supposed to do something different, but I don't know what it is."

Despite his self-effacement, Rick exhibited the vanity of most sex symbols. Astigmatism ran in the Nelson family, but he stubbornly refused to wear glasses. He couldn't read menus without holding them at an angle and squinting at the type, and he occasionally bumped into walls. In his forties Rick's hair was snow white, but he dyed it and avoided chlorine-treated swimming pools—a zealously guarded secret.

"It took him a long time to admit it to me," said Greg McDonald, remembering how Rick agonized for the better part of an evening before asking self-consciously, "Uh, Greg? You've got to do something for me . . ." Now and then someone was dispatched to a local drugstore for more Miss Clairol Light Ash Brown.

"The last three years," said Alan Bush, "I watched Rick grow old." At home, unshaven and clad in his towel, "You'd see the gray hairs and the gut. But as soon as he walked out of the house, you didn't see that age anymore."

A video documentary from one of Rick's last tours attests to how vigorous he still looked on stage. *Ricky Nelson in Concert,* originally slated to air as a television special on 143 stations in January 1986 but postponed following Rick's death,[1] was taped in front of an enthusiastic crowd at Los Angeles's Universal Amphitheatre on August 22, 1985. His mother, brother, uncle, and children (except Sam, prohibited by Kris from attending) were in the audience, along with singers Jan and Dean, Anita Bryant, Randy Newman, and John Fogerty.

Dressed in a black shirt unbuttoned at the neck, a thin white tie, white pants, and a lightly checked jacket, Rick projects the cool confidence of his character Colorado from *Rio Bravo.* John Wayne's drawled remark about the young cowhand—"I'd say he's so good he doesn't feel he has to prove it"—perfectly describes Rick's demeanor. Except for a slight paunch accentuated by the white pants, he appears unchanged.

---

[1] The show was reedited and released the summer after Rick's death as a nine-song home video. *Ricky Nelson in Concert,* coproduced by Greg McDonald and Jeff Kranzdorf, reached the top twenty of *Billboard*'s Top Music Videocassettes chart and later went platinum, selling over one million copies.

Most striking of all is how even while singing "oldies," Rick lights up the songs as if originating them on the spot, hands cupping the microphone, brow creased in concentration. There is no sense of nostalgia, only of the moment.

"This was not a guy going through the motions," praised Fogerty. "This was a guy putting his heart into the music." When Rick and the band struck up "Poor Little Fool," the Jordanaires adding their rich harmonies, Fogerty observed, "everybody played it as if they were sixteen years old and it meant the whole world."

Rick split the bill with Fats Domino, whose renowned eccentricities enlivened the three-week tour. A compulsive man (all eight Domino children have first names beginning with the letter *A*), Domino ate only his own Creole cuisine, carrying with him a Crockpot and trunks full of utensils. The ample pianist also required one room solely for his wardrobe and upon checking in fastidiously arranged his shoes in a tidy semi-circle.

Domino's ten-piece band had its share of colorful characters, one of whom pulled a gun on Rick's road manager. Clark Russell had found a pair of cheap sunglasses on the band's private jet and, not realizing they belonged to this musician, wore them to soundcheck at the Sands Hotel in Las Vegas. While positioning a stage monitor, Russell felt someone tap his shoulder, turned around, and found himself starring down the barrel of a revolver.

"Bobby Neal and I pleaded with the guy to put down the gun," said Greg McDonald. "Meanwhile, one of Fats's horn players kept yelling, 'Shoot the motherfucker!' "

Domino felt avuncular affection for Rick, insisting he harmonize with him on "I'm Walkin' " during Domino's half of the show. Although Rick was the headliner, out of respect he let the Fat Man close every night. "Never argue with a legend," he explained to old friend Sharon Sheeley before the Amphitheatre concert. "But you're the best," she said. Rick smiled. "Maybe. But who's gonna argue with that ten-piece band?"

Rick always deferred to his idols, offering to open for Carl Perkins, whom he finally met in September after thirty years of emulating his rockabilly sound. The occasion was a recording reunion of Perkins and former Sun Records labelmates Jerry Lee Lewis, Roy Orbison, and Johnny Cash at the American Sound Studio in Memphis. For the grand finale, an en-masse rendition of John Fogerty's "Big Train (From Memphis)," the quartet invited Rick, Fogerty, June Carter Cash, the Judds, Dave Edmunds, Sun's Sam Phillips, and several others to join them.

Waiting for the session to begin and feeling somewhat anxious, Rick wandered alone into an adjacent room that had been turned into a Presley museum. He was both amused and appalled by the glass cabinets containing spoons, cups, and plates all bearing Elvis's likeness; a life-size cardboard cutout of The King; and a giant china statue of Nipper, the RCA Records mascot. Then he floated back into the main room.

When introduced to Perkins, Rick said, "I've admired you for a long time."

"Thank you, man, 'cause I really feel the same way about you." The two shook hands and hugged each other.

"One of the last things Ricky said to me," recalled Perkins, "was, 'I really would like to open some shows for you next year, Carl.' I said, 'You've got your horse before the cart—*I'll* open for *you*.' But Ricky said, 'No way.' That was very special, and when I heard about the accident, it really tore me up."

Rick's sons Matthew and Gunnar turned eighteen that September and immediately moved back in with their father. Since their separation, Rick and Kris had joint legal custody of the twins, while Sam continued living with Tom and Elyse Harmon, coming to call his maternal grandfather "Pop." Although Rick was out of the country touring Australia and Great Britain much of fall 1985, friends say that having the two boys live with him further elevated his mood. Tracy remembered her father saying happily, "I feel like I have a home again."

Through Tracy, the Nelsons' show-business legacy had entered its fourth consecutive generation. At age five she landed a small role in *Yours, Mine, and Ours,* a 1968 comedy starring Henry Fonda and Lucille Ball, and by the early 1980s she appeared frequently on television. Rick was tremendously proud of his daughter and admired her self-reliance. Unlike him, Tracy embarked upon her career with little help from her parents, working as a hostess at a Burbank coffee shop to earn the money for a summer drama workshop in England.

In 1982 she dropped out of Barnard College to play vacuous Valley Girl Jennifer DeNuccio on the critically acclaimed TV sitcom *Square Pegs,* and was actually shooting the series before Rick knew anything about it. On the road, whenever he caught an episode, he called the band members into his room to watch, beaming.

The twins, blond, quintessentially good-looking California teenagers, were also following in Rick's footsteps, albeit over their mother's strenuous objections. With Matthew on bass and Gunnar on drums, they led a band of their own that rehearsed upstairs at the Torreyson house.

When they were fourteen, Rick's manager arranged their first public performance, opening for their father at the Magic Mountain amusement park near Los Angeles. "Naturally," said McDonald, "Kris got mad."

Just like Rick at that 1957 Hamilton High School assembly, once the boys heard the applause, "You could see the lights go on in Matthew's and Gunnar's eyes," recalled McDonald. "They were going to be singers."

In a music-industry first, the twins would become the third consecutive generation of singing Nelsons to reach number one.[2] Billed simply as Nelson, their debut 1990 single, "(I Need Your) Love and Affection," topped the charts fifty-five years after Ozzie and Harriet did it with "And Then Some." Rick, of course, went to number one twice.

---

[2] The Boone family accomplished a similar feat, but not with three generations of blood relatives: first, Red Foley, with 1950's number one "Chattanoogie Shoe Shine Boy"; then his *son-in-law* Pat Boone, who placed six singles at number one between 1955 and 1961; and Boone's daughter Debby, with "You Light Up My Life" in 1977.

Rather than please Kris, the twins' phenomenal success widened the distance between them and their mother. For a triumphant homecoming show at the Universal Amphitheatre, the entire Nelson clan turned out to lend support. *Almost* the entire clan.

"You'll notice Mom's not here," Matthew commented to a backstage visitor afterward. "Everytime one of our records makes the charts, we get into a fight." He observed wistfully, "I guess we've become Pop to her."

When they were younger, the boys didn't fully comprehend the extent of their father's early fame and significance. "Rick wasn't considered hip by their peer group," said McDonald. "If you'd asked them to name all their dad's hits, they might have gotten to five. But then rockabilly started happening again, and they and their friends all began discovering Rick's music and became fans. Suddenly he was this legendary figure inside his own house. Rick got a real kick out of that."

In addition to their own material, back in 1985 Matthew and Gunnar's group performed a new song of Rick's, the rockabilly-style "Do You Know What I Mean." It was slated as the first single from the album he was recording. One night he called the studio to say he'd be late; he and Helen planned to catch the boys' show at Madame Wong's West. "Do you realize how unusual that is?" bassist Pat Woodward remarked. "Rick *never* goes to clubs." Arriving at their reserved table, they found Kris sitting there with her current boyfriend. Rick, somewhat shaken, watched the show with Helen from the other side of the room.

It was the first time he'd seen his ex-wife since the divorce. The relationship—if it can be called that—remained as combative as ever, Kris venting her ire through legal threats. And action.

"If the check [for spousal and child support, totaling $90,000 a year] was one second late," said Bill Hoyt, "she would slap an injunction on Rick. He made his payments; they just weren't always timely. We did the best we could." Weary of keeping creditors at bay and covering bank overdrafts, Hoyt resigned as Rick's business manager.

Arriving home from the road one time, Rick entered his house to find that Kris had illegally carted off his furniture. He had to obtain a restraining order against her and borrow furnishings from Harriet. Jordanaire Ray Walker recalled his shock at walking into the Torreyson house for the first time:

"Here was this well-known superstar, and the place was practically empty. Rick said, 'Have a seat, guys, if you can find one. She didn't leave me much.' Then he laughed. He was living beneath what you'd expect a person like him to live, but it didn't seem to matter to him."

Some suspect that like the prince who swapped identities with the pauper, Rick secretly enjoyed this austere life-style. No longer wealthy, he could blend in more with those he felt most comfortable among, his musicians. "You've got as much money as I do," he'd say, though naturally none of them believed him.

"Rick had very few material needs," said accountant Gary Olsen. "He still wore clothes he'd had for five, ten years. He drove a 1973 Ford Pantera, but it was a twenty-thousand-dollar car, not a two-hundred-thousand-dollar car." For insight into Rick's values, when he and Kris first separated, he'd moved his most prized possessions to David's house for safekeeping: two acoustic guitars, his collection of gold records, and a Tiffany lamp.

He did treasure the red Pantera with the black interior, though. Knowing this, Kris once had it impounded, alleging nonpayment of child support. Rick returned from a tour and called Alan Bush.

"Alan, do you have my car?" he asked, perplexed.

"No."

"Uh, well, it's gone."

The pool maintenance man found the court order floating in the water the next morning and handed it to Helen, saying, "I think you might want this."

252

That fall Rick learned that with the proceeds from having sold the Flynn residence, he was within about $40,000 of climbing out of the red. He came home from a business meeting "with the biggest grin on his face," recalled Bush, "and he said, 'I'm finally free! We just settled everything up with Kris, and I'm on my own. I'm in the plus column. I don't have to worry about her anymore.' We popped a bottle and started celebrating." (After Rick's death, some newspapers inaccurately claimed he'd been millions of dollars in debt, their reports based on the assumption that the estate would be found liable in a number of exorbitant lawsuits filed against it in early 1986.)

For the first time in ten years Rick could scale back on road work and formulate a long-range career plan. The constant touring imposed a hardship on the band members, all of whom, with the exception of young Ricky Intveld, had families at home. Bobby Neal, with a wife and two children back in Arkansas, especially felt the strain. After seven years with Rick, he planned to sit down with his employer come the new year and discuss his future.

As for Rick's own future, he envisioned it this way: Ideally, acting on a television series again and touring during the summer, just like in the old days. Time and circumstances had worn away much of his early distaste for acting. He'd taped several series pilots, but none sold. "I've done more pilots than a TWA stewardess," he used to quip.

Rick felt ambivalent about most of the scripts sent to him but was banking on NBC's *High School U.S.A.*, which cast him as Pete Kinney, principal of Excelsior Union High. Harriet played his wisecracking secretary. Coincidentally, the pilot (featuring cameos by Jerry Mathers, Paul Petersen, and other denizens of 1950s–1960s sitcoms) was shot at the same Norwalk, California, school as Tracy's former series *Square Pegs*.

Even for network television, the hourlong comedy was silly and sophomoric, and it was not picked up for fall 1984. The following year Rick appeared in his last pilot, *Fathers and Sons*, playing a truant divorced father who abandons his son on the

253

beach to pick up a woman. It did not escape Rick that Kris might have called it good typecasting. NBC passed on that one as well. But Rick enjoyed a high "Q rating," indicating strong popularity among viewers, and in time probably would have found a suitable show.

Especially when you consider the climate of cultural nostalgia that would grip America in the late 1980s. Between digital compact-disc reissues of classic rock & roll and a plethora of retro radio stations to play them (not necessarily a healthy development), Baby Boomers who hadn't frequented record stores since Ringo Starr's hairline began receding were now purchasing the music of their youth in the new format. Adding to this frenzy for the good old days, Jerry Lee Lewis, Richie Valens, and Chuck Berry all became the subjects of major motion pictures.

Suddenly artists from the 1950s and 1960s were in demand again, their concert fees rising. In 1985 Rick grossed an average of $12,500 nightly; by 1990 he'd easily have doubled that figure. The quality of his bookings was improving, too, with fewer club dates and more small concert halls, fairs, and arena-size 1950s package shows.

"Things were looking up again for Rick," said Gordon Stoker. "Everywhere we went we had big crowds and were well received." Mothers who'd screamed for Rick twenty-five years ago now brought along their own teenagers, who "acted like they'd just found some new sound," said Ray Walker. This satisfied Rick most of all. "It means that it's solid music," he stressed in an interview, "not just nostalgic stuff."

Rick radiated optimism about the upcoming year, in which he would be releasing a new album recorded with the Jordanaires and with Jimmie Haskell back behind the board. The arranger, producer, composer, and conductor—a three-time Grammy Award winner—had seen little of Rick since the mid-1960s.

He'd originally been brought in to remix another LP, *All My Best,* more a financial venture than an artistic one. Initially marketed via television on Silver Eagle Records in 1985, then distributed by MCA Records a year later, it is essentially a greatest-hits collection but contains new, near-identical versions of Rick's finest. *All My Best* went on to sell nearly one million copies.

Rick, conceding at last that he needed a producer's objective ear, called Haskell and said, "Jimmie, let's make records the way we used to."

Which is what they did on the new album, bypassing state-of-the-art technology in favor of tube microphones, live echo chambers, an antiquated three-track tape machine, and the same mixing board from United Recorders studio B where Rick waxed so many classics in the early 1960s. Haskell went so far as to contact James Burton to overdub some solos after the first of the year.

So that Rick could record free of record-company dictates, Greg McDonald decided to finance the production himself, then sell it to a label. The day Rick died, Curb Records was finalizing a contract.

"It was a thrill to have Rick with our company," said founder Mike Curb, a onetime lieutenant governor of California who claims to own most of Rick's early 45s. "In my last conversation with him, he indicated that he was ready to go in a progressive country direction, which would have fit in well with our artist roster." Curb Records is home to such successful new-country acts as Hank Williams, Jr., the Judds and Sawyer Brown.

Speculating on how Rick might have fared in the country field, Curb said, "I think he would have been very successful, because he didn't have to change his music at all to be accepted. His hits from the fifties and sixties, and then particularly 'Garden Party' and the Stone Canyon Band records had a definite progressive-country feel, which was the direction country music took in the nineteen eighties."

Ten tracks stood at various stages of completion, most requiring instrumental overdubs, and two, Rick's final, polished vocals. But even in their rough form, they reclarify his musical identity.

In spirit the unreleased LP recalls the original *Memphis Sessions,* containing gutbucket rock & roll (the Beatles' "One After 909," Jerry Fuller's "You Got Me Gone") and heartbreaking ballads. Rick's voice took on an appealing graininess in his later years and ached with yearning on quieter numbers like "Lucky Boy" and "As Long As I Have You."

Most affecting of all is his version of Buddy Holly's tender "True Love Ways." He'd covered it once before, in Memphis. But that tape was collecting dust in an Epic Records vault, and Rick liked the song so much that he decided to do it again. He'd been moved to sing it the first time after seeing the movie *The Buddy Holly Story,* which closes emotionally with "True Love Ways."

Holly was also on his mind that week in 1979 because Rick was appearing at the second annual Buddy Holly memorial concert held at Clear Lake, Iowa's Surf Ballroom. It was there that the twenty-two-year-old Texan had given his last performance exactly twenty years before, on February 2, 1959. Early the next morning, he, J. P. "the Big Bopper" Richardson, and Richie Valens died when their chartered plane plunged into a snow-covered pasture shortly after takeoff.

Musicians' humor leans toward the black and profane, but it's an unspoken rule that you don't joke about air disasters. In a trifling incident that would acquire macabre significance seven years later, Rick was singing "True Love Ways" when guitarist John Beland drew and held up to the control-room window a cartoon depicting Buddy Holly, his glasses smashed. The caption read, "Buddy Holly at the Moment of Impact." Rick burst out laughing, spoiling that take, as well as most of those to follow. However, on the plane ride back from Clear Lake, he reflected solemnly on Holly's fate. "Boy," he said, "that must be a terrible way to die."

The day after Christmas 1985, a smiling Rick breezed into Hollywood's Conway Recorders to rerecord "True Love Ways." He'd enjoyed a particularly merry Christmas Eve at home with all four children, Harriet and David, and Helen. Though some strain remained, the two brothers had smoothed out most of their differences. Helen's sister Marti was also there.

"It was really fun and very warm," she recalled. "They had the Christmas tree decorated. I remember Rick looking at it and saying, 'I've got to thank Helen for this, because she did it all.' "

Helen almost always came to the studio with Rick, but she stayed home packing the couple's bags for a quick tour. Instead of running until two, three in the morning as usual, this night's session would have to wrap up by eleven-thirty so that the group could catch the flight out.

Holly's original "True Love Ways," issued after his death, was drenched with violins, saxophone, drums, and harp. Rick interpreted it intimately, studio lights dimmed, with just acoustic guitar and bass. The performance, taped live, is a haunting one, and not merely because it is Rick's final recording.

His voice opens the song starkly—"Just you know . . ."— the guitar and bass falling in on ". . . why . . ." Sounding as if he's in the room with the listener, Rick caresses the simple lyrics, letting the *s* in *ways* linger on his tongue.

He wanted to retake several lines, but it was getting late. Time to head to the airport.

"Great vocal," Jimmie Haskell called out as Rick slipped on his black leather jacket.

"Yeah, it came off pretty well," he replied. "Well, see you next week, Jimmie. We'll work some more on it."

Fifteen

As its affectionate nicknames "Gooney Bird," "Placid Plodder," and "Bucket of Bolts" suggest, the Douglas DC-3 is hardly graceful. It waddles down runways, groaning and creaking, then staggers into the air, wings flexing as if attached to the fuselage with springs. But since its maiden voyage in 1935, the twin-propeller DC-3 has earned its reputation as the most dependable aircraft in aviation history.

Tales of its air-worthiness invite skepticism: One smacked a mountaintop during heavy turbulence, losing several feet off its wingtip, yet landed safely. Another withstood a bomb explosion in its baggage compartment. And yet another flew on just one wing after a midair collision with a larger Lockheed Hudson bomber during World War II.

The prospect of guiding a DC-3 lights up a pilot's eyes. "I'd wanted to fly one since I was three years old," said Ken Ferguson,

Rick's private copilot. "To me it epitomized *airplane*." Because it can carry a large load economically, the bulky craft makes excellent transportation for traveling rock & roll acts. However, its tendency to vibrate, belch smoke, and gush oil frequently unnerves those not fond of flying.

Surprisingly, given his youthful death-defying exploits on the racetrack, the trapeze, and in the bullring, Rick dreaded airplanes, as did his mother. On landings and takeoffs he unconsciously fingered the cross that Harriet had given him. Sometimes he tossed back a shot of liquor. Ferguson recalled how on departure days Rick carefully studied the local TV weather forecasts.

"He'd buttonhole me and say, 'What about this storm front over Tennessee? How's that going to affect us?' Sometimes it was a little embarrassing," Ferguson admitted with a laugh, "because he knew more about the weather conditions than I did."

Despite his fear, Rick snobbishly refused to travel by bus. In May 1985, after years of leasing private jets and flying commercially, Rick decided he needed his own plane. Though he could ill afford one, the convenience was worth it to him. He and Brad Rank, who'd piloted Rick's chartered flights since 1983, fell instantly in love with a 1944 DC-3 that had belonged to the DuPont family and later to Jerry Lee Lewis.

"It was a magnificent airplane in tremendous condition," said Ferguson, "with real low airtime and all sorts of extras the average DC-3 doesn't have. There were only nine of them in corporate service at that time. The next day I got a phone call from Brad saying they'd made a deal on it." Unlike the cramped Jet Commander he'd been using, the DC-3 comfortably sat fourteen people, its immaculate interior featuring two triple-seat divans, two doubles, four singles, kitchen, bathroom and bar. "A traveling house," Ferguson called it.

Although vintage DC-3s usually require high maintenance, Rick's seemed beset by mechanical mishaps. In August, bound for Hemet, California, from San Francisco, the craft had to make an emergency landing in Salinas when the left radial engine's oil line blew. Another time, while taking off from the Hollywood-Burbank Airport, Brad Rank forgot to turn on the oil pump, blowing an engine. Yet he handily piloted the DC-3 over the San Gabriel Mountains and set it down on the other side in Lancaster. The band, muttering curses, had to push the plane off the runway.

In September a malfunctioning sparkplug blew Rick's opportunity to participate in the first Farm Aid concert organized in Champaign, Illinois, by Willie Nelson and John Cougar Mellencamp. The nationally telecast all-day benefit starred Bob Dylan, Tom Petty, George Jones, Don Henley, and other major acts. Taxiing down the runway in Memphis, the right engine sputtered and died. An irate Greg McDonald, who for financial reasons had argued against Rick's purchasing the $138,000 craft, kicked it and yelled, "Sell this damn thing to the first person who walks by!"

As much as Rick didn't like to fly, "He felt safe on the plane," said Willy Nelson, reinvolved with his cousin's career since 1982, "because he knew they could land it anywhere. And he had a whole escape plan to get out of it." Not everyone felt so secure inside the aging craft. When Rick once offered Jerry Lee Lewis a ride, its former owner is said to have replied, "I may be crazy, but I ain't *that* crazy." It became a safety concern among the band members as well, although to what degree is unclear.

Ricky Intveld's brother James, still bitter toward Rick's management, claimed, "Nobody wanted to fly on that plane. It was always breaking down. Rick liked it because he thought it was a cool old plane, but the truth was, the plane was a tank; a piece of shit. My brother used to call from the road and say, 'The plane's cheesing out. I don't want to get on it. What do I do?' Bobby, Andy, Patrick, Ricky [Intveld], and I hardly ever talked about the music anymore, we talked about the plane."

Returning from Australia via commercial airliner in mid-October 1985, the group was informed that Rank and Ferguson would meet them in Houston with the repaired DC-3. Rather than board it, pianist Chapin quit for a few days (a denied pay raise also influenced his decision) but quickly reconsidered. James Intveld contends that the others, including Bobby Neal, also contemplated leaving the band because of the plane, an allegation the late guitarist's wife refutes.

"That didn't have anything to do with Bobby's decision," said Phyllis Neal. "I know that a lot of the guys picked against the plane. They hated it. I really don't know why."

Copilot Ferguson heatedly repudiates charges that the band feared the DC-3. "None of them said to me they hated the airplane or didn't think it was safe. Frankly, the disquiet wasn't with the airplane itself, it was with Brad and the way he ran the airplane." Following the crash, in which Ferguson suffered severe burns, "There was a lot of loose talk in the papers about the plane being in bad condition, and that simply was not true," he said. "I would not have flown it if it were. Certainly there were areas I would have liked to see improved—I wanted new radios, things like that—but they were not areas of major safety concern."

It was an irritable group that assembled at the airport the night of December 26. Nobody welcomed being on the road Christmas week, including Rick. "That was one of the few times he actually said, 'I really don't want to go out,'" recalled Greg McDonald, adding, "The only reason Rick went on that tour was because Kris had her attorney send him a letter saying he owed her money. She'd figured out in her arithmetic that he was behind in his payments, which we later found out he wasn't."

Besides unhappiness over being away during the holidays, a premonition of doom pervaded the usually jovial entourage. Ken Ferguson had felt it all week. While packing his bags for the trip, the copilot's roommate, a flying buddy, barged into his room. "Ferg, don't go," he blurted.

"What do you mean, don't go?"

"You're scared to death. You've been walking around this apartment like a caged animal for days. I've never seen you like this before, and I don't think you should go."

"I was full of foreboding and so distraught that I literally ruined Christmas for my family," reflected the veteran flier. "I was nervous. Terribly. But I couldn't pinpoint why. None of us could. It was just a nonspecific disquiet very much associated with the group being on the road." Ferguson had been plagued by these thoughts since June, which is when Tracy Nelson began having the same presentiments about her father.

According to Ferguson, Ricky Intveld's parents later mentioned to him that their boy acted strangely over Christmas. Harriet Nelson likewise remarked on Rick's unusual behavior. "When he was home for Christmas," she told Ferguson, "it was as if he were doing things for the last time, as if he were saying good-bye."

The seven passengers included Rick, Helen, the four musicians, and road manager/soundman Clark Russell, who'd previously worked in that capacity for Rick in the mid-1970s. Band members were nearly as fond of the burly, bearded thirty-eight-year-old as they were of Rick. "An unbelievable character," Dennis Larden called him. "Intelligent, worldly. If you were on the space shuttle and all the systems went down, Clark is the guy you'd want."

Russell and the others at least took consolation in the fact that this would be a short itinerary, taking the band to Orlando, Florida; Guntersville, Alabama; and Dallas, for a New Year's Eve extravaganza. The dates in Guntersville, a town of seven thousand, were a favor to former band member Pat Upton. He'd opened a club there called P. J.'s Alley. Rick had agreed to play at no fee, just a percentage of the door to pay his band.

Wherever it landed, Rick's DC-3 never failed to attract aviation enthusiasts, and the small Guntersville airport was no exception. Iris Harris from nearby Fort Payne, there working on her private pilot's license, was excited by the arrival of both Rick Nelson and a vintage DC-3.

"He was really nice," she remembered. "I asked him if I could see the inside of the aircraft, and he said, 'Come on in.'" Rick, proud of the plane, always liked to show it off. Bob Lock, a pilot friend of Harris's and a Boeing Aircraft engineer, said, "The pilots were very proud of it too. It was a beautiful airplane, well kept." Lock gave Rank and Ferguson a lift to the local Holiday Inn where the band was staying.

Rick put on two shows Saturday night at P. J.'s Alley, a converted brick warehouse and tire store that held 240. The local fire department ticketed Pat Upton for overcrowding, but able to charge a club-record $12 admission for someone of Rick's stature, he didn't much mind paying the fine.

With the club closed on Sunday, Rick and Helen drove around town, stopping at picturesque Lake Guntersville and paying a visit to Upton's family. "I was surprised," said Upton, "because Rick never went places." He observed, "Rick really seemed in a good mood. He was real positive about the music he was doing."

On Monday, December 30, Rick gave what would be his final performance, closing with Buddy Holly's "Rave On." As the crowd cheered, he unhooked his guitar, smiled, and shouted, "Rave on for me!" Afterward he patiently signed autographs for an endless line of fans that included Iris Harris, tickled that Rick remembered her from the other afternoon. Many fans have since contacted her, offering to buy her autographed cocktail napkin and photographs of Rick and Helen at the airport. "But they're my treasures," she said.

Tuesday morning at around 8:30,[1] the sleepy entourage arrived at the airport. All were disheartened to learn they'd be delayed, first by fog and then by a minor mechanical problem: a clogged primer line preventing the left engine from starting.

Some published reports claimed that while waiting for the line to be fixed, the musicians griped about the plane's condition. Not true, said airport operator Greg Leach. "We sat and talked

[1] All times are Central Standard Time.

263

all day long about how it was such a gorgeous airplane even though it was so old. As a matter of fact, one of the band members said, 'It takes money to fly on a Lear, but it takes *style* to fly on a DC-3.' "

Leach and Ricky Intveld drove into town and brought everyone back lunches of hamburgers and homemade onion rings, and when the young drummer admired an old military officer's hat hanging on a wall, Leach gave it to him. Intveld eagerly tried it on, saying, "Watch for our next music video; I'm gonna wear this hat in it."

En route to Dallas, the DC-3 was to stop in Memphis and pick up Bobby Neal's wife. The guitarist, concerned over the delay, called home from a pay phone. "You're here already?" asked Phyllis Neal, looking at the clock. It was 11:00 A.M.

"No, we're still in Guntersville; something's wrong with the plane."

Realizing the group might be late for its show, she told him, "Bobby, don't bother landin' the plane in Memphis. Y'all go on to Dallas when you're ready to leave, and I'll have a big New Year's dinner ready when you get in."

Phyllis Neal went out for a while. When she returned mid-afternoon the phone machine contained a message from her husband: "Phyllis, I'm still in Guntersville. We're gettin' ready to take off. Boy, we're runnin' real late. I just wanted to call and tell you and the kids that I love you, and I'll see you in the morning." In the confusion after the crash, the message got erased.

"I think about that a lot," Phyllis said ruefully, "that it was my very last message from Bobby." For a time, she tormented herself with guilt, believing that if she'd only insisted they pick her up in Memphis . . . well, perhaps the crash might have been avoided somehow. "Now I feel different," she said. "I feel that I was blessed, in a way."

Pat Upton had said his good-byes to the band at the airport in the morning before driving up to Huntsville to return equipment he'd rented for Rick's three shows. Passing by the airport on his way home several hours later, he was surprised to see the plane sitting on the runway. "They were just getting ready to take off," he remembered. "Rick said he'd like to come back to Guntersville. The last thing I saw was Bobby Neal waving to me out the cockpit window." At around 1:00 the DC-3 lumbered into the gray sky and disappeared west into the horizon.

At 5:08, approximately one hundred twenty miles east of their destination, copilot Ken Ferguson radioed the Fort Worth Air Route Traffic Control Center. "I think I'd like to turn around, uh, head for Texarkana here," he said tersely. "I've got a little problem . . ."

Mike Sullivan, waiting at Dallas's Love Field to collect Rick and the band and drive them to the Park Suite Hotel, was growing fidgety. It was past 5:00, New Year's Eve revelers would begin arriving at the hotel within the hour, and his headline attraction was still somewhere in the air. When at first it wasn't clear if Rick's DC-3 would be available, the promoter had booked them on Continental Airlines. He still holds copies of the tickets.

Earlier in the day Sullivan had spoken to Clark Russell from Guntersville. "I don't know if we'll ever get the hell out of here," the road manager told him. "Brad is out there, and they're doing all sorts of stuff to the engine. I hope we make it."

"Clark, don't even talk that way," he replied nervously. "You've *got* to be here."

Sullivan, president of the Starforce International entertainment company, had already sunk two months of preparation and $50,000 for promotion into the festivities at the Park Suite, a new luxury hotel located just off the LBJ Freeway. He'd constructed a twenty-five-foot stage in the center of the tower-type building so that guests could guzzle champagne and watch the show from their balconies. All two hundred eighty suites were sold out at $169.95 each, and an additional five hundred patrons had paid for seats on the floor.

265

It promised to be a memorable evening. "An event," said Sullivan.

"Fort Worth, just any field will do, we've got a problem here."

Sixty seconds after requesting clearance for Texarkana, straddling the Texas-Arkansas border twenty miles to the east, pilot Brad Rank indicated he could not keep the DC-3 aloft long enough to make it there. His voice betrayed unmistakable alarm, as did the voice that startled Rick's manager at home in Palm Springs. In the event of an emergency with aircraft N711Y, the flight plan listed Greg McDonald as the person to contact.

The caller, identifying himself as an officer with the Texas Department of Public Safety, was speaking over a two-way radio as he sped along a country road, trying to follow the DC-3's erratic path. "The plane is on an emergency-landing pattern near Texarkana," he said. "It's smoking, and it's coming down!" McDonald, not believing what he heard, did not think to tell the officer whose plane it was. Not that it mattered.

"You're going to have to stand by." For thirty agonizing minutes Rick's manager kept the receiver pressed tightly to his ear, envisioning the worst. Every so often the officer came back on the line to shout, "Don't leave the phone, don't leave the phone, this is an emergency!"

At 5:11 either Rank or Ferguson radioed again, gasping for breath: ". . . smoke in the cockpit . . . have smoke in the cockpit . . ." No more transmissions followed. The dense smoke billowing in from the cabin totally obscured both pilots' vision. Rank managed to steer the craft only by poking his head out the blackened cockpit window and frantically looking for a spot to land.

Burning debris from the fuselage rained to the ground six hundred feet below, igniting grass fires in a DeKalb, Texas, pasture. Farmer Don Lewis, grazing his cattle, peered into the sky and saw the crippled plane, with smoke trailing from its right side and "making a funny noise." It disappeared over the trees, as Rank tried in vain to set down the DC-3 on a highway, then reappeared from the east. Craning his neck, Lewis muttered, "Put it down, boy, and get the heck out of there."

In Marin County, California, former Stone Canyon Band bassist Stephen Love was driving home when suddenly "I got this incredible heat flash in my body," forcing him to pull off the road. He sat there stunned, wondering, *My God, what's going on?* And in Houston, Rick's loyal fan Francine "Frenchy" Falik, then in her late thirties and a writer for the *Houston Post*, sat behind the wheel of her car "when all of a sudden it hit me that Rick was coming to Texas.

"I get these feelings, they're real," she insisted, "and I was so excited. It was as if he'd come down and told me that he was coming." At approximately the same time, 5:14, Rick's plane vanished from the Fort Worth air-traffic controller's radar screen.

As Don Lewis watched in horror, the DC-3 severed two power lines, snapped a utility pole, plowed into a tree, shearing off its left wing, and finally plunged into a wooded area two hundred yards from a farmhouse. Both pilots scrambled out their cockpit windows, tumbling ten feet to the ground, then turned around to look at the wreckage. Ken Ferguson told investigators from the National Transportation Safety Board, "Flames and smoke was all that one could see," and that the cabin area "appeared to be an inferno." Fearing an explosion, he hobbled away from the craft as quickly as he could.

From up to two hundred yards away, eyewitnesses could feel the searing heat of flames that leaped as high as seventy-five feet. According to Lewis, when fire trucks from the little town of DeKalb arrived on the scene, "They wouldn't let anyone near the plane." The fiery tomb, holding seven bodies inside, was left to burn and smolder all night. Eerily, the DC-3's left propeller kept spinning until finally engulfed by the blaze.

The officer from the Texas Department of Public Safety finally got back on the line with a terrified Greg McDonald. "The plane has crashed," he said. "There are two survivors on the ground. We don't know who they are. We think they're the pilots." Then, abruptly, "Hold on!" For the next twenty minutes McDonald listened anxiously as ambulance and fire-engine sirens wailed in the background.

Had one of his sons not been seriously injured in a hiking accident the month before, McDonald and his family would have been on the DC-3 themselves. Rick had talked him out of joining the group in Orlando. "Stay home with little Greg," Rick scolded his manager. "Don't feel obligated to come out just for a couple of shows." On another phone line McDonald began the grim task of informing the families that the plane had gone down but that fatalities had not yet been firmly established.

"Let me know. I'll tell the kids," Kris snapped and hung up. Harriet accepted the news stoically. "Please call me back as soon as you find out for sure," she said softly. Both she and McDonald clung to the thin hope that perhaps at the last minute Rick and Helen had decided to take a commercial flight to Dallas. Unfortunately, before McDonald received official confirmation that Rick had indeed perished in the crash, Harriet heard her son's death reported on the TV news.

She immediately called St. Michael Hospital in Texarkana, where the two survivors were taken. They were the two pilots, she was told. Brad Rank was listed in good condition. Ken Ferguson, his skin so badly scorched that St. Michael helicopter pilot Bob Ellison "thought he was a Negro," was in serious condition and later rushed to a burn center in Little Rock, Arkansas. Harriet expressed to hospital authorities her hope that the two men would recover.

Besides being heartbroken, she was angry. "I can't believe they would handle Rick's death this way," she cried to Mike Sullivan. In a statement issued later, Harriet said, "It's very cruel of them to let me find out about my son's death through a blurb on national television." The Texas Department of Public

Safety defended its actions, claiming it was policy to make victims' identities public whether or not families have been notified.

Matthew Nelson also learned of his father's death through the media. He was in his car, happily listening to "Garden Party" on the radio. Then an announcer sadly intoned, ". . . A tribute to Rick Nelson, killed in a plane crash earlier today." The teenager started screaming. Both he and Gunnar were to have accompanied their father east, but Rick abruptly and without explanation changed his mind, telling them they could come along on another short trip instead.

All around the country, those whose lives Rick had touched most closely were devastated. Charley Britt, a newscaster at WRDW-TV in Augusta, Georgia, had to go on the air and inform viewers his friend of twenty-five years was dead. The first thing that flashed through his mind was how Rick always talked about the two ways he didn't want to die: either in a fire or in a plane crash. "I just thought, *How ironic, that this way of dying should happen*," Britt recalled.

Certainly the horrible manner in which Rick lost his life made it even more painful to bear.

"He didn't deserve that," said Sharon Sheeley, returning by boat from Catalina Island when she heard the news over a portable television. "I sat there thinking, *It can't be my Ricky, it must be some football player*." She bit deeply into her hand, which still bears a scar, and reflected on how thirty years earlier "a little fan with braces bullshitted this beautiful kid" into recording her song "Poor Little Fool."

In Birmingham, Alabama, another of Rick's early songwriters, Baker Knight, broke into uncontrollable sobs. "That's the first time that ever happened to me," he said. That night in his study he noticed that a picture of a bullfighter—which always reminded him of Rick—had fallen off the wall.

Back at the Dallas Park Suite Hotel, guests had been preparing for the evening's gala. Now shocked cries reverberated through the building. Radio personality Ken "Hubcap" Carter from old-ies station KLUV, there to broadcast Rick's concert, an-nounced, "I've got some bad news for those listening on the radio and here in the audience. The plane carrying Rick Nelson from Alabama crashed tonight."

Only about a quarter of the patrons demanded refunds; the rest stayed to listen to local entertainers sing Rick's music in tribute. Upon finishing his show elsewhere in town, country star Johnny Lee headed over to the Park Suite to perform, as did several other name attractions. The mood, though, re-mained somber. "People were trying to have a good time," said Carter, "but they couldn't."

At midnight, there was a toast and a moment of silence in memory of the late Rick Nelson.

It had been a long-running Nelson-family joke that "It's Late" should have been Rick's theme song. Stone Canyon Band mem-bers cracked that Rick observed "Nelson Standard Time," always arriving about a half-hour behind schedule. The problem grew so acute that at one point he'd received counseling.

So it seemed consistent that Rick's remains were lost in transit from Texas to California, delaying funeral arrangements by several days. "We can't find Rick," David had to explain to condolence callers. Harriet commented how fitting it was—and how Rick would have found it hilarious—that he should literally be late to his own funeral.

Between the day of the fatal accident, December 31, and the funeral, January 6, Kris rocked the already distraught family by threatening to sue for part of Rick's life-insurance money. Based on an agreement reached after the divorce settlement, it was supposed to have gone to their four children. Rather than battle in court, David let her have the money from one of Rick's two policies.

Kris further outraged the clan by trying to wrest control of the estate from David, appointed administrator in a Last Will and Testament that Rick drew up four months before his death.[2] Rick bequeathed his entire estate to his children, explicitly failing to provide for his ex-wife, his illegitimate son, Eric Crewe, and Helen Blair. Two weeks after the funeral a Los Angeles Superior Court Judge would reject Kris's bid.

Her legal disputes with David and her children created tremendous tension at the funeral, held on a blue-skied Monday at Hollywood's Forest Lawn Memorial Cemetery. "Nobody wanted Kris to be there," Alan Bush said, adding, "The kids really didn't want her there. Matthew and Gunnar wouldn't even get in the car with her; Tracy had to calm them down."

Kris emerged pale-faced from a limousine, aware of the hostility directed at her. A family member's accusation that she feigned grief seems harsh, however. One has to believe that despite her vindictiveness Kris felt an eternal bond with Rick, her first love, her husband of over fifteen years, and the father of her four children.

As seven hundred tearful fans watched, two hundred fifty mourners from all phases of Rick's life filed into the white-spired red-brick Church of the Hills, where David and June had been married. They included "Colonel" Tom Parker, Connie Stevens, Angie Dickinson, dozens of actors, writers, and crew members from the Nelson show, and many, many musicians.

David prepared a moving memorial service celebrating Rick's

---

[2] The original copy of Rick's will never turned up, and so a photocopy was filed in court as a lost will. According to attorney Barbra Reinecke, Rick signed the three-page document in her presence backstage at the Universal Amphitheatre concert in August 1985. "Obviously there was no copy machine there," she explained, "so I made a copy in my office the next day and mailed it to Rick."

Or so she thought. When David Nelson called for the will, Reinecke went to the safe in which she stored such papers and found the photocopy. "That's when I realized I must have sent the original to Rick and put the photocopy in my safe. So they probated the photocopy. There was no question; it's his signature."

In his will, Rick additionally directed that Greg McDonald continue to manage and make all creative decisions concerning his name, likeness, and show business properties, except for *The Adventures of Ozzie and Harriet*. Although this provision specifically stated that McDonald "shall be paid the usual fee of 15 percent of all gross revenues," inexplicably it aroused intense resentment among certain family members for several years.

life. The ceremony began on a bizarre note, however, when the same Rev. Francis J. Parrish who'd presided over Rick and Kris's 1963 wedding rhapsodized about the happy couple, stirring murmurs of resentment among the congregation.

"He talked about, 'When I first met Rick and Kris . . . ,' as if they'd been happily married all that time," said Charley Britt. "That kind of bothered me. I didn't understand it."

David read a condolence from President Ronald Reagan (whose politics, incidentally, Rick despised). He prefaced the Lord's Prayer with a remembrance of how when he and Rick were kids, their father played hide-and-seek with them at bedtime, then kneeled with them in singing the Lord's Prayer. All of Rick's children delivered eulogies, Tracy calling her father "a quiet and honorable man" and drawing laughs when she said, "The man had class. He was an artist. He was wise. And he loved ice cream." Sam read from an American Indian poem.

Most emotional of all was Matthew and Gunnar singing Rick's "Easy to Be Free," bringing tears to everyone's eyes. "One of them said, 'I don't want to see any of you crying, because Pop wouldn't have wanted that,'" Gordon Stoker remembered. "I thought that was such a sweet thing." At the family's request, he and the Jordanaires sang several spirituals, their voices close to breaking on "Peace in the Valley" and "Just a Closer Walk With Thee."

The Jordanaires were slated to join Rick in Dallas for New Year's Eve, but the plans unraveled at the last minute. When it was first broadcast that Rick and four band members had been killed, "our phones started ringing," said Ray Walker, "because people thought it was us." Stoker added, "I always wondered why we were spared."

Harriet's strength throughout was an inspiration. "I was amazed at the lady's ability to carry on," recalled Jimmie Haskell, badly shaken by Rick's death. "There she was, reassuring her relatives, when she had just experienced a severe loss." At one point, some youngsters in the congregation broke down crying. "Harriet, always being this gracious lady, got up, went over and hugged them, to reassure them that everything was all right."

Helen Blair's name was not uttered once at his funeral, a slight that bothered some. "It was as if she had no more importance in Rick's life than a friend," said Lee Miller, recording engineer on his last two albums. Obviously troubled throughout her life, Helen has not been allowed to find peace in death either. Her parents refuse to bury her remains, which greatly upsets older sister Marti Ditonto. "I don't even talk to them now," she said wistfully. John and Ruth Blair brought a $2 million wrongful death suit against Rick's estate, one of over seventy-five lawsuits filed, totaling more than $21 million.

The funeral ended as strangely as it began, Kris and Tracy getting into a fight over Kris's plans to sue for the life-insurance money. "She threw Tracy down," said Alan Bush, "and started hitting her with her purse." Kris did not return with the others to David's house after the ceremony but did attend the private burial days later. Fueling David's anger, she arrived late.

Rick was laid to rest on a gentle slope overlooking the San Fernando Valley, several steps from the graves of his father and his maternal grandmother. Following the brief graveside prayer and interment, David could no longer contain his rage. Turning on Kris, he screamed, "Murderess!"

Sixteen

Although Rick had avoided controversy throughout his life, the media saw in his tragic death an opportunity to "expose" the Boy Next Door.

On January 15, 1986, the *Washington Post* front page blared, "Drug-Related Fire Suspected in Rick Nelson Plane Crash." Page six's jump head was more specific: "Cocaine Use Suspected in Nelson Plane Crash." The story itself, not nearly as sensationalistic as its headline suggested, reported responsibly that onboard drug use was *one of several* possibilities federal investigators were considering as having caused the fire that killed Rick, forty-five; Helen Blair, twenty-nine; Bobby Neal, thirty-eight; Pat Woodward, thirty-five; Andy Chapin, thirty-three; Ricky Intveld, twenty-three; and Clark Russell, thirty-eight.

The National Transportation Safety Board's (NTSB) investigation would ultimately take a year and a half, impeded by a lack of physical evidence due to the plane's near-total destruction. It was briefly speculated that one or more of the passengers had been freebasing cocaine, a process whereby the powerful drug is mixed with an alkaline solution and ether, then cooked over a flame. This leaves pure free-based crystals, which are heated in a glass waterpipe and drawn deeply into the lungs.

Of all methods of taking cocaine, freebasing produces the most potent high. It speeds the drug to the brain in a mere six to seven seconds, twice as fast as injecting it intravenously, and more than twenty times quicker than snorting it. Because the substances involved are so flammable, and the user so euphoric, freebasing can also be hazardous. In 1980 comedian Richard Pryor accidentally set his shirt on fire while smoking the drug and suffered life-threatening burns over the upper half of his body.

Despite the implications of the *Post*'s headline, any evidence suggesting freebasing was purely circumstantial. Investigators found no drug paraphernalia in the wreckage, although the media treated the discovery of eighteen aerosol cans as a virtual indictment. (Aerosol propellants are sometimes used as solvents.) These were hardly contraband but standard traveling accessories for entertainers: hair sprays and deodorants.

And while toxicology reports did reveal small amounts of cocaine or its metabolite, benzoylecgonine, in the blood and urine of Rick, Woodward, and Chapin, no toxicological test can determine either the method or the time of ingestion, as cocaine remains detectable in urine up to three days after the last dose.

When in February 1986 the NTSB made public the results of these two toxicology studies, conducted by the Civil Aeromedical Institute in Oklahoma City and the Center for Human Toxicology at the University of Utah in Salt Lake City, it cautioned that no conclusions could or should be drawn. The safety board quickly discounted the freebase theory altogether.

But as far as millions of readers were concerned, Rick Nelson, in a drug-induced stupor, carelessly set fire to his plane eight thousand feet in the sky, killing himself and six others. The story was especially shocking given its subject, who for years epitomized an era of innocence.

As the toxicology reports clearly verified, Rick did take drugs. In addition to cocaine, the tests also uncovered traces of THC, marijuana's main psychoactive ingredient, as well as the painkiller Darvon. In determining the extent of his use we must take into account society's attitudes toward drugs, which, coincidentally, began shifting toward a more conservative, sensible position right about the time Rick was killed.

Like many of his peers Rick began dabbling with substances in the 1960s. A touring musician who lived among Hollywood's so-called beautiful people in an era of rampant experimentation, he was extremely susceptible. And not that it should be this way, but intoxicants and rock & roll have gone hand in hand ever since the music began.

Denial is common among families of drug users, but for most of his life Rick's use was mild enough that according to Connie Nelson, "If there was a drug problem, Harriet and David were not aware of it. I think you would have trouble convincing them there was." Gordon Stoker of the Jordanaires becomes indignant when the subject of Rick and drugs is even mentioned. "We worked with him for two years before he died, and we saw no evidence of that," he said firmly. "Complete lies."

Kris's allegations during the divorce that her husband had a "severe drug problem," were lawyerly hyperbole. And her claims that Rick permitted "wild parties to take place in his home at all hours, during which drugs are always taken," and that the children were "literally in physical danger" from the "drugged and unpredictable persons" there, were laughable. Rick didn't throw parties of any kind, and if the kids were in such danger, why did she send Matthew and Gunnar to temporarily live with Rick in 1981, when she'd been granted legal custody of the twins?

The fairest way to gauge Rick's usage is by relating the accounts of those who spent the most time with him—his fellow musicians. Their descriptions, offered reluctantly, sound a similar theme: Drugs were present, but they weren't a "problem." Miles Thomas, the Stone Canyon Band's first road manager, recalled that when he, Allen Kemp, Pat Shanahan, and Randy Meisner met Rick in 1969, "We were wondering about drugs, because we all smoked pot. We wanted to play it real straight, figuring he'd be real straight; turns out he wasn't at all. We all wound up being one big traveling party on the road."

Singer-songwriter Eric Andersen, a friend in the late 1960s and early 1970s: "He was a pothead; liked getting high. I remember we took mescaline and went to a Rolling Stones concert. He'd never done anything like that. We sat up there watching Mick Taylor playing, Keith Richards, and we almost rocked right out of the balcony."

Jay White, bassist from 1973 to 1977 and again in 1983: "I didn't see a lot of it [drugs]. I mean, I saw a little cocaine here and there, and participated in some of it too. We were pretty much left to do what we damn wanted, which was smoke pot, maybe toot a little coke on the airplane back and forth, behind the stage before the job. But that's about all I saw."

Another band member from the mid-1970s insisted anonymously, "No one was going off the deep end. Obviously any sort of use is abuse, but it never became a real problem. It did not control Rick's life. Back at the hotel after gigs there were no party animals. There might be a toot, a toke, nothing maniacal. It was pretty casual."

John Beland, guitarist from 1978 to 1980: "I had a bout with cocaine, which I'm not ashamed to say. Rick did a little bit too, but he didn't abuse it. We all did it back then, and it was real chic, if you remember, in the late seventies. That's all we did. It kind of kept us going sometimes. It wasn't the right thing to do, but we did it. It was never abused. I never saw Rick once be less than professional as soon as he hit the stage."

Pat Upton, vocalist-guitarist from 1979 to 1982: "I can honestly say that I'm aware Rick did cocaine. To what extent, I don't know, because he never involved me or members of the band. He didn't come around and offer it to us or ask us for it. Whatever he did, he kept to himself."

One reason Rick didn't share with the others was that he rarely had enough to share. "For Rick to have a gram of cocaine was a big deal," said Paul Rose, his friend from 1979 on. "He didn't have the pocket money, for one thing. Rick wasn't an angel, but he wasn't an addict. Nothing harder than cocaine; a line here, a line there. He never freebased in his life." Rick's attitude toward drugs, said Rose, basically came down to, "If they were there, great, and if they weren't, great."

Once Helen Blair became Rick's companion, though, his will-power was tested every day, and toward the end of his life he found it harder to resist temptation. "Helen promoted the co-caine," Rose contended, as did others close to the situation. "She was strung out on drugs and would hound everybody—bellmen in hotels—to get them. Under the pretense of getting them for Rick, of course," he added, "which made it that much easier. Her whole life was drugs."

Did Rick Nelson have a drug problem? By most anybody's definition, absolutely. Did it greatly affect his life's outcome? No. Contrary to Kris's portrayal after his death, their marital problems went far deeper than codependency. His career may have suffered somewhat, although one suspects that Rick's amotivational syndrome in his early forties had less to do with smoking a garden herb than it did with "Garden Party."

Most important of all, recreational drug use did not alter Rick's basic humanity and kindness. "He was still the same good-hearted person, he still cared for people and all," said Tom Brumley, who grew so upset with Rick for using drugs at all, "that played a big part in my quitting the band," he admitted.

"Rick Nelson was one of the greatest guys in the world; he didn't need that stuff." Does anybody? But Rick was no drug casualty. He was never, to quote road manager Clark Russell's favorite saying, "rolling in the gutter with no arms." And he did not in any way contribute to his own death.

On May 21, 1987, the National Transportation Safety Board finally released its report on the accident involving aircraft N711Y. As had been suspected for some time, based on the pilots' statements and examination of the wreckage, everything pointed to a malfunctioning or faultily repaired Janitrol gasoline heater. It was located aft of the lavatory on the right side, which sustained the most severe damage.

The heater had acted erratically before, once in Memphis in September 1985 and several times in the days prior to the fatal flight. Bobby Neal called his wife from Orlando on December 27, 1985, and remarked, "God, I just about burned my ass on that plane." Then, phoning from Guntersville the next day, he complained, "We are freezing to death on that plane! It is so cold. The heater's just not working right." Copilot Ken Ferguson said under oath before the NTSB that pilot Brad Rank had examined it in Alabama the day before the crash but "found nothing of note."

Ferguson's testimony came on March 19, 1986, following his release from the hospital. During those two and a half months, "Harriet was in almost constant touch with my sister and was very concerned about my welfare," he said gratefully. The badly burned copilot's voice had been reduced to a whisper, and it would be another three months before he regained use of his hands. Today his voice is still hoarse, and recurring bouts of pneumonia make it difficult for him to fly. The NTSB found major discrepancies between Ferguson's statements and those of Rank, who appeared before investigators on January 22, 1986.

Several people associated with Rick contend that Rank, then thirty-four, was not popular with the band. "He had an exaggerated conception of his own importance," said one, while another claimed that the aviator seemed to ingratiate himself too much with the musicians for Rick's taste. Rank's version of the events of December 31, 1985, goes like this:

During the flight, he went into the cabin and noticed smoke drifting from the area where Rick and Helen sat. "Instead of investigating that smoke," said the report, "the pilot stated that he went through the baggage compartment to the cabin heater. He said that the heater shield was cool to his touch, and that he saw neither smoke nor fire near the heater. However, he said that he did activate one of the two fire extinguishers attached to the heater.

"He then left the heater area and moved through the cabin, opening the cabin fresh-air inlets on his way back to the cockpit." Rank claimed that when he returned to his seat, Ferguson had already contacted the Fort Worth Air Route Traffic Control Center, and that shortly thereafter the cockpit began filling with smoke.

Ferguson told a much different story:

After the DC-3 was airborne, the heater began to "act up," causing the overheat light on the cockpit control panel to flash. When this happened more than once, the crew turned off the heater, waited, then turned it back on. But the overheat light blinked again. Finally, Rank went to the rear of the plane to try to get it working properly and instructed his copilot, several times, to turn it on.

"One of the times," Ferguson stated, "I refused to turn it on. . . . I was getting nervous. I didn't think that we should be messing with that heater en route. I had discussed this with Brad on previous flights . . . and he turned it on again. . . . Once again, it either shut off, or the overheat light came on; [it] went through the same cycle.

"The last time Brad went aft in the tail, he was aft for not very long, came out and signaled to me to turn it on again, which I did. Several minutes after that Pat Woodward . . . came forward to me and said, 'There is smoke back here in the cabin . . .'"

Ferguson's most damning allegation against Rank concerned the aftermath of the crash landing. After the copilot retreated from the fiery plane, so badly burned that "he had skin hanging off him," according to farmer Don Lewis, Rank hustled over, sat Ferguson on the ground, and repeated urgently, *"Don't tell anyone about the heater, don't tell anyone about the heater . . ."*

Investigators wrote in their report: "If the copilot's statement about the repeated attempts to relight the cabin heater are accurate, then the captain's repeated attempts to troubleshoot and relight the heater apparently resulted in a fire in the area of the heater. There were other potential ignition sources in the area of the heater, such as airplane electrical wires; however, after examination of these systems, none could be identified as having ignited the fire."

Because the wreckage was so completely destroyed, no definitive conclusions about the source of ignition could be reached. But the NTSB did chastise Rank for not closing the fresh air vents (he opened them), not having passengers and crew use supplemental oxygen, and not attempting to fight the fire with the cockpit's handheld extinguisher, all standard emergency procedures. "While these actions, if taken in a timely manner, may not have prevented the loss of the airplane," it said, "they would have enhanced the potential for survival of the passengers."

Ironically, at the time of the accident, Rank was hailed for his masterful landing of the burning aircraft. The seven passengers died not from impact but from smoke inhalation and thermal burns, the official cause of death given by the Dallas County medical examiner. It is likely that by the time the plane touched ground, they had already perished. Their remains were discovered huddled against the bulkhead. Horrifyingly, a recurrent nightmare of Rick's—in which he found himself trapped in a room, with no way out, no escape—had come true.

In February 1990 Rick's children, Ken Ferguson, and the families of Andy Chapin, Pat Woodward, Clark Russell, and Ricky Intveld[1] received a total $4.5 million out-of-court settlement from Duncan Aviation, which repaired the heater; Mid-

---

[1] Helen Blair's parents also received a small settlement, as did Phyllis Neal, who filed a separate action in Texas.

land Ross Corp., which designed the heater; Century Equipment Company, which sold Rick the DC-3; and over a dozen other defendants. A spokesman for Duncan, however, insisted the settlement in no way implied liability.

For those who knew Rick and his band, the fatal accident was doubly tragic because of the insinuations of onboard drug abuse, creating sad epitaphs for those involved. "It put such a cloud over Rick's and everybody else's memories," complained former Stone Canyon Band member Steve Duncan, since 1987 drummer for Chris Hillman's Desert Rose Band. "That's bugged me to this day. It was torture for the families. They were dragged through the mud for months." By the time the NTSB report came out, a year and a half after the plane went down, "nobody saw it or heard it. You ask anybody, and the freebase thing always comes up."

The Nelson family's once sterling reputation was further tarnished when, in a highly publicized 1987 trial, Mark Harmon took Kris to family court to gain custody of Sam. Harmon charged his oldest sister was incapable of mothering the boy, who was then living with Harmon and his new wife, actress Pam Dawber, while Kris underwent drug rehabilitation.

Though a sideshow atmosphere pervaded the weeklong trial, one poignant moment emerged: A psychiatrist who'd interviewed the thin thirteen-year-old related a dream of Sam's in which he and his late father reunite inside an airplane. In a drawing, Sam depicted his mother as a dragon, and complained to the psychiatrist about Kris's mood swings and how she prevented him from seeing his siblings. Harmon abruptly dropped the custody bid, however, after Kris's attorney hinted he might produce witnesses who'd snorted cocaine with Dawber.

Amid the scandalous publicity came an encouraging sign: the twins escorting their mother to and from the Los Angeles Superior Court, evidence that after a bruising couple of years the family's wounds might be healing. Rick, never one for conflicts, would have been pleased. Late that year Tracy, who had recently married longtime beau actor Billy Moses and whose career was in high gear, was diagnosed with Hodgkin's disease, further drawing everyone together. Happily, following surgery, chemotherapy, and radiation, she was pronounced cured.

Harriet came out of seclusion to be with her only grand-daughter, living next to Tracy in Century City for a time. "She's just an unbelievably strong lady," Ken Ferguson observed, "a very, very powerful human being. I think she's indestructible." And forgiving. While Kris was in drug treatment, Harriet sent flowers and a card expressing her love.

"I know Kris stepped hard on some family toes, but she and Harriet are close," said Connie Nelson. "These are big people, and they can overlook the mistakes that are made and are credited to youth, jealousy, unhappiness, whatever."

David is not so forgiving about the past, saying only, "My mother doesn't want to know [the things Kris did to Rick]. I do." After some difficult years personally and professionally in the mid-1970s, David, now a grandfather, is happy in his marriage and his work, running his own production company, Casablanca Productions, and directing TV commercials, series episodes, and the occasional low-budget film. Over the years he's directed former *The Adventures* cast members Don Defore, Parley Baer, and Hal Smith. All compare him favorably to his father. In 1987 David directed and starred in a moving one-hour tribute to Rick, *Rick Nelson: A Brother Remembers*, for which he rummaged through twenty-seven hours of Nelson family footage, much of it never seen before.

The special aired on cable's Disney Channel, which was already running *The Adventures of Ozzie and Harriet* twice a day. After a decade of watching single-parent TV-sitcom families tackle socially relevant problems, the Baby Boomer generation was once again finding comfort in Ozzie Nelson's depiction of what the nuclear family could be like. And so it goes.

A few summers after Rick's death, at a Nelson family barbecue, Harriet sat chatting with Rick's old friend Mary Jo (Sheeley)

Collins. "It was like going to a barbecue at the Kennedys, I imagine," said Mary Jo, once married to Larry Collins of the Collins Kids, "with that kind of family closeness you don't see anymore. Rick's kids were there, and cousins and uncles."

While she and Harriet reminisced, Matthew and Gunnar walked up and handed their grandmother a bouquet of roses. "Oh, thank you!" she exclaimed, giving each a kiss. "Would you do me a favor and take these into the kitchen and put them in water?" With the boys out of earshot, Harriet giggled and whispered to Mary Jo, "You know, I still don't know which one is which.

"Oh, Gunnar!" she called.

"Yeah, grandma?"

"Never mind."

One almost expected to hear Ozzie yell, "Cut!," and for Rick to break into song.

On January 21, 1987, Rick was inducted into the Rock & Roll Hall of Fame, then still housed in a state of mind rather than in an actual edifice. Rick would have found the event's formal tone antithetical to rock & roll's spirit, but he would have been heartened to know his Sun Records idols Carl Perkins and Roy Orbison were among the fourteen other inductees that year.

Upon hearing that Rick was to be instated in the second annual ceremony, John Fogerty volunteered to act as inductor. "I made it very clear that I wanted to be the one to do it. I just felt very strongly about it." For Fogerty, Rick stood not only as a musical inspiration but a personal role model.

"Rick was a guy who seemed to have handled success," he reflected. "He didn't become a jerk, a drunk, a bum, a mean person. He didn't end up wild and crazy like Jerry Lee Lewis. He was a classy guy throughout and handled himself with grace. I think sometimes in this business that thrives on uniqueness, we tend to forget that people who remain classy and very human are also setting an example, that you can make good rock &

roll and not have to be crazy. That became a very basic tenet of what I aspired to be. I wanted to be a guy like that."

At the ceremony, held at the Waldorf-Astoria Hotel in New York, Rick's three oldest children joined Fogerty on stage. Matthew and Gunnar, clad in tuxedos, with flowing manes, and Tracy, in an elegant black dress, all read tributes to their father and his music.

Fogerty spoke passionately about Rick's commitment to rock & roll, calling him a pioneer. "As far as I'm concerned, he made some of the greatest rockabilly records of all time," Fogerty declared. To Sam Phillips, sitting among the distinguished crowd, he said, "Sam, he gave you a run for your money, I think," and while Phillips nodded in agreement, a hush filled the room. As *Rolling Stone* magazine publisher and Hall of Fame vice chairman Jann Wenner had noted earlier in his introduction, the "critical myopia that dogged his career" continued to haunt Rick's memory, even on this day.

"He wrote the lines to 'Garden Party,'" Fogerty continued, "a couple of which were, 'If memories were all I sang, I'd rather drive a truck.' And it's what he firmly believed."

Rick truly did. To the very end.

Discography

SINGLES

Release dates are from Verve, Imperial, Decca, MCA, Epic, and Capitol record catalogs. (Verve Records catalog does not include exact release dates. Imperial Records catalog has exact release dates only for singles issued after mid-1960, with the exception of "A Wonder Like You" b/w [backed with] "Everlovin'.")

Where release dates are not available, the date the record first appeared on *Billboard* magazine's "Best Sellers in Stores" chart and subsequent "Hot 100" chart is given (for both A sides and B sides, if different). Highest-charting side is listed first, even if originally intended as B side. The number in parentheses indicates highest chart position, also according to *Billboard;* noncharting A sides are denoted by (--).

"A Teenager's Romance" [Verve 10047], released April 24, 1957 (#2); b/w "I'm Walking" (#4).
"You're My One and Only Love" [Verve 10070], first charted September 16, 1957 (#14); b/w "Honey Rock."

"Be-Bop Baby" [Imperial 5463], first charted October 7, 1957 (#3); b/w "Have I Told You Lately That I Love You?" (#29).

"Stood Up" [Imperial 5483], first charted December 30, 1957 (#2); b/w "Waitin' in School" (#18).

"Believe What You Say" [Imperial 5503], first charted April 7, 1958 (#4); b/w "My Bucket's Got a Hole in It" (#14).

"Poor Little Fool" [Imperial 5528], first charted July 7, 1958 (#1); b/w "Don't Leave Me This Way."

"Lonesome Town" [Imperial 5545], first charted October 20, 1958 (#7); b/w "I Got a Feeling," first charted October 13, 1958 (#10).

"Never Be Anyone Else but You" [Imperial 5565], first charted February 23, 1959 (#6); b/w "It's Late," first charted March 2, 1959 (#9).

"Just a Little Too Much" [Imperial 5595], first charted June 29, 1959 (#9); b/w "Sweeter Than You," first charted July 6, 1959 (#9).

"I Wanna Be Loved" [Imperial 5614], first charted November 30, 1959 (#20); b/w "Mighty Good" (#38).

"Young Emotions" [Imperial 5663], first charted April 25, 1960 (#12); b/w "Right by My Side," first charted May 2, 1960 (#59).

"I'm Not Afraid" [Imperial 5685], released August 8, 1960 (#27); b/w "Yes Sir, That's My Baby" (#34).

"You Are the Only One" [Imperial 5707], released November 16, 1960 (#25); b/w "Milk Cow Blues" (#79).

"Travelin' Man" [Imperial 5741], released April 4, 1961 (#1); b/w "Hello Mary Lou" (#9).

"A Wonder Like You" [Imperial 5770], first charted October 2, 1961 (#11); b/w "Everlovin' " (#16).

"Young World" [Imperial 5805], released February 1, 1962 (#5); b/w "Summertime" (#89).

"Teen Age Idol" [Imperial 5864], released July 25, 1962 (#5); b/w "I've Got My Eyes on You (And I Like What I See)."

"It's Up to You" [Imperial 5901], released November 23, 1962 (#6); b/w "I Need You" (#83).

"That's All" [Imperial 5910], released December 20, 1962 (#48); b/w "I'm in Love Again" (#67).

"You Don't Love Me Anymore (And I Can Tell)" [Decca 31475], released March 11, 1963 (#47); b/w "I Got a Woman" (#49).

"Old Enough to Love" [Imperial 5935], released March 26, 1963 (#94); b/w "If You Can't Rock Me" (#100).

"A Long Vacation" [Imperial 5958], released May 23, 1963 (--); b/w "Mad Mad World."

"String Along" [Decca 31495], released May 30, 1963 (#25); b/w "Gypsy Woman" (#62).

"There's Not a Minute" [Imperial 5985], released July 22, 1963 (--); b/w "Time After Time."

"Fools Rush In" [Decca 31533], released September 9, 1963 (#12); b/w "Down Home."

"Today's Teardrops" [Imperial 66004], released October 15, 1963 (#54); b/w "Thank You Darlin'."

"For You" [Decca 31574], released December 30, 1963 (#6); b/w "That's All She Wrote."

"Congratulations" [Imperial 66017], released February 2, 1964 (#63); b/w "One Minute to One."

"The Very Thought of You" [Decca 31612], released April 20, 1964 (#26); b/w "I Wonder (If Your Love Will Ever Belong to Me)."

"Lucky Star" [Imperial 66039], released May 14, 1964 (--); b/w "Everybody but Me."

"There's Nothing I Can Say" [Decca 31656], released August 17, 1964 (#47); b/w "Lonely Corner."

"Happy Guy" [Decca 31703], released November 23, 1964 (#82); b/w "Don't Breathe a Word."

"Mean Old World" [Decca 31756], released March 8, 1965 (#96); b/w "When the Chips Are Down."

"Yesterday's Love" [Decca 31800], released June 7, 1965 (--); b/w "Come Out Dancin'."

"Say You Love Me" [Decca 31845], released August 30, 1965 (--); b/w "Love and Kisses."

"Your Kind of Lovin' " [Decca 31900], released January 31, 1966 (--); b/w "Fire Breathin' Dragon."

"You Just Can't Quit" [Decca 31956], released May 30, 1966 (--); b/w "Louisiana Man."

"Things You Gave Me" [Decca 32026], released October 17, 1966 (--); b/w "Alone."

"They Don't Give Medals (To Yesterday's Heroes)" [Decca 32055], released December 5, 1966 (--); b/w "Take a Broken Heart."

"Take a City Bride" [Decca 32120], released April 24, 1967 (--); b/w "I'm Called Lonely."

"Suzanne on a Sunday Morning" [Decca 32176], released August 14, 1967 (--); b/w "Moonshine."

"Dream Weaver" [Decca 32222], released November 13, 1967 (--); b/w "Baby Close Its Eyes."

"Promenade in Green" [Decca 32284], released March 11, 1968 (--); b/w "Don't Blame It on Your Wife."

"Don't Make Promises" [Decca 32298], released May 1, 1968; b/w "Barefoot Boy."

"She Belongs to Me" [Decca 32550], released August 25, 1969 (#33); b/w "Promises."

"Easy to Be Free" [Decca 32635], released February 9, 1970 (#48); b/w "Come On In."

"I Shall Be Released" [Decca 32676], released April 20, 1970 (--); b/w "If You've Got to Go, Go Now."

"We've Got Such a Long Way to Go" [Decca 32711], released July 6, 1970 (--); b/w "Look at Mary."

"How Long" [Decca 32739], released August 31, 1970 (--); b/w "Down Along the Bayou Country."

"Life" [Decca 32779], released January 18, 1971 (--); b/w "California."

"Thank You Lord" [Decca 32860], released July 19, 1971 (--); b/w "Sing Me a Song."

"Gypsy Pilot" [Decca 32906], released November 22, 1971 (--); b/w "Love Minus Zero/No Limits."

"Garden Party" [Decca 32980], released June 19, 1972 (#6); b/w "So Long Mama."

"Palace Guard" [MCA 40001], released January 8, 1973 (#65); b/w "A Flower Opens Gently By."

"Lifestream" [MCA 40130], released September 17, 1973 (--); b/w "Evil Woman Child."

"Windfall" [MCA 40187], released January 28, 1974 (--); b/w "Legacy."

"One Night Stand" [MCA 40214], released March 18, 1974 (--); b/w "Lifestream."

"Try (Try to Fall in Love)" [MCA 40392], released April 28, 1975 (--); b/w "Louisiana Belle."

"Rock and Roll Lady" [MCA 40458], released September 15, 1975 (--); b/w "Fade Away."

"You Can't Dance" [Epic 850458], released September 30, 1977 (--); b/w "It's Another Day."

"Gimme Little Sign" [Epic 850501], released February 3, 1978 (--); b/w "Something You Can't Buy."

"Dream Lover" [Epic 850674], released February 27, 1979 (--); b/w "That Ain't the Way Love's Supposed to Be."

"Almost Saturday Night" [Capitol 4962], released January 12, 1981 (--); b/w "The Loser Babe Is You."

"It Hasn't Happened Yet" [Capitol 4974], released January 26, 1981 (--); b/w "Call It What You Want."

"Believe What You Say" [Capitol 4988], released March 16, 1981 (--); b/w "The Loser Babe Is You."

"Give 'Em My Number" [Capitol B5178], released October 29, 1982 (--); b/w "No Fair Falling in Love."

"You Know What I Mean" [MCA 52781], released February 24, 1986 (--); b/w "Don't Leave Me This Way."

"Dream Lover" [Epic 34–06066], released May 27, 1986 (--); b/w "Rave On."

ALBUMS

For albums that charted on *Billboard* magazine's Best Selling Pop Albums chart, release date (or, if not available, date record first appeared) is given. For noncharting albums whose exact release dates are missing from record-label catalogs, month and year are given based on various sources. The number in parentheses indicates highest chart position, also according to *Billboard;* noncharting albums are denoted by (--). The second of two catalog numbers, where applicable, indicates stereo release.

Ricky [Imperial LP 9048/LP 12392], first charted November 11, 1957 (#1).

Teen Time [Verve MGV-2083], released November 1957 (--) Various artists: Rick Nelson, Randy Sparks, Jeff Allen, Gary Williams, Rock Murphy, Barney Kessel. Rick's selections: "I'm Walkin," "A Teenager's Romance," and "You're My One and Only Love." By Barney Kessel: "Honey Rock" (B side to Rick's second Verve single, "You're My One and Only Love").

Ricky Nelson [Imperial LP 9050/LP 12393], first charted July 28, 1958 (#7).

Ricky Sings Again [Imperial LP 9061/LP 12090], first charted February 2, 1959 (#14).

Songs by Ricky [Imperial LP 9082/LP 12030], first charted September 28, 1959 (#22).

More Songs by Ricky [Imperial LP 9122/LP 12059], first charted August 29, 1960 (#18).

Rick Is 21 [Imperial LP 9152/LP 12071], first charted May 29, 1961 (#8).

Album 7 by Rick [Imperial LP 9167/LP 12082], first charted April 14, 1962 (#27).

Best Sellers by Rick Nelson [Imperial LP 9218/LP 12218], first charted March 2, 1963 (#112).

It's Up to You [Imperial LP 9223/LP 12223], first charted May 4, 1963 (#137).

290

For Your Sweet Love [Decca DL 4419/DL 74419], released May 27, 1963 (#20).

Million Sellers [Imperial LP 9232/LP 12232], released July 1963 (--).

A Long Vacation [Imperial LP 9244/LP 12244], released in October 1963 (--).

Rick Nelson Sings "For You" [Decca DL 4479/DL 74479], released December 9, 1963 (#14).

Rick Nelson Sings for You [Imperial LP 9251/LP 12251], released October 1963 (--).

The Very Thought of You [Decca DL 4559/DL 74559], released August 3, 1964 (--).

Spotlight on Rick [Decca DL 4608/DL74608], released November 23, 1964 (--).

Best Always, Rick Nelson [Decca DL 4660/DL 74660], released April 19, 1965 (--).

Love and Kisses [Decca DL 4678/DL 74678], released November 15, 1965 (--).

Bright Lights and Country Music [Decca DL 4779/DL 74779], released May 30, 1966 (--).

On the Flip Side [Decca DL 4836/DL 74836], released December 19, 1966 (--).

Soundtrack to "ABC Stage 67" TV special; various artists: Rick Nelson, Joanie Sommers, Joanie Sommers and the Celestials, Donna Jean Young, Peter Matz. Rick's selections: "It Doesn't Matter Anymore," "They Don't Give Medals (To Yesterday's Heroes")," "Take a Broken Heart," "Try to See It My Way" (with Joanie Sommers).

Country Fever [Decca DL 4837/DL 74837], released April 17, 1967 (--).

Another Side of Rick [Decca DL 4944/DL 74944], released November 13, 1967 (--).

Perspective [Decca DL 5014/DL 75014], released February 2, 1969 (--).

Rick Nelson in Concert [Decca DL 75162], first charted February 21, 1970 (#54).

Rick Sings Nelson [Decca DL 75236], released September 3, 1970 (#196).

Rudy the Fifth [Decca DL 75297], released October 4, 1971 (--).

Garden Party [Decca DL 75391], released November 27, 1972 (#32).

Windfall [MCA 383], released January 14, 1974 (#190).

Intakes [Epic KE-34420], released September 21, 1977* (--).

* Dates are approximate, as Epic Records assigned its albums release *weeks,* not exact days.

291

Playing to Win [Capitol SOO-12109], released January 15, 1981 (#153).
Memphis Sessions [Epic FE 40388], released May 27, 1986.*
All My Best [Silver Eagle SED-1035/MCAD-6163/PTL 17011–2], re-
leased 1986 (marketed via television only in 1985) (--).
Ricky Nelson Live, 1983–1985 [Rhino R2–71114], released May 1989
(--). (Originally released on Silver Eagle in 1986.)

ESSENTIAL BEST-OFS

Ricky Nelson (Legendary Masters Series No. 2) [United Artists UAS-9960],
released October 15, 1971 (--).
Greatest Hits [Rhino RNLP 215], released September 1985 (--).
Ricky Nelson: All-Time Greatest Hits [Curb Records, D2-77372], released
January 7, 1991 (--).

EXTENDED-PLAY SINGLES (EPs)

Neither Verve nor Imperial Records catalogs contain exact release
dates for EPs. For those that made *Billboard* magazine's Best Selling
Pop EPs chart, date record first appeared is given; for those that
did not, approximate release date is given, based on various sources.
The number in parentheses indicates highest chart position according
to *Billboard;* noncharting EPs are denoted by (--). *Billboard* initiated
its EP chart on October 7, 1957, and discontinued it on October 17,
1960; therefore no chart positions are available (NC) after that date.

[Verve EVP-5048], released 1957 (--); "I'm Walkin," "A Teenager's
Romance," "You're My One and Only Love," "Honey Rock."
[Imperial IMP 153], first charted November 25, 1957 (#1); "Honey-
comb," "Boppin' the Blues," "Be-Bop Baby," "Have I Told You
Lately That I Love You?"
[Imperial IMP 154], released 1957 (--); "Teenage Doll," "If You Can't
Rock Me," "Whole Lotta Shakin' Goin' On," "Baby I'm Sorry."
[Imperial IMP 155], released 1958 (--); "Am I Blue," "I'm Confessin',"
"Your True Love," "True Love."
[Imperial IMP 156], first charted August 4, 1958 (#3); "Shirley Lee,"
"There's Good Rockin' Tonight," "Someday," "I'm Feelin' Sorry."
[Imperial IMP 157], released 1958 (--); "Down the Line," "Don't Leave
Me This Way," "I'm in Love Again," "My Babe."
[Imperial IMP 158], first charted June 30, 1958 (#1); "Unchained

---

* Dates are approximate, as Epic Records assigned its albums release *weeks*, not exact
days.

Melody," "I'll Walk Alone," "There Goes My Baby," "Poor Little Fool."

[Imperial IMP 159], first charted January 12, 1959 (#1); "Be True to Me," "One of These Mornings," "Lonesome Town," "It's Late."

[Imperial IMP 160], released 1958 (--); "Restless Kid," "Believe What You Say," "It's All in the Game," "You Tear Me Up."

[Imperial IMP 161], released 1959 (--); "Old Enough to Love," "Tryin' to Get to You," "Never Be Anyone Else but You," "I Can't Help It."

[Imperial IMP 162], first charted September 28, 1959 (#1); "You Never Know What You're Missing," "I've Been Thinkin'," "So Long," "You're So Fine."

[Imperial IMP 163], released 1959 (--); "One Minute to One," "Blood from a Stone," "Half Breed," "Just a Little Too Much."

[Imperial IMP 164], released 1959 (--); "Don't Leave Me," "That's All," "A Long Vacation," "Sweeter Than You."

Ricky Sings Spirituals [Imperial IMP 165], released 1960 (--); "Glory Train," "I Bowed My Head in Shame," "If You Believe It," "March with the Band of the Lord."

[Decca ED-2760], released May 27, 1963 (NC); "I Will Follow You," "Let's Talk the Whole Thing Over," "One Boy Too Late," "Pick Up the Pieces."

Four You [Epic 3E 36868], released February 27, 1981* (NC); "Almost Saturday Night," "Lay Back in the Arms of Someone," "That's All Right," "Rave On."

LITTLE LP SERIES

Rick Nelson Million Sellers [Imperial 4–2232], released 1963 (NC); "Travelin' Man," "Never Be Anyone Else but You," "It's Late," "Young Emotions," "Hello Mary Lou," "Yes Sir, That's My Baby."

All chart positions are based on *Billboard* magazine's weekly record sales charts and are compiled in a series of books by Joel Whitburn's Record Research. These books are available by writing: Record Research, P.O. Box 200, Menomonee Falls, Wisconsin 53051.

---

* Date is approximate, as Epic Records assigned its EPs release *weeks*, not exact days.

Bibliography

BOOKS

Alger, Horatio. *Strive and Succeed* ("Julius," or "The Street Boy Out West," and "The Store Boy," or "The Fortunes of Ben Barclay"). New York: Holt, Rinehart and Winston, 1967.

Blumenthal, John. *Hollywood High*. New York: Ballantine Books, 1988.

Bronson, Fred. *The Billboard Book of Number One Hits*. New York: Billboard Publications, Inc., 1985.

Brooks, Tim. *The Complete Directory to Prime Time TV Stars, 1946–Present*. New York: Ballantine Books, 1987.

———, and Earle Marsh. *The Complete Directory to Prime Time Network TV Shows, 1946–Present*. 3rd ed. New York: Ballantine Books, 1985.

Browne, Joy. *Nobody's Perfect*. New York: Simon & Schuster, 1988.

Busnar, Gene. *It's Rock 'n' Roll*. New York: Wanderer Books, 1979.

Buxton, Frank, and Bill Owen. *The Big Broadcast*. New York: The Viking Press, 1972.

Christgau, Robert. *Any Old Way You Choose It*. Baltimore: Penguin Books, Inc., 1973.

294

_____. *Christgau's Record Guide*. New York: Ticknor & Fields, 1981.

Clifford, Mike. *The Harmony Illustrated Encyclopedia of Rock*. New York: Harmony Books, 1983.

Colman, Stuart. *They Kept on Rockin'*. Poole, Dorset, England: Blandford Books, Ltd., 1982.

Current Biography Yearbook(s) (1940–1988). New York: The H. W. Wilson Company, 1940–1988.

Dundy, Elaine. *Elvis and Gladys*. New York: Dell Publishing Co., Inc., 1985.

Dunning, John. *Tune in Yesterday*. Englewood Cliffs, New Jersey: Prentice-Hall, Inc., 1976.

Ehrenstein, David, and Bill Reed. *Rock on Film*. New York: Delilah Books, 1982.

Eisner, Joel, and David Krinsky. *Television*. Jefferson, North Carolina; London: McFarland & Company, Inc., Publishers, 1984.

Eliot, Mark. *Rockonomics*. New York: Franklin Watts, 1989.

Escott, Colin, and Martin Hawkins. *Sun Records*. New York: Quick Fox, 1980.

Evory, Ann, and Peter M. Gareffa, eds. *Contemporary Newsmakers, 1985*. Detroit: Gale Research Company, 1986.

Flynn, Errol. *My Wicked, Wicked Ways*. New York: G. P. Putnam's Sons, 1959.

Gareffa, Peter M., ed. *Contemporary Newsmakers, 1986*. Detroit: Gale Research Company, 1987.

_____. *Contemporary Newsmakers, 1987*. Detroit: Gale Research Company, 1988.

Gilbert, Bob, and Gary Theroux. *The Top Ten*. New York: Simon & Schuster, 1982.

Glines, Carroll V., and Wendell F. Moseley. *The DC-3—The Story of a Fabulous Airplane*. Philadelphia: Lippincott, 1965.

Helander, Brock. *The Rock Who's Who*. New York: Schirmer Books, 1982.

Hendler, Herb. *Year by Year in the Rock Era*. Westport, Connecticut: Greenwood Press, 1983.

Hesse, Hermann. *Siddhartha*. New York: New Directions Publishing Corporation, 1951.

Hounsome, Terry. *Rock Record*. 3rd ed. New York: Oxford, England: Facts on File Publications, 1987.

Houston, David. *Jazz Baby*. New York: St. Martin's Press, 1983.

Katz, Ephraim. *The Film Encyclopedia*. New York: Thomas Y. Crowell, Publishers, 1979.

Kelley, Kitty. *Nancy Reagan*. New York: Simon & Schuster, 1991.

Kiersh, Edward. *Where Are You Now, Bo Diddley?* Garden City, New York: Dolphin/Doubleday, 1986.

Lamparski, Richard. *Whatever Became of . . . ?* Fourth in a series. New York: Crown Publishers, Inc., 1973.

_____. Lamparski, Richard. *Whatever Became of. . . ?* Fifth in a series. New York: Crown Publishers, Inc., 1974.

MacDonald, J. Fred. *Don't Touch That Dial.* Chicago: Nelson-Hall, Inc., Publishers, 1979.

Mason, Michael, ed. *The Country Music Book.* New York: Charles Scribner's Sons, 1985.

McCallum, John D., and Charles H. Pearson. *College Football U.S.A. 1869–1971.* New York: Hall of Fame Publishing/McGraw-Hill Book Company, 1972.

McNeil, Alex. *Total Television.* New York: Viking Penguin, Inc., 1980.

Miller, Jim, ed. *The Rolling Stone Illustrated History of Rock & Roll.* New York: Rolling Stone Press/Random House, 1976.

Mitz, Rick. *The Great TV Sitcom Book.* New York: Richard Marek Publishers, Inc., 1980.

Moffatt, Michael. *The Rutgers Picture Book.* New Brunswick, New Jersey: Rutgers University Press, 1985.

Moody, Raymond A., M.D. *Elvis After Life.* Atlanta: Peachtree Publishers, Ltd., 1987.

Muirhead, Bert. *The Record Producers File.* New York: Sterling Publishing Co., Inc., 1984.

Murrells, Joseph. *Million Selling Records.* New York: Arco Publishing, Inc., 1984.

Nash, Robert Jay, and Stanley Ralph Ross. *The Motion Picture Guide.* Chicago: Cinebooks, Inc., 1985.

Nelson, Ozzie. *Ozzie.* Englewood Cliffs, New Jersey: Prentice-Hall, Inc., 1973.

Nite, Norm N. *Rock On, Volume 1.* New York: Harper & Row, Publishers, 1982.

Ochs, Michael. *Rock Archives.* Garden City, New York: Doubleday & Company, Inc., 1984.

Pareles, Jon, and Patricia Romanowski, eds. *The Rolling Stone Encyclopedia of Rock & Roll.* New York: Summit Books, 1983.

Pollock, Bruce, ed. *Popular Music* (volumes 7, 8, and 9). Detroit: Gale Research Company, 1984, 1985, and 1986.

_____. *When Rock Was Young.* New York: Holt, Rinehart and Winston, 1981.

Rice, Tim, Jo Rice, Paul Gambaccini, and Mike Read. *British Hit Singles.* 5th ed. Enfield, Middlesex, England: Guinness Superlatives, Ltd., 1985.

Rijff, Ger. *Long Lonely Highway*. Ann Arbor, Michigan: The Pierian Press, Inc., 1987.

The Rolling Stone Index 1967–1979. New York: Rolling Stone Press, 1983.

Schessler, Ken. *This Is Hollywood*. La Verne, California: Ken Schessler Publishing, 1989.

Shannon, Bob, and John Javna. *Behind the Hits*. New York: Warner Books, Inc., 1986.

Shapiro, Nat. *Popular Music* (volumes 1, 3, and 6). New York: Adrian Press, 1964, 1967, and 1973.

Shaw, Arnold. *The Rock Revolution*. London: Crowell-Collier Press, 1969.

_____. *Black Popular Music in America*. New York: Schirmer Books, 1986.

_____. *The Rockin' '50s*. New York: Hawthorn Books, Inc., 1974.

Shore, Michael. *The Rolling Stone Book of Rock Video*. New York: Rolling Stone Press, 1984.

Simon, George T. *Simon Says*. New Rochelle, New York: Arlington House, 1971.

_____. *The Big Bands*. New York: Macmillan Publishing Co., Inc., 1974.

Smith, Joe. *Off the Record*. New York: Warner Books, 1988.

Steinberg, Corbett S. *TV Facts*. New York: Facts on File, Inc., 1980.

Thomas, Bob. *Joan Crawford*. New York: Simon and Schuster, 1978.

Tobler, John, and Stuart Grundy. *The Guitar Greats*. New York: St. Martin's Press, 1984.

Tosches, Nick. *Hellfire*. New York: Dell Publishing Co., Inc., 1982.

Vellenga, Dick, and Mick Farren. *Elvis and the Colonel*. New York: Delacorte Press, 1988.

Ward, Ed, Geoffrey Stokes, and Ken Tucker. *Rock of Ages*. New York: Rolling Stone Press/Summit Books, 1987.

Weinberg, Max, with Robert Santelli. *The Big Beat*. Chicago: Contemporary Books, Inc., 1984.

Whitburn, Joel. *Top Pop Artists & Singles, 1955–1978*. Menomonee Falls, Wisconsin: Record Research, 1979.

_____. *Top Pop Singles 1979*. Menomonee Falls, Wisconsin: Record Research, 1980.

_____. *Top Pop Singles 1980*. Menomonee Falls, Wisconsin: Record Research, 1981.

_____. *Top Pop Singles 1981*. Menomonee Falls, Wisconsin: Record Research, 1982.

_____. *Top Pop Singles 1982*. Menomonee Falls, Wisconsin: Record Research, 1983.

_____. *Top LPs 1945–1972.* Menomonee Falls, Wisconsin: Record Research, 1973.

_____. *Top LPs 1973.* Menomonee Falls, Wisconsin: Record Research, 1974.

_____. *Top LPs 1974.* Menomonee Falls, Wisconsin: Record Research, 1975.

_____. *Top LPs 1975.* Menomonee Falls, Wisconsin: Record Research, 1976.

_____. *Top LPs 1976.* Menomonee Falls, Wisconsin: Record Research, 1977.

_____. *Top LPs 1977.* Menomonee Falls, Wisconsin: Record Research, 1978.

_____. *Top LPs 1978.* Menomonee Falls, Wisconsin: Record Research, 1979.

_____. *Top LPs 1979.* Menomonee Falls, Wisconsin: Record Research, 1980.

_____. *Top LPs 1980.* Menomonee Falls, Wisconsin: Record Research, 1981.

_____. *Top LPs 1981.* Menomonee Falls, Wisconsin: Record Research, 1982.

_____. *Top LPs 1982.* Menomonee Falls, Wisconsin: Record Research, 1983.

_____. *Music Yearbook 1983.* Menomonee Falls, Wisconsin: Record Research, 1984.

_____. *Music Yearbook 1984.* Menomonee Falls, Wisconsin: Record Research, 1985.

_____. *Joel Whitburn's Pop Memories, 1890–1954.* Menomonee Falls, Wisconsin: Record Research, 1986.

Worth, Fred L., and Steve D. Tamerius. *All About Elvis.* New York: Bantam Books, 1981.

SELECTED NEWSPAPER AND PERIODICAL ARTICLES

Adler, Michael. "Striped Panties Killed Romance, Dancer Declares." *New York Mirror,* March 8, 1933.

Arvidson, Cheryl, and Ford Fessenden. "Co-Pilot Cites Heater in Nelson Plane Crash." *Dallas Times Herald,* July 30, 1986.

Atlas, Jacoba. "The American Dream—Part Two." *Melody Maker,* February 3, 1973.

Bacon, James. "Ozzie Nelson Gains Rating as 'Genius' in Hollywood." New Brunswick *Daily Home News,* March 26, 1961.

Baltin, Will. "Ozzie Nelson, Rutgers Graduate, Back in Town; Autograph Hunters Besiege Orchestra Pilot as His Band and Harriet Hilliard Appear in Park." New Brunswick *Daily Home News*, February 19, 1934.

Barry, Milt. "Ozzie Nelson Remembered." *The Sun-Bulletin*, June 8, 1975.

Berges, Marshall. "Home Q&A/Kristin & Rick Nelson." *Los Angeles Times*, June 6, 1974.

Borie, Marcia. "Come On, Rick, What Do You Want to Do Tonight?" *Photoplay*, March 1959.

_____. "When You Pray, You Have to Believe God Listens." *Photoplay*, March 1961.

_____. "David Nelson and June Blair: No Two People Ever Started Life Further Apart . . ." *Photoplay*, July 1961.

_____. "Rick Nelson's Special Memory of Elvis." *Elvis Presley/A Photoplay Tribute*, 1977.

Boyd, Kathleen. "Ozzie Nelson's Success Due to Knowledge of Audiences." New Brunswick *Sunday Times*, December 3, 1933.

Breslin, Rosemary. "All in the Family." New York *Daily News*, February 4, 1986.

Callahan, Mike, Bud Buschardt, and Steve Goddard. "Both Sides Now: Rick Nelson." *Goldmine*, August 1980.

Carter, Tom. "After Growing Up on 'Ozzie and Harriet,' David Nelson Finds Real-life Adventure." *Chicago Tribune*, February 24, 1981.

"Celebrity Visit With Kris & Rick Nelson." *Good Housekeeping*, May 1978.

Chadwick, Bruce. "Ricky's Reunion." New York *Daily News*, November 11, 1983.

Cloonan, Richard T. "Rick Nelson Reaches Out for a Wider World in Music." *New York World-Journal Tribune*, December 4, 1966.

Cohen, Scott. "Rick & Tracy Nelson." *Interview*, September 1984.

Considine, Shaun. "Wow, Has Little Ricky Changed." *The New York Times*, January 23, 1972.

Cromelin, Richard. "Rick Nelson Starts Anew." *Los Angeles Times*, January 25, 1981.

Dalmas, Herb. "Ozzie, Harriet & Family." *Coronet*, July 1954.

Darrach, Brad. "Life After Ozzie & Harriet." *People Weekly*, September 7, 1987.

Davidson, Sara. "The Happy, Happy, Happy Nelsons." *Esquire*, June 1971.

Dawidziak, Mark. "One for His Brother." New York *Daily News*, July 28, 1987.

Demaret, Kent. "Rick Nelson, 1940–1985." *People Weekly*, January 20, 1986.

Denton, Charles. "Era of Teenage Idols a Show Biz Sensation." *New York Journal-American*, July 26, 1959.

Dougherty, Steve. "The Adventures of Billy (Moses) and Tracy (Nelson): Stars Engage in a Romantic Pas de Deux." *People Weekly*, December 16, 1985.

Dumont, Lou. "Historical Tape Recordings: Ozzie and Harriet." *Hobbies*, May 1979.

Eells, George. "Ozzie and Harriet's Ricky and David." *Look*, May 19, 1953.

Everett, Todd. "Rick Nelson: Light Years Away From 'Ozzie and Harriet' and Still Moving." *Stereo Review*, July 1973.

"Ex-Amateur Makes Good!" New Brunswick *Sunday Times*, March 13, 1936.

Flythe, Jr., Starkey. "Eric Hilliard Nelson (Alias Ricky) Celebrates Twenty-five Years in Show Business." *The Saturday Evening Post*, April 1974.

Forsling, Elizabeth. "Ozzie and Harriet." *Pic*, August 1947.

Fox, Hazel Hitchcock. "Four on TV Stairs Together." *The Christian Science Monitor*, October 8, 1953.

Freeman, Paul. "Brother Dave Pays Tribute to Rick Nelson." *San Francisco Chronicle*, November 15, 1987.

Fricke, David. "Ricky: TV's Teen Dream Knew How to Rock." *Rolling Stone*, February 13, 1986.

Garrison, Peter. "Falling Stars." *Flying*, February 1988.

Goldberg, Michael. "Ricky Nelson: 1940–1985." *Rolling Stone*, February 13, 1986.

Goldstein, Pat. "A '50s Teen Angel, A '60s Fade Out, A '70s Rock Re-entry." *The Washington Star*, October 14, 1977.

Goodwin, Betty. "Tracy Nelson Gets Revenge." *TV Guide*, May 21, 1983.

Gould, Jack. "Comment and Comedy." *The New York Times*, October 29, 1944.

———. "Programs in Review." *The New York Times*, November 30, 1947.

———. "Radio and Television." *The New York Times*, October 6, 1952.

Graham, Sheilah. "Ricky: 6-Foot-1, 168-Lb. Star." *New York Mirror*, February 1, 1959.

Grayden, Robin. "The Boy Next Door Went A-Walkin'." *Melody Maker*, July 7, 1979.

Grein, Paul. "Nelson Upholds Family Tradition at No. 1." *Billboard*, September 29, 1990.

Gross, Ben. "Ozzie Nelson Defends Teen-Agers." *New York Sunday News*, February 26, 1961.

_____. "Ozzie Nelson Gives Secret of Happy H'wood Marriage." *New York Sunday News*, March 5, 1961.

Gutman, Barry. "Nelson Regaining His Old Popularity." *News of Delaware County*, October 24, 1977.

Hendrickson, Paul. "At the Stardust, Ricky's Girls Attend Their God." *The National Observer*, May 31, 1975.

Henniger, Paul. "An Upbeat Grandmother Who Likes to Race Cars." *Los Angeles Times*, November 17, 1982.

Hopkins, Jerry. "Records." *Rolling Stone*. July 12, 1969.

Hopper, Hedda. "No Rocky Road for Ricky," New York *Daily News*, October 5, 1958.

"How Long Can Rick Keep His Secret?" *TV and Movie Screen*, February 1959.

Hyams, Joe. "Life in a Fishbowl." *New York Herald Tribune*, June 1, 1955.

_____. "Daring Young Men," *New York Herald Tribune TV Magazine*, January 24, 1960.

_____. "Presley Back, Ricky Nelson Unafraid." *New York Herald Tribune*, March 7, 1960.

Jackovich, Karen G. "Proving She's No Square Peg, Ozzie and Harriet's Granddaughter Tracy Nelson Takes to the Tube." *People Weekly*, December 13, 1982.

Johnson, Bob. "What Makes Ricky Tick?" *TV Guide*, December 28, 1957.

_____. "Facts Behind the Fan Clubs." *TV Guide*, January 29, 1960.

"Just Like the Kids Next Door? . . . Not Those Nelson Boys." *TV Guide*, December 27, 1958.

Krebs, Albin. "Ozzie Nelson, Entertainer, Dead at 68." *The New York Times*, June 5, 1975.

Ladd, Bill. "It Takes Fast Footwork to Produce Nelson Show Around Boys' Schedules." *Louisville Courier-Journal*, June 12, 1959.

_____. "Nelsons Change, but the Show Keeps Rolling." *Louisville Courier-Journal*, February 25, 1962.

Leary, Jack. "Success Can't Spoil Him." *New York Sunday News*, September 17, 1961.

Levy, Bonnie. "Rutgers Friends, Associates Remember, Mourn Ozzie Nelson." New Brunswick *The Home News*, June 4, 1975.

Lewis, Randy. "Rick Nelson, Now Signed to Epic Records, Discusses New LP and His 20 Years in Rock." *Cash Box*, October 29, 1977.

"Like Ozzie, Like Son." *TV Guide*, November 20, 1953.

Lindbloom, Ronald E. "Working Vacation for Nelsons." *Newark News,* June 10, 1956.

Mackin, Tom. "Nelson Takes Poke at Pressure Groups." *Newark Evening News,* July 14, 1963.

Mahoney, Marie. "All in the Family." *The Austin Chronicle,* February 13, 1987.

Marsh, Beatrice. "Rick—Why Dare Death?" *Photoplay,* November 1960.

Maynard, John. "For the 2 Nelson Kids, $800 an Hour = $3 in Cash." *Pictorial Review,* July 12, 1953.

McGee, David. "Rick Nelson Looks Back on His Career in Music." *Record World,* March 21, 1981.

McLellan, Dennis. "Harriet Nelson: Laughing Through Tears." *Los Angeles Times,* August 27, 1981.

McMahon, Ernest E. "Band Leader: Ozzie Nelson Ignored a Dean's Advice and Became Famous." *RAM,* April 1937.

McMahon, Regan. "Rick Nelson: Back to Schooldays." *BAM,* January 16, 1981.

Menze, Mary E. "Ozzie and Harriet Make an Old-Fashioned Home in Hollywood." *American Home,* April 1946.

"Miss Harriet Hilliard Becomes Bride of Ozzie Nelson, Famous Orchestra Leader—Simple Home Wedding." *Ridgefield Park Bulletin,* October 11, 1935.

"Music and Marriage Will Mix." Chicago *Down Beat,* May 1, 1943.

Nachman, Gerald. "And Ricky Nelson As Himself." *New York Post,* January 23, 1966.

"Nelson Orchestra Star Shows Alma Mater How." New York *Daily Mirror,* April 18, 1931.

Nelson, Harriet. "The Men in My Life." *Look,* November 11, 1958.

_____. "My Heart Belongs to My Three Men." *Ladies' Home Companion,* June 1953.

Nelson, Rick. "Everything Happens to Me." *Photoplay,* May 1958.

_____, as told to Warren Hall. "Make Friends With Your Parents." *American Weekly,* January 4, 1959.

_____. "Were You the Girl in the Gingham Dress." *Photoplay,* January 1960.

"Normality and $300,000." *Newsweek,* November 17, 1952.

Obrecht, Jas. "Q/A: Rick Nelson." *Guitar Player,* September 1981.

O'Brian, Jack. "Ozzie and Harriet Prove Parents Can Be Talented!" *Pictorial TView,* July 1, 1956.

Okon, May. "Everybody Works in This Family." *New York Sunday News,* March 28, 1954.

_____. "Those Nelson Boys." *New York Sunday News*, August 4, 1957.

_____. "Teen-age Crush." *New York Sunday News*, November 9, 1958.

"Old '21-Job Ozzie'." *TV Guide*, August 18, 1962.

O'Leary, Dorothy. "Radio Version of Nelson Family Life Born of Fact and Fiction." *The New York Times*, March 30, 1947.

"One Family's Triumph." *Newsweek*, August 26, 1957.

"Ozzie and Harriet: They Never Leave Home." *Look*, October 24, 1950.

"Ozzie Nelson Is Understander When He's Not Leading Band." *New York World-Telegram*, December 7, 1940.

Parsons, Louella O. "They Live in a 'Glass House.' " *Pictorial TView*, March 13, 1955.

Perry, Scott. "Rick(y) Nelson's Pushing Back Up." Nashville *Tennessean*, October 8, 1977.

Pietschmann, Richard J. "So Stop Calling Him a Poor Little Fool." *Los Angeles*, April 1981.

Popson, Tom. "Rick Dusts Off the Old Equipment—and Heads Back to Rockabilly." *Chicago Tribune*, May 13, 1984.

Porter, Del. "Garden Boos Spur a Rick Revival." *Rolling Stone*, November 23, 1972.

Pryor, Thomas M. " 'Ozzie and Harriet': Life With the Nelsons Is Now on Video." *The New York Times*, November 23, 1952.

Radovsky, Vicki Jo. "Rick." *US*, May 26, 1981.

Rea, Steven X. "Rick Nelson Returns to Rock." *Philadelphia Inquirer*, January 13, 1984.

Reid, James. "Watch Harriet Hilliard's Smoke!" *Motion Picture*, June 1936.

Ross, Don. "The Nelson Adventures Are Essentially True." *New York Herald Tribune*, September 19, 1954.

"Rutgers Football Star Talks to N.B.H.S. Team at Banquet." New Brunswick *Daily Home News*, December 8, 1926.

Rutkoski, Rex. "Rick Nelson: 'You've Got to Please Yourself.' " *Valley News Dispatch*, March 23, 1981.

Scheurer, Philip K. "Ozzie's Harriet Embodies Youth, Serenity in Work." *Los Angeles Times*, January 15, 1960.

Scott, Vernon. "Hop 'n Holler Set's New Hero Is Pathetic People Bleater." *New York Journal-American*, July 22, 1958.

_____. "A Nice Normal Family." *TV Guide*, September 21, 1963.

Seldes, Gilbert. "Domestic Life in the Forty-ninth State." *Saturday Review*, August 22, 1953.

Servi, Vera. "Rick Nelson Making It in New Career, With Roots in Past." *Chicago Tribune*, November 26, 1972.

Shanley, J. P. "Ozzie Nelson—Practical Parent." *The New York Times,* June 9, 1957.

Sharbutt, Jay. "New Tune for Harriet Nelson." *Los Angeles Times,* August 31, 1976.

Shearer, Lloyd. "The Fabulous Nelsons." *Parade,* March 2, 1958.

Sheeley, Shari. "What Makes a Nice Boy Change Like That?" *Photoplay,* January 1960.

Shipp, Randy. "Rick Nelson: The Rock Star Who Came Back." *Christian Science Monitor,* April 20, 1978.

Smith, Cecil. "Prime Times Puts Ozzie Back in Business." *Jersey Star Ledger,* August 26, 1973.

———. "From Superteen to Supersick Role." *Los Angeles Times,* January 27, 1972.

Snyder, Camilla. "Only an Acre, But to the Rick Nelsons It's a Farm." *The New York Times,* August 29, 1973.

Stern, Daniel. "A Day With Rick Nelson." *Photoplay,* January 1958.

Stump, Al. "Meet Hollywood's Most Exciting Family." *American Magazine,* October 1955.

Sutton, Lawrence. "Ozzie Nelson: Rutgers Favorite Son Reminisces." *The Rutgers Daily Targum,* April 3, 1973.

Tamarkin, Jeff. "Rick Nelson, Pioneer Rock 'n' Roll Teen Idol." *Goldmine,* February 14, 1986.

"Teen-ager Rocks Teen-agers." *Life,* December 1, 1958.

"The Full Nelson." *Time,* February 16, 1948.

"The Great Competitor," *Time,* December 14, 1953.

"The Nation's Second Best-Known Family." *TV Guide,* July 29, 1961.

"The Nelson Touch." *Newsweek,* April 28, 1947.

"The Nelsons and How They Grew." *TV Guide,* October 15, 1956.

Thomas, Bob. "Talented and Rich." *Newark Evening News,* July 11, 1958.

———. "Ozzie Nelson Comes Back." New Brunswick *Daily Home News,* October 30, 1967.

Toepfer, Susan. "Rick and Col. Parker: Back to Square One." New York *Daily News,* October 20, 1977.

"Top Families." *People Weekly,* October 27, 1986.

Tuber, Keith. "Rick Nelson Still Riding Rock 'n' Roll Roller Coaster." *Los Angeles Herald-Examiner,* January 2, 1981.

Tusher, Bill. "I Dig My Brother's Wife." *Photoplay,* September 1961.

"TV's Youngest Comic." *TV Guide,* May 15, 1953.

Van Horne, Harriet. "Homey Is the Word That Fits Nelsons." *New York World-Telegram,* November 21, 1952.

Van Matre, Lynn. "The Latest Nelson Rating Finds Rick(y) All Grown Up." *Chicago Tribune,* November 19, 1976.

Weiner, Debra. "Rick Nelson: Still Little Old Me." *The Soho Weekly News,* November 3, 1977.

Whitall, Susan. "Lonesome Town Cheers Up: Rick Nelson Goes Back on the Boards." *Creem* Magazine, June 1981.

Wilkins, Barbara. "The Rick Nelsons Come of Age." *People Weekly,* May 27, 1974.

Williams, Richard. "Nelson's Victory." *Melody Maker,* April 3, 1971.

_____. "Nouveau Rick." *Melody Maker,* February 26, 1972.

Young, Bob. "All-American Family Feud." *Newsday,* August 25, 1987.

Zimmerman, Ray. "Harriet Hilliard 'Hates' Life of Hollywood Star." New Brunswick *Sunday Times,* March 22, 1936.

Zito, Tom. "Rick Nelson: At 31, Mellowing." *Washington Post,* October 8, 1971.

Zurawik, David. "America's First Teen Idol." *Newsday,* January 2, 1986.

Index

308

311